Unionism in the United Kingdom, 1918–1974

Also by Paul Ward

RED FLAG AND UNION JACK: Englishness, Patriotism and the British Left,
1881–1924

Unionism in the United Kingdom, 1918–1974

Paul Ward

First published 2005 by
PALGRAVE MACMILLAN
Houndmills, Basingstoke, Hampshire RG21 6XS and
175 Fifth Avenue, New York, N.Y. 10010
Companies and representatives throughout the world

PALGRAVE MACMILLAN is the global academic imprint of the Palgrave
Macmillan division of St. Martin's Press, LLC and of Palgrave Macmillan Ltd.
Macmillan® is a registered trademark in the United States, United Kingdom
and other countries. Palgrave is a registered trademark in the European
Union and other countries.

ISBN-13: 978–1–4039–3827–5   hardback
ISBN-10: 1–4039–3827–X   hardback

This book is printed on paper suitable for recycling and made from fully
managed and sustained forest sources.

A catalogue record for this book is available from the British Library.

Library of Congress Cataloging-in-Publication Data
Ward, Paul, 1964–
   Unionism in the United Kingdom, 1918–1974/ Paul Ward.
      p. cm.
   Includes bibliographical references and index.
   ISBN 1–4039–3827–X (cloth)
      1. Great Britain–Politics and government–20th century. 2. Northern
Ireland–Politics and government–1969–1994. 3. Scotland–Politics and
government–20th century. 4. Ireland–Politics and government–20th
century. 5. Wales–Politics and government–20th century. I. Title.

DA566.7W27 2005
320.441′049–dc22   2004056893

10   9   8   7   6   5   4   3   2   1
14 13 12 11 10 09 08 07 06 05

Printed and bound in Great Britain by
Antony Rowe Ltd, Chippenham and Eastbourne

For Jackie

Contents

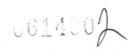

Abbreviations

CEMA	Council for the Encouragement of Music and the Arts
CLG	Commonwealth Labour Group
CLP	Commonwealth Labour Party
CPGB	Communist Party of Great Britain
EMB	Empire Marketing Board
FCO	Foreign and Commonwealth Office
IRA	Irish Republican Army
ILP	Independent Labour Party
NILP	Northern Ireland Labour Party
NLS	National Library of Scotland
NPS	National Party of Scotland
NLW	National Library of Wales
PRONI	Public Record Office of Northern Ireland
RWG	Revolutionary Workers' Group
SNP	Scottish National Party
UWUC	Ulster Women's Unionist Council

A note on terminology

There is plenty of room for misunderstanding in the use of upper and lower case letters in a book such as this. There is a difference between Unionism and unionism. Upper case has been used in this book for Unionism where it refers to parties designating themselves as such in their official names, as did the Conservative Party in the United Kingdom between the 1880s and 1920s. In Scotland the 'Unionist' label was retained as the party's primary name until the 1960s. In Northern Ireland, a variety of parties continue to call themselves 'Unionist'. Where I use lower-case for unionism it refers to general support for the constitutional Union between the four nations of the United Kingdom. Similarly, Labour refers to the British Labour Party, whereas labour means the general labour movement without denoting membership of particular organizations.

In each chapter, where any confusion may arise, an early note spells out the chosen use of name for the person under discussion.

I have used Northern Ireland and Ulster interchangeably following accepted usage in unionist circles. I have used Derry and Londonderry depending upon which group I have been discussing.

Acknowledgements

In the normal course of events this book might have taken five years to complete but thanks to the support of my colleagues at Huddersfield University and the Arts and Humanities Research Board research leave scheme I was able to have a full year's sabbatical. Such intensity of research and writing is extremely rewarding but entails great debts. Keith Laybourn, Katherine Lewis and Bill Stafford have provided academic advice and friendship. Chas Loft more than filled my shoes while I was on leave. Annette Heydon cast her gaze upon the imperfections of the text. I would also like to thank John Turner and Martin Daunton. I would like to express my gratitude to the various history secretaries, especially Liz Trayte, who have provided the daily kindnesses that have enabled me to spend more time on writing books than form-filling. I have also been lucky to have had the chance to write some sections of this book in various locations within and without the Union. Enjoyable respites were had in Spain and Germany, and I would like to express my thanks to Elizabeth Woodward Smith and Alan Floyd at the University of A Coruna and Geoff and Renate Sparkes in Braunschweig for their hospitality. The final stages in seeing this book to production were undertaken while I was Fulbright-Robertson Visiting Professor of British History at Westminster College, Fulton, Missouri. Thanks are owed to the benefactors of this valuable professorship and also to the faculty at Westminster who provided such a friendly atmosphere in which to work.

I owe gratitude to staff at the University of Manchester John Rylands Library, National Library of Wales (especially Dr J. Graham Jones), National Library of Scotland (where Alan Bell was especially helpful), Belfast Linen Hall library, Queen's University Belfast Library, and the Public Record Office of Northern Ireland. The people staffing the inter-library loans service at the University of Huddersfield library were particularly helpful and efficient. Permission to quote material in the Lloyd George Papers was kindly granted by the National Library of Wales. Permission to publish material from the Public Record Office of Northern Ireland was kindly given by the Deputy Keeper of the Records. Permission to include material from the National Library of Scotland was kindly granted by the Trustees of the National Library of Scotland. I am also grateful to Mrs Eleri Huws and Ms Sioned Williams for permission to quote material from the papers of Dr Huw T. Edwards. I am grateful to Luciana O'Flaherty and Dan Bunyard at Palgrave, as well as Helen Ang and Shirley Tan for dealing with the copy-editing of this book.

I acknowledge a major debt to the researches of the previous biographers and historians of the people discussed in this book. It could not have been written without the work of Graham Walker, Diane Urquhart and J. Graham Jones among others.

Gill Mellor kindly looked after the children allowing valuable writing time. Georgia doesn't think that I am working if I am at home and considers me to be on holiday when I visit an archive away from home, yet remains my most affectionate critic. Oscar played quietly with his trains. First and last, though, my love and thanks go to Jackie.

Supported by A · H · R · B

arts and humanities research board

Introduction: Unionist Lives

The problematic nature of the multi-national United Kingdom has been recognized for a long time. The United Kingdom is not a single nation but different nations held together by various Acts of Union. Wales was incorporated with England in 1536 and 1543, Scotland became part of Great Britain in 1707 and Ireland's Act of Union, passed in 1800, came into operation in 1801. In 1921, the United Kingdom, for the first time in four hundred years, saw its geographical extent diminished through the Government of Ireland Act of 1920 and the Anglo-Irish Treaty of 1921. Six counties in north east Ireland were named Northern Ireland and retained within the United Kingdom, but the formation of the Irish Free State in the south meant that the territorial area of the Union was reduced for the first time in centuries. The union of nations that constituted the United Kingdom was, therefore, a dynamic relationship given to ebb and flow according to the political economy of national identity in the four nations.

While nations are a collective outcome of imagination, the act of imagining is the sum of millions of individual mental processes, which in the United Kingdom has been complicated by the co-existence of several nations within the same state. Modern British history, as Kenneth Morgan notes, has been 'an exercise in pluralism'.[1] Some commentators have argued that the United Kingdom has been an artificial nation-state, shown in the inability of the inhabitants of the territory to agree on a single collective description for their homeland.[2] This in turn has led to the assumption that the United Kingdom was and is a fundamentally unstable state form heading towards its demise.

In this book I examine the lives of eight individuals to understand how the United Kingdom was imagined in a specific historical setting and how personal identities were transmitted into national and Union

1

identities through a sense of common interest and allegiance. This bio-graphical approach has the advantage that it enables emphasis to be placed on the complex and multiple nature of individuals' identities and allows changes in identity to be mapped with some precision. The biographies are not complete. I consider only aspects of their political and personal lives relating to the Union. There is little discussion, for example, of the day-to-day running of government departments or of constituency politics.

The individuals consist of three Scottish, three Welsh and two Northern Irish politicians who were active during the decades of the mid-twentieth century. Walter Elliot was a Conservative MP between 1918 and 1958. He was a cabinet minister in the 1930s, and was Secretary of State for Scotland between 1936 and 1938. Tom Johnston was a Labour MP from the 1920s to the 1940s. He was Secretary of State for Scotland during the Second World War. Lady Priscilla Tweedsmuir (Baroness Tweedsmuir of Belhevie from 1970) was a Conservative MP between 1946 and 1966 and was a member of the Conservative governments of 1959 to 1964 and 1970 to 1974. Gwilym Lloyd-George and Megan Lloyd George were the fourth and fifth children of David Lloyd George, 'the Welsh wizard' and Prime Minister between 1916 and 1922. Both became MPs under his political leadership in the 1920s, although subsequently their careers took different paths. Megan resigned from the Liberal Party and joined Labour in 1955, while Gwilym, having served in the wartime coalition as Minister of Fuel and Power, stood as a 'National Liberal' in 1945 and accepted office under Winston Churchill in the 1950s. He was appointed Home Secretary, which gave him responsibility for Welsh affairs. Huw T. Edwards was a leading trade unionist in north Wales. He was a Labour councillor and stood for parliament but was not elected. He was appointed chairman of the Council of Wales in 1948, and sat on other appointed bodies, such as the Welsh Tourist Board. Harry Midgley was a leading member of the Northern Ireland Labour Party in the 1930s. In 1943 he became the first non-Unionist to serve in the Northern Ireland government. Dehra Parker was elected a member of the Northern Irish parliament in 1921 for the Unionist Party, and was the only woman to serve in the Northern Irish government before that parliament was suspended by the Conservative government of Edward Heath in 1972.

In the main, the political careers of these individuals came to an end in the late 1950s and the mid 1960s, within what Christopher Harvie has called 'the moment of British nationalism' that ended around 1970.[3] Tweedsmuir's career continued for a further decade, providing an opportunity to examine the ability of an individual to cope with quite significant challenges to her sense of identity.

All these individuals reflected upon their political lives within the context of the Union. As members of the smaller nations of the United Kingdom, they were all well aware of its multi-national nature.[4] Each considered the means by which the tensions entailed in relationships inside a single state might be resolved. Examination of these individuals suggests that the mid-twentieth century did not encompass the beginnings of the unravelling of the United Kingdom, but instead was a period during which unionist identities continued to be formed.

The mid-twentieth century has been seen as a fairly uncomplicated and stable yet transitory period. Harvie's description of it as only a 'moment' has the clear implication that it was short-lived and in the past. Likewise David Marquand has argued that 'the legitimacy, the authority and the efficacy of the British state were on a rising curve from around 1920 to around 1950; and ... from around 1960 to the present day they have been on a declining curve.' David Powell has argued that 'the decades between the 1920s and the 1960s offer an atypical interlude of stability in the domestic relation of the British nations with their central government'.[5] Because of its 'momentary' nature (it was a long moment), the period is usually given historical consideration only in order to draw attention to the subsequent 'break-up of Britain' from the late 1960s onwards. I argue that the continuing formation of unionism in the mid-twentieth century created a remarkably solid edifice. It was the outcome of numerous negotiations between multiple identities that took place in the minds of all those engaged in politics within the multi-national state.[6] The Union was stable but not static. Its constant renegotiation was evidence of its strength.

Support for the Acts of Union had come to be defined as 'Unionism' in the late nineteenth century as the Liberal leader William Gladstone was personally converted to supporting Irish Home Rule. Both within his party and without, his opponents branded themselves as 'Unionists', defenders of the constitutional status quo in relation to Ireland. The Liberal Party fractured when 93 of its MPs voted against the first Irish Home Rule Bill. These rebels subsequently entered an electoral alliance with the Conservative Party. This process has been seen as part of the drift of property towards the politics of class when the Conservative Party consolidated itself as the protector of property rights. In Ireland, Scotland and Wales the land and national questions were entwined with those of class. Land reform by the Liberals in the 'Celtic fringe' was part of their response to the plurality of the United Kingdom. Hence the drift of property towards the Conservatives was also about the national question. The Conservatives recognized this in changing the name of their party to the Unionist Party. The party in England reduced the emphasis on Unionism in the 1920s, as the 'problem' of Ireland and Ulster ceased to haunt them and they turned to the politics of anti-socialism.[7] The Scottish party, however, retained the name until 1965, and the Northern Irish party, which formally broke from the British Conservatives in 1974, has continued to use the name.

Many individuals throughout the 'Conservative' party described themselves with different labels for decades after 1886, reminders of their Unionist past and continuing commitment. The Liberal Unionists only formally merged with the Conservative Party in 1912 and retained their influence. Neville Chamberlain continued to call himself a Unionist into the 1930s and as late as 1948 there were twenty-three constituency associations affiliated to the National Union of Conservative and Constitutional Associations with 'Liberal' in their title.[8] This indicates that Unionism was often more than just Conservatism. This was confirmed by the ability of the party to make inroads into some working-class areas to a much greater extent than might be expected within the paradigms of the politics of class. The politics of the Union could be used to attract the support of many working-class voters in Lancashire, the West Midlands and the West of Scotland who were Unionists rather than Conservatives.[9]

Furthermore unionism was much more widespread than Unionism alone.[10] Many historians have pointed out that while Unionism is associated with the Conservative Party, unionism is the belief that Scotland, Wales, Northern Ireland and England should all remain part of the United Kingdom.[11] As such, unionism can be found in each of the all-British political parties. Gladstone saw concessions to Irish national identity as a means of strengthening the Union. In 1880 he told the House of Commons that

> Those who endangered the Union with Ireland were the party that maintained there an alien church, an unjust land law ... and *the true supporters of the union* are those who firmly uphold the supreme authority of parliament, but exercise that authority to bind the three nations by the indissoluble tie of liberal and equal laws.[12]

Gladstone believed that the Union could accommodate and be strengthened by national diversity. The Liberal Party throughout the twentieth century continued to adhere to such a position, though pursuing devolution was rarely its priority. The Labour Party enthusiastically shared this approach before 1924, but its entry into government suggested that an all-British policy directed centrally from Westminster might hasten social progress rather more than devolving power away from the centre. In that sense, Labour's unionism was never static but developed and receded in response to its political fortunes. In each of the main parties, therefore, there was a determination to see the continued existence of the United Kingdom as a unitary nation-state. Unionism was as diverse as the United Kingdom itself, and it is this diversity and the variety of forms of Unionism that I examine in this book.

Unionism entailed a form of establishing relationships between the various parts of the United Kingdom. It was a dynamic force, seeking to find equilibrium in the inner-outer relationship, between the 'peripheries' and the 'core'.[13] None of the individuals discussed in this book considered their relationship to England/London as being that of colony to metropolis but rather they saw themselves in relationships between equals. They believed they had something distinctive yet not subordinate to offer to the Union.

None of them considered the Union as the only point of identification in their lives. They fitted a variety of identities together, so that the Union/British nation was not an abstract concept, but was part of their everyday lives and cultural being. There were direct connections between their personal, political and national identities. Their lives were lived within the Union and the Union was internalized. This can be seen in their membership not only of political parties but in their wider involvement in civil society. Graeme Morton has suggested that 'Because the state in Great Britain enshrined more than one civil society there was no coherent British nation-state, no coherent and overwhelming sense of Britishness. In contrast, and importantly so, this disjuncture provides the sustenance of four national identities.'[14] The latter part of his interpretation is certainly useful in understanding how differences between civil societies contributed to a sense of nationhood separate from a monolithic Britishness, but Britishness invoked a sense of similarity of objectives to which the different civil societies sought to progress. The position of civil societies within the Union was complex. Scotland had separate legal, educational and religious systems and Wales had a range of separate cultural institutions, while Northern Ireland had a separate and subordinate state. The individuals discussed in this book operated within these separate civil societies. So, for example, Tom Johnston was editor of a Scottish left-wing newspaper, the *Forward*, and after 1945 chairman of the Scottish Tourist Board. Yet he, like many of the others discussed in this book, also participated in a civil society that crossed the internal borders of the United Kingdom. He was president of the British Electrical Development Association between 1958 and 1960 and a member of the board of governors of the British Broadcasting Corporation. Civil societies in the United Kingdom were both national and transnational, encouraging Scottishness, Welshness and Northern Irishness alongside Britishness.

Benefits were gained for each nation-society through negotiation with the single multi-national polity at Westminster. Negotiations were frequently uneven and operated with different methods, so that the existence of the Northern Ireland parliament meant that a regional government negotiated with the United Kingdom government. Scotland's negotiations, from 1884 onwards, were conducted between the Scottish Secretary (from 1926 a Secretary of State) and the British cabinet. The situation in Wales was different again, and changed throughout the twentieth century. While in the 1950s there had been a minister within the Home Office responsible for Welsh affairs, the office of Welsh Secretary with a post in the cabinet was only established in 1964.

The relationship was not straightforwardly one between Scotland, Wales and Northern Ireland on the one hand and England on the other. David Lloyd George, a Welshman, clearly had Union interests at heart when he negotiated the Anglo-Irish Treaty in 1921. Nearly half of the twentieth-century British Prime Ministers have had significant connections with nations other than England.[15] The allocation of resources to the different parts of the United Kingdom depended on establishing broad based alliances across territorial boundaries. This encouraged the development and enabled the success of parties that were pan-British, crossing internal borders. In Scotland and Wales, the negotiations for distribution of resources frequently took place within the parties that could win parliamentary control at Westminster. All-British politics acted as an essential integrative force. The Government of Ireland Act of 1920 and the Anglo-Irish Treaty of 1921 severed Northern Ireland from the party system. Ulster Unionists had not wanted devolution but accepted it because it seemed to provide them with a safeguard for their identity. The Unionists recognized that sovereignty continued to rest at Westminster. This lessened the likelihood of tension between Belfast and London, because 'the pressures that led to devolution in Northern Ireland were not, as is usually the case, centrifugal, but centripetal'.[16] However, the Unionists voiced mistrust of the British Liberal and Labour parties, because their pluralism sympathized with Irish nationalism. Anxiety in Unionist Northern Ireland about what Britain might do reinforced the sense of separation from British politics, which encouraged politics based on ethno-sectarianism rather than those based on social and economic policies related to social class.

The British world within which most of these individuals operated was not confined to the archipelago off the north-west coast of continental Europe, but extended, with the British Empire, to the four corners of the globe.[17] Each of the individuals devoted differing amounts of attention to the issue of Empire and global politics, but nonetheless all were forced at certain points to confront the imperial nature of their polity. The Union related to the nations in the United Kingdom but the association of new nations in the Empire and Commonwealth provided some of these individuals with models for development, whether national or social. The Union made the Scottish, Welsh and Northern Irish partners in the imperial project, and in differing degrees all the individuals discussed in this book consented to that partnership. The United Kingdom's global position and power in the mid-twentieth century was seen as a benevolent force. In the Empire, Britishness was associated with a genius for government and the desire to pass on its knowledge and skills to the colonized. The Union enabled Scotland, Wales and Northern Ireland to participate in a global enterprise that would have been far beyond their capabilities outside the Union. Most of the individuals I discuss consciously drew attention to the distinctive contributions their sub-nations played in the Empire and foreign policy, and particularly in the First and Second World Wars. The benefits of the Union were not solely economic but spiritual as well. As part of the Union, a global role was open to these small nations, which could represent themselves as part of a progressive international power and defenders of liberty and democracy.

This does, of course, raise the question of the end of Empire as the major contributor to the 'break up of Britain' in the last three decades of the twentieth century. David Marquand has seen this as the crucial factor forcing the questioning of the Union and what it means to be British. He has argued that 'The British state was, by definition, a global state ... whig imperialist Britain was Britain :.. Empire was not an optional extra for the British ... it was their reason for being British as opposed to English or Scots or Welsh'.[18] I argue that Empire was important to nearly all those discussed in this book but it was never fundamental to their identities. Lady Priscilla Tweedsmuir, for example, renegotiated her support for the Union in the context of decolonization and the United Kingdom's turn to Europe without abandoning a belief in the potential for a global British role.

The individuals whom I discuss represent the diversity of unionism in the middle of the twentieth century. Some were Conservatives (Elliot, Tweedsmuir, Parker), some had Liberal origins (the Lloyd Georges), some were, or had been, socialists (Johnston, Edwards, Midgley). All have been selected because, while they were prominent figures, they never held the highest political posts. In United Kingdom politics, the highest offices have tended to draw their holders increasingly towards a Britannic approach. David Lloyd George did retain a sense of Welshness, Stanley Baldwin's Englishness was seen as central to his political being, Ramsay MacDonald continued to espouse a folkish Scottishness. Nevertheless the major concerns of all three were with the governance of the United Kingdom (and its imperial possessions and partners). In many ways this provides greater evidence for the dominating influence of the Union and Britishness within the multinational context of the UK. However, it often seemed that holding office as Prime Minister diminished the significant contribution of sub-national identities. The prominent but subordinate status of the individuals discussed in this book enabled them to hold on to distinctive sub-national identities within their unionism, allowing for greater discussion of the connections and tensions between their multiple identities of place. Individuals from Scotland, Wales and Northern Ireland, rather than England, have been selected in order to demonstrate that unionism was a product of the peripheries as well as of the core. Unionism was not simply Englishness enlarged. Some of the individuals were more oriented towards the United Kingdom than others. For example, Elliot wanted to operate at the highest levels of United Kingdom politics, while Parker saw her orbit as being entirely around Northern Ireland. Gender and class identities also come into play. It is probably unrepresentative to consider three women out of eight individuals because this is disproportionate to the contribution of women in high politics and civil society in the mid-twentieth century. Moreover, Parker was the only woman to serve in Northern Ireland government and Tweedsmuir was one of only a handful of women Conservative MPs. Nonetheless, it is necessary to consider the ways in which unionism was gendered and this certainly does not mean just for women. Masculinities played significant, though often unspoken, roles in unionist politics, not least through military service. When Elliot was excluded from Winston

Churchill's wartime government in 1940 he (and other appeasers) rejoined the army in an attempted restoration of the manliness of their patriotism.[19] Horizontal class identities also overlay vertical union and national identities. Edwards and Johnston consciously devoted themselves to the working class, while Parker and Elliot were from different landed backgrounds. Social origins and adherences affected the way in which they viewed the Union.

There is some disparity in the treatment of each individual, resulting from the differing quantities and qualities of source material available. Private papers are available for Elliot, Tweedsmuir, the Lloyd Georges and Edwards. Johnston left few papers, and none at all are available for Parker. Academic biographies have been written about Johnston and Midgley (both by Graham Walker), and Megan Lloyd George. Some shorter scholarly essays about Gwilym Lloyd-George have been written by J. Graham Jones. There is a biography of Elliot written by a friend. Johnston and Edwards wrote memoirs, as did the husband of Lady Tweedsmuir. There is little writing on Parker, who remains the most elusive of all these individuals. Her invisibility emphasises the masculinist nature of Northern Ireland Unionism.

The last three decades of the twentieth century have been described as signifying a crisis of Britishness and the break-up of Britain.[20] This has encouraged a teleological approach to the early and mid-twentieth century, as the origins of political nationalisms in Wales and Scotland are sought. Richard Weight, for example, has published an 800-page book that examines the period since 1940 to explain 'why the British people stopped thinking of themselves as British and began to see themselves instead as Scots, Welsh and English'.[21] Such approaches presume that the 'unravelling' of the United Kingdom in the late twentieth century was the outcome of an inevitable process, and this has created a research context that looks for incompatibilities in the multiple identities necessarily adopted within the multinational state. In addition, recent historiography has tended to focus separately on the 'four nations' of the United Kingdom, with emphasis being placed on the differences and separate development of politics in Scotland, Wales and Northern Ireland.[22] This book, on the other hand, seeks to explore the 'British' nature of politics in the United Kingdom. There was a sense of consent among this range of disparate political figures that the Union was something worth defending. Their political lives reveal that a sense of common interest accounted for the persistence of the United Kingdom in the twentieth century.

1
Scotland and the Union

In a multinational state, relations between the constituent nations are always likely to be dynamic rather than static, even when they appear remarkably tranquil. Between the 1920s and 1960s, there were almost no demands for separation from the United Kingdom from within Scotland, and few demands even for Home Rule, as a legislative assembly subordinate to the United Kingdom parliament has been described. Demands for reform were episodic rather than part of any consistent campaign. The Union between England and Scotland was accomplished in 1707, and was dynastically resisted by the Jacobites, followers of the Stuarts, in 1715 and 1745. There had been substantial anti-Scottish agitation by John Wilkes and his supporters in the late eighteenth century, but by the mid-nineteenth century the relationship between the two nations had settled down into one of apparent mutual benefit.[1] Tranquillity, however, is relative and, like dynamism, has a history. The tranquillity of the Union relationship rested on the continued recognition of Scottish difference from England within the Union. As Graeme Morton has remarked about the relationship in the nineteenth century: 'Scots be not Britons, but be Scots *and* Britons.'[2] Scottish national identity had not been absorbed within a new and monolithic British identity but had come into a negotiable relationship with a more extensive identity. The Scottish bargaining position was certainly strengthened by the maintenance of distinctive Scottish institutions in religion, education and law, which enabled the continued existence of a separate Scottish civil society.[3] This provided a basis for a civil identity, which on the one hand rested on the operation of politics at a local level, and on the other hand rested on national (Scottish) politics that took place in London. Walter Elliot, Tom Johnston and Lady Priscilla Tweedsmuir provide representative

10

examples of Scottish politicians who reconciled the process of acting for Scotland through negotiation of their lives and politics through British parties and institutions. The intention of this chapter is to provide the historical and political background for the subsequent discussion of the lives of Elliot, Johnston and Tweedsmuir. It outlines the reasons for the weakness of nationalism in Scotland, while making no assumptions that this represented a diversion from what should have been. It does so by examining the way in which the Liberal, Labour and Conservative parties were able to represent the diverse varieties of political Scottishness in twentieth century Britain.

In the nineteenth and twentieth centuries, there were significant factors that created tensions within the Union between Scotland and England, but these were certainly outweighed by those factors that emphasized a common 'British' destiny. While 'nationalist' organizations came and went in the nineteenth and early twentieth centuries, it was not until the 1930s that a more or less permanent nationalist party emerged. The existence of an effective separatist party, providing a feasible alternative to the Union, would, of itself, have been an essential agent in straining the Union. However, by the middle of the twentieth century, much nationalist effort was expended on explaining why the Scottish National Party, formed in 1934, had failed despite its belief that most Scottish people held a distinct Scottish national consciousness. Some blamed the eccentricities of individual Scottish nationalists, or the tendency for most people to 'live from day to day'.[4] Others considered that while 'Every second Scot will tell you he is "a Scottish Nationalist at heart"' there was 'the fact that the average Scot is unconsciously Anglicised ... He wants Home Rule, but he doesn't want to be a Nationalist!'[5] In April 1945, Dr Robert McIntyre had been elected for Motherwell for the SNP, but his victory can be seen as an anti-government vote in the context of wartime coalition politics rather than a sincere endorsement of separatist nationalism. Independent candidates had experienced remarkable success in all parts of the United Kingdom because of the electoral truce between the main parties. McIntyre was defeated in the general election of July 1945 that swept Labour into government in a shift to the left in England, Wales and Scotland.[6] The SNP did not witness inexorable advance but persistent weakness. Membership in 1934 was claimed at 10,000, while in the late 1940s it was only 4,000, with many Nationalists operating in Dr John MacCormick's 'Scottish Convention'. This succeeded in gathering two million signatures on a Covenant for Home Rule but its numerical success can perhaps be accounted for as a protest against government from its natural opponents rather than as nationalist triumph. Certainly in 1950 and 1951, the working-class vote in Scotland was consolidated behind the British Labour Party despite its rejection of the Covenant.

The Nationalists' failure was only in small part due to its own actions. There were too many elements of unity in the United Kingdom for separatism or even legislative devolution to make headway and for a nationalist party to move out from the political margins. Despite protests over royal titles, the monarchy was a force for Anglo-Scottish unity throughout the nineteenth and twentieth centuries. Indeed, protests about royal titles were themselves not expressions of nationalism so much as a desire for consideration of Scottish distinctiveness within the Union. In 1953, when Queen Elizabeth's title had to be considered in terms of the revision of the relationship of the United Kingdom to its former imperial possessions, many in Scotland protested that because Elizabeth I had not ruled Scotland then this new Elizabeth should not be crowned Elizabeth II. This was neither an anti-royal nor anti-British position to take, but a desire to prevent 'a gross injustice to Scotland' within the Union.[7] The solution within Scotland was to ensure that pillar boxes, almost the only place in which Britons came face to face with the royal numeral, bore the inscription 'ER' rather than 'EIIR' as they did elsewhere in the UK.

The political space for nationalists was reduced even more significantly by the existence of political parties that considered themselves to be 'British'. Even the Communist Party designated itself as a party of Great Britain, and it had some of its most significant support in Scotland and Wales.[8] The major parties, however, were more important in maintaining the Union.

In the third quarter of the nineteenth century, the Liberal Party was dominant in Scotland. The party was a coalition of social groups, aristocratic, middle and working class, held together by religion, free trade and reform, as was the party in England and Wales. The bond was reinforced by recognition of the distinct national aspirations of the party's supporters.[9] In the 1880s, the Highland politics of the Crofter MPs challenged Liberalism only to find themselves absorbed within the party once at Westminster, not by some conspiratorial design but because the party was genuinely if reluctantly responsive to pluralist demands. Under William Gladstone and Herbert Asquith, 'the Liberals were good at managing and absorbing Celtic separatism, turning a potentially destructive force into an important asset for both the stability of the United Kingdom and the electoral success of their own party'.[10] In the nineteenth century, the Liberals did well, often functioning as the party of Scottish aspirations. The split in the party over Irish Home Rule strengthened Conservatism by leavening it with Liberal Unionism. Despite the temporary success of the efforts of the Young Scots to revive Liberalism in the Edwardian period, the Liberals declined in Scotland as elsewhere in the UK as class politics and the First World War added to their troubles. Between 1918 and 1987, the Liberals only won more than ten Scottish seats in the general elections of 1923 and 1929.[11] Throughout the mid-twentieth century, the Liberals had a policy of Scottish Home Rule but little support.[12] Scottish nationalism alone was not enough to secure Scottish votes.

Labour certainly benefited from the Liberal decline. They had contributed to the Liberals' troubles in many ways. In late Victorian and Edwardian Britain, they inherited the mantle of the pluralist party, professing the class politics of the cities as well as the distinctive demands for Scottish Home Rule. Michael Keating and David Bleiman have argued that 'support for Home Rule in the early days was an integral part of the character of the Scottish Labour Party, part of its shared background with radicalism'.[13] This relationship continued through Tom Johnston's formation of the Highland Land League in 1909, the Clydeside MPs distinctive Scottishness between the wars and the Home Rule Bills of 1924 and 1927.

It would however be a mistake to consider only those parties committed to establishing a legislature to confirm Scottish nationality as capable of advance within Scotland. Labour's position continued to improve in Scotland after 1924 when Ramsay MacDonald as first Labour Prime Minister had displayed his lack of concern with Home Rule for his native land by not allowing the 1924 Home Rule bill parliamentary time. Instead, Labour became the party of housing and employment, which seemed to be more achievable within a planned British economy rather than a decentralized Scottish economy. The political career of Tom Johnston provides an opportunity to examine the reconciliation of Scottish identity operating within British Labour politics.

The Liberals in the nineteenth century and Labour in the twentieth did well because they could operate as both British and Scottish parties simultaneously. They may have agitated most for political devolution when they were in opposition but they could best achieve more for Scotland when they were in government. The Young Scots, for example, wanted to secure Home Rule for Scotland on the one hand and the election of a Liberal government for the United Kingdom on the other. They were hostile to English candidates in Scottish seats and represented a distinctively Scottish interest, yet championed British Liberalism.[14]

The Conservatives, because of appalling electoral performance in Scotland in the late twentieth century, have widely been considered to have been a party waiting for its own demise, unable to represent Scotland because its focus was too much on the English-dominated United Kingdom. Yet, like the Liberal and Labour parties, the Unionist party as it was officially called in Scotland between 1912 and 1965 was also a 'multinational "coalition" party'.[15] The Scottish Unionists did their best to benefit from the Liberal decline. In the 1920s they called effectively on a shared anti-socialism with former Liberals.[16] In 1931, there were proportionally more Liberals and National Liberals in Scotland than in England, as the Unionists continued to build a 'national' coalition against Labour.[17] The moderate and progressive Conservatism of inter-war Unionists such as Walter Elliot, Noel Skelton, Bob Boothby and the Duchess of Atholl was frequently palatable to Liberals. John Maclay exemplified the success of former Liberals in the party and the tolerance shown towards them. He stood in elections as 'National Liberal and Conservative,' which did not prevent him serving as Secretary of State for Scotland between 1957 and 1962, when he would alarm political acquaintances with the phrase, 'I'll have to find out what the Tories think.'[18]

This also signified the extent to which the Conservatives had built a coalition to oppose tampering with the Union. This had emerged in opposition to Irish Home Rule in 1886. Ireland, or more specifically Ulster, was close to Scotland, both geographically and politically, and hostility to Catholic Home Rule in Ireland could be mobilized as hostility to Irish immigrants in Scotland.[19] But the Conservatives' subsequent success, while enabled by the coalition with Liberal Unionism, was not wholly parasitic upon it. Conservatism was also able to sustain itself in Scotland by its appeal to Scottishness. British Conservatism was in many senses associated with 'Englishness'. Some leaders were exclusively English considering the 'periphery' with contempt. Lord Salisbury remarked of an invitation to Scotland that 'it's a long way off and it's an awful climate'.[20] Such insensitivity allowed the opponents of Conservatism to associate the image of the party with aristocratic Englishness, even within serious historical writing. Jack Brand's interpretation of the leaders of Scottish Conservatism was that 'The majority of these leaders might be of Scottish origin but they were largely educated in England and their orientation was towards the centre of government which was, obviously, in London.'[21] James Kellas has supported such assumptions with evidence about the education of Conservative Scottish Secretaries. Of the fifteen in office between 1895 and 1990, thirteen had had some part of their education in England. Only two, Walter Elliot and Malcolm Rifkind, had been wholly educated in Scotland. Six, including these two, had had some part of their education in Scotland.[22] This begs a series of questions. Did education in England make them English or British in outlook? Did they become Anglo-Scottish (and the balance within this hyphenated identity could be varied)? And should such an Anglo-Scottish identity be compared more closely to Anglo-Irishness or Anglo-Welshness?

Vernon Bogdanor, from his vantage point at the end of the 1970s, suggested that the Conservative Party had no consistent policy on devolution towards Scotland and Wales.[23] A lack of consistent policy does not, however, always signify a lack of consistent thought. As well as the sustenance of the institutions of the United Kingdom (monarchy, Empire and Church), Scottish Conservatives consistently sought to uphold Scottish post-Union institutions. The Church of Scotland and the Scottish legal system were natural homes for the conservative-minded, and Conservatives such as Walter Elliot championed the Scottish education system. Conservatives also granted new institutions to Scotland. It was a Conservative government that set up the office of the Scottish Secretary in 1885; it was a Conservative government that raised the status of this office to cabinet rank as the Secretary of State for Scotland in 1926. Conservative-dominated governments raised the number of under-secretaries and ministers within the Scottish Office in the 1920s and 1950s. The Conservative-dominated National government transferred the Scottish Office from London to Edinburgh in the 1930s.[24] The Checklands have commented that 'It was a curious circumstance that the Conservatives did more to recognize Scottish claims than the Liberal Party so favoured by the Scots.'[25] But it is only curious if one starts from the premise that Unionism and Scottishness were in some way incompatible, and that premise was, for much of the late nineteenth and twentieth centuries, untenable. As the discussion of Walter Elliot in this chapter will show, de-centralization of power was seen as a strong stick with which to beat the socialism of Labour as London-based government.

The Conservatives and even more so the Liberal Unionists had confidence in their Scottishness based on its acceptance by a substantial part of the Scottish electorate.[26] A brief narrative of the outcome of elections in Scotland reveals long-term Unionist success. What concerns us most here is the share of the vote given to Unionist candidates rather than the number of seats won because the first-past-the-post system can mask levels of support for minority parties. In 1906, a bad year for the Unionists across the UK, the party secured 38.2 per cent of the vote. They recovered slightly in December 1910 to 42.6 per cent, but the Liberals still achieved more than 53 per cent of the vote and Labour got 3.6 per cent. Before 1914, therefore, an unpopular policy of Tariff Reform and a 'progressive' alliance held the Unionist vote down but four out of ten Scottish voters still supported Unionist candidates.

In 1918 the Unionists and their coalition allies secured 49.9 per cent of the vote in Scotland. The 1920s were a decade of three-party politics, and the Unionists' fortunes depended on the health of Liberalism. In 1922, the first election in which Ireland was removed from British politics since the 1880s, the Unionists took 42 per cent of the vote, compared to 21.5 per cent for the Liberals and 32.2 per cent for Labour. There was 'a significant working-class Unionist vote in Glasgow' despite Labour's advance in the city.[27] The following year, Tariff Reform returned to haunt the party and its vote fell to 31.6 per cent. It recovered to 40.8 per cent in 1924, compared to Labour's 41.1 per cent. The election of 1929, when the party got 35.9 per cent, was the Unionists' worst electoral performance until February 1974. Otherwise the 1930s to the 1960s saw Scotland providing the Unionists with results comparable to the rest of the United Kingdom. Fighting on a National (that is, UK) ticket in 1931 and 1935, the Unionists achieved 54.5 per cent and 49.8 per cent respectively in Scotland. In 1945, the year of Labour's first landslide, the Unionists stood up better in Scotland getting 41.1 per cent compared to 40.3 per cent in England. The three subsequent elections saw major advances, from 44.8 per cent in 1950, to 48.6 per cent in 1951 and 50.1 per cent in 1955. This was effectively as a single party even though 8.6 per cent of the vote had been cast for 'National Liberals' like John Maclay.

Historians have identified 1959, when the Unionist vote fell to 47.2 per cent, as the beginning of divergence from 'British' politics and the decline of Unionism.[28] Richard Finlay, however, warns that the weakness of Unionism should not be prematurely located. 'A case,' he argues, 'could be made that the Conservative decline before 1974 in Scotland was more apparent than real.'[29] In the three elections after 1959 the Unionists still retained the support of four out of every ten Scottish voters. In the two elections of 1974 the party did very badly. The vote in February was 32.9 per cent and in October it was only

24.7 per cent. Three out of four Scottish voters now rejected Unionism (though not necessarily unionism). However, the Labour Party too had seen its vote decline. Its poorest performance since 1935 had been 44.5 per cent of the Scottish vote, yet in the elections of 1974 it secured just over 36 per cent. The SNP and to a lesser extent the Liberals were taking votes from both major parties. Even at this late stage, the Conservative vote in Scotland recovered to 30 per cent in 1979 in the wake of the failure of the devolution referendum.[30]

The dominance of Unionism in Scotland between the 1920s and the 1950s should tell against the presumption of the inevitability of the incompatible nature of Unionism and Scottishness. Kellas has pointed out that the Conservative and Unionist Party 'has always been the party of British nationalism: of the Union and the Empire'.[31] For much of the twentieth century this did it little harm and may well have been a force for good in many elections. Unionism certainly provided a popular alternative rallying cry to socialism and Labour in Scotland.

British Unionists generally considered that the movement of history was towards bigger political units. Lord Salisbury in the late nineteenth century thought that progress meant the absorption of lesser nationalities and that nationalism was anachronistic: 'It is the agglomeration and not the comminution of states to which civilization is constantly tending; it is the fusion and not the isolation of races by which the physical and moral excellence of the species is advanced.'[32] Walter Elliot applied such thinking to Scotland in his 1945 election address declaring that 'We hold by the Treaty of Union' because 'This is no time to break up a union anywhere in the world, where small units have proved in so many cases simply snares for their inhabitants.'[33] Yet most Unionists also believed, at the same time, that the aggregation of states within the UK did not mean the merging of identities to create a single and exclusive British identity. Lord Robert Cecil explained in 1910 that 'under the British Crown, though there are many races, there is but one nationality,' but this did not mean that he expected that a single nationality or Crown meant a lack of diversity.[34] Likewise, Joseph Chamberlain's view that 'the separate nationalities of Welsh, Scots and English were now merely local divisions of the developing British/English imperial race' did not preclude the continued existence of those 'local divisions'.[35] Unionism was aware of difference and it tolerated a range of identities as long as they remained subordinate to British national identity and that they were not expressed through politics.

Unionists could see national distinctiveness generating positive benefits for the Union. In the case of Scotland, the mutual and beneficial relationship between that nation and the leadership of Unionism is apparent in the form of A.J. Balfour.

> If I consider the case I know best (namely my own) [he wrote], I find that within a general regard for mankind, which I hope is not absent nor weak, I am moved by a feeling, especially patriotic in its character for a group of nations who are the authors and guardians of western civilization, for the subgroup which speaks the English language, and whose laws and institutions are rooted in British history, for the communities which compose the British Empire, for the United Kingdom of which I am a citizen, and for Scotland, where I was born, where I live, and where my fathers lived before me. Where patriotisms such as these are not forced into conflict, they are not only consistent with each other, but they may mutually reinforce each other.[36]

Balfour's inter-locking racial, linguistic and historical collectivities strengthened rather than weakened each other. Unionism not only accommodated diversity within the United Kingdom but often welcomed it. The flirtation of some senior Edwardian Unionists, including Austen Chamberlain, Lord Selborne and Walter Long, with federalism and 'Home Rule all round' as a solution to the starkness of Irish Home Rule provides ample evidence of a Unionist belief in the diversity of the United Kingdom. There was a belief that the range of identities in the British Isles could be politically accommodated without jeopardising the continued existence of the United Kingdom.[37]

For many Conservatives, Unionism was a force that allowed the expression of regionalism within the United Kingdom. Neil Evans has argued that 'The United Kingdom ... exhibits a strong degree of integration, though it achieves this partly by means of tolerating diversity.'[38] Such a judgement can equally be applied to the Unionist Party in the first three quarters of the twentieth century.

As well as the monarchy and politics providing integrative forces in Scotland, historians have drawn extensive attention to the way in which Scottishness could be articulated within the framework of the British Empire. 'And,' as Michael Fry, argues in his exhaustive survey of the issue, 'Scots believed they possessed better ideas about Empire than the English, who notoriously had acquired it in a fit of absence of mind.'[39] While the Unionists succeeded in associating themselves most with the Empire, perhaps to their electoral cost in the late twentieth century, no party had a monopoly on imperialism. Elements of the British and Scottish left also embraced imperialism. Lord Rosebery, Liberal Prime Minister in the 1890s, led the Liberal Imperialist wing of the party and saw the Empire as the mission of the British, enabling Scottishness to survive within the greater whole.[40] Among the Clyde-siders, John Wheatley and Tom Johnston saw the Empire providing benefits for the Scottish working class.[41] Even where imperialism was not fully embraced the context of politics and culture in all parts of the United Kingdom was imperial. The meanings of Empire and imperialism were often disputed, but this was as variants of the fact of Empire rather than as significant opposition to that fact.

If the impact of Empire was profound then so would be the end of Empire, its dissolution between 1947, when India and Palestine were jettisoned and 1967, when the United Kingdom abandoned its 'East of Suez' policy. Elliot and Tweedsmuir both participated in the re-adjustment of British policy to decolonization. They did so, though, without losing their faith in the Union. This was possible because both were convinced that the United Kingdom continued to have a global future ahead of it. Elliot thought it possible to build a 'Third British Empire' that would take the changing world situation into account and Tweedsmuir turned her attention to European integration. She believed that Britain's imperial role could be reconciled with the turn to Europe. The end of Empire did not, therefore, meant the end of British global pretensions. As John Darwin has argued, for those involved in the process, 'Decolonization was the continuation of empire by other means.'[42]

There were, therefore, powerful processes in Scotland holding the Union together. The Unionism of the Conservatives was electorally dominant for a remarkably long period. Their vote did fall after 1959 but it was not until the 1970s that the reduction began to look ruinous. The Labour Party was, anyway, full of unionists. Both parties considered it possible to combine political unionism with at least some measure of administrative and civil devolution. There was no national-ist challenge waiting to breakthrough. The main parties could generally accommodate the desires for national distinctiveness. These desires were not external to the parties. The parties were not English creations imposed on the Scottish people. They were British parties, built in Scotland as in England and Wales. Elliot, Johnston and Tweedsmuir wanted to secure material, social and cultural resources for Scotland. They adhered to British parties in order to do so. The SNP remained weak until the mid-1960s. Only 5 per cent of the Scottish electorate voted for it in 1966. In October 1974, nearly one in three Scottish voters, 30.4 per cent gave it their support. This was staggering growth. But 1974 was not representative. Disillusion with both the Conservative and Labour resulted in protest vote that elsewhere in Britain went to the Liberals. There was, of course, a substantial support for nationalism from the 1970s onwards, but the SNP still remained one political representative of Scottishness among others. By 1979, the Conservatives regained an additional 7 per cent share of the vote and Labour a further 5 per cent. There was substantial restructuring of the political field in Scotland in the 1970s and after. The strength of nationalism, however, should not be overestimated. Scottish nationality continued to find expression in the British parties.

2
Scotland and Westminster: The Unionism of Walter Elliot (1888–1958)

Walter Elliot was the leader of Scottish Conservatism in the 1930s. He was a Lowland Scot, concerned with the affairs of state of the United Kingdom as an imperial power. Within Scotland, he was most concerned with Roxburghshire in the rural Borders where he lived, Lanark where he had business interests, and the Glasgow constituency of Kelvingrove, which he represented as a Member of Parliament for most of his political career. In the United Kingdom, his concerns resided at Westminster, where he was an MP from 1918 to 1957 (with only two brief interludes outside parliament in 1923 to 1924 and 1945 to 1946). He held a variety of government posts. He was Parliamentary Under-Secretary of State of Health for Scotland in 1923, Parliamentary Under-Secretary for Scotland between 1924 and 1929, and Financial Secretary to the Treasury between 1931 and 1932. In 1932 he was promoted to the cabinet as Minister of Agriculture and Fisheries. Between 1936 and 1938, still in the cabinet, he returned to the Scottish Office, this time as Secretary of State. In 1938 he was appointed as Minister of Health, a post that he held until the fall of Neville Chamberlain as Prime Minister in May 1940. While he was in Churchill's shadow cabinet in the late 1940s he was not offered any government post commensurate with his seniority and instead he played the part of backbench elder statesman until his death in 1958.

Few politicians in the middle decades of the twentieth century failed to come face to face with the imperial nature of the United Kingdom. The Empire was an important issue in Elliot's political career. He found himself chairman of the research committee of the Empire Marketing Board in the 1920s, concerned with issues of imperial agriculture in the 1930s, higher education in West Africa in the 1940s, and the incipient problems and opportunities of decolonization in the 1950s. For Elliot, the Union was the adhesive that bound together Scotland and the Empire. This chapter examines each of these three concerns to explore the juxtaposition of Elliot's personal and national identities.

Elliot and Scotland

Walter Elliot was born in Lanark in 1888 into a successful and prosperous farming family.[1] His father was a forward-looking and modern agricultural businessman who ran a large sheep farm called Harwood with six hundred acres of arable land at Bonchester Bridge near Hawick in the Scottish Borders. He also established a successful agricultural auctioning business in Lanark. Walter Elliot retained this farm and business throughout his life, and it not only provided income but also kept him attached to the particular locality that he always considered to be his portion of Scotland. Elliot's was a lowland non-Celtic Scottishness.[2] In his sympathetic biography of Elliot, Colin Coote, editor of the *Daily Telegraph* and close friend of Elliot for four decades, wrote that 'farming was in his blood'.[3] The depths of Elliot's attachment to Bonchester Bridge were shown when Churchill failed to offer him a government position during the Second World War. Elliot returned to the army in which he had served during the Great War and as deputy assistant adjutant general of Western Command he organized arrangements to deal with refugees in the event of a German invasion. Letters to his wife Katharine implored her for more news from their farm. In the midst of war he associated his patriotism with a particular locality.

That patriotism was on his mind was clear. Stationed in Chester, one of his letters during the summer of 1940 remarked that 'England this morning was looking very lovely after the rain, and proper to fight for. We shall give the old Hun a great knock if he comes.'[4] But his interest was more in Harwood. On the 16 August, he wrote: 'I got your letter from the Hawick Mart and very charmed I was to have it. I could almost smell the strong animal smell, and feel the shouldering about amongst the sheep. I note the prices. Templehall isn't so much up, but there seems to be a whacking rise in the Lurgie Cheviots from 14/9 to 23/-.'[5] The next day he wrote: 'Meanwhile I am interested in the Harwood news. Chiefly pleased by the news of getting in the Redsmuir hay, which will be a sheet anchor in the winter. The turnips were bound to be all right, but I am glad to hear of them. The rape and day-nettles is a characteristic crop of that field.'[6] These letters were not necessarily unconsciously written, for as early as 19 July 1940 he told Katharine that he was 'keeping the Scottish letters for a little bunch in the Harwood book "Harwood in War-time."'[7] In his moment of depression over being excluded from government, Elliot had turned to Scotland and farming for consolation.

Elliot always considered that farming was more than of just personal importance. In particular, he recognized its importance for Scotland, criticizing another MP in 1951 for not raising agriculture in a House of Commons' debate on the Highlands. 'No debate on Scottish affairs,' he said, 'even a general one, would be complete without a certain study of agriculture.'[8] And as Minister of Agriculture in the early 1930s, he considered agriculture of British national and imperial importance. In his 'maiden' speech as minister, he referred to the anxiety occasioned by the depression and political crisis. People were beginning to

> fear that something is happening to break the spring of this nation, and that if you lose agriculture, you not only lose your industry; you lose your life. If a nation loses the art of producing food from its soil it is not as if it loses some kind of skill or other, it is as though a man loses the power to breathe.[9]

Elliot was connected to Scotland in many other ways. He was educated entirely within the country, culminating in eight years at Glasgow University, where he studied sciences and medicine. He was editor of the *Glasgow University Magazine*, president of the Union, and a member of the Fabian Society. If he had found moderate politics, he had also found patriotism. He was a member of the Officer Training Corps and in April 1913 joined the Special Reserve of the Royal Army Medical Corps. While his life had been 'Scottish' his membership of the British Army meant that he was called up in August 1914 when the United Kingdom declared war on Germany after the violation of Belgian neutrality. By December 1914, Elliot had been promoted to medical officer to the Royal Scots Greys on the Western Front.[10] He showed particular bravery and was awarded two Military Crosses in 1917 for providing medical aid under heavy shelling, first at Arras in February and then in November at the Battle of Cambrai. The appreciation of his fellow officers was displayed when they presented him with a 'miniature reproduction of the Scots Grey in Princes Street, Edinburgh' in August 1918.[11] The statue had been erected in 1906 to signify Scotland's commemoration of one of its regiments in the British Army, and now Elliot was honoured in imitation of that national commemoration for his individual patriotism and bravery. The First World War increased Elliot's engagement with the Union, drawing his attention towards British issues in tandem with his ontinuing concerns with Scotland.

In December 1918 Elliot stood for the parliamentary seat of Lanark and won. Elliot's political life henceforth took him to the centre of the Union. There is an apocryphal story associated with Elliot's entry into politics that is used to signify the moderate nature of his politics. Asked to stand for the seat his reply was reputed to have been 'Yes, which side?'[12] However, it is clear that Elliot was already a unionist; his Scottish life had been accommodated with the structures of the UK, and when he moved from military to political service it was a British role that he sought. This did not mean that he became any the less 'Scottish' at that point. Coote considered that both 'Scotland and Westminster made the major fibres of his being.'[13]

Unionists did very well in the khaki election of 1918, securing just under half the vote. As Christopher Harvie argues, 'They were the patriotic party of the "Anglo-Scottish" Empire – ex-officers as agents, ex-servicemen in the British Legion.'[14] Elliot continued to use his military rank throughout his political career and a senior civil servant in the Scottish Office serving under him in the 1930s wrote that Elliot's 'mind was indelibly marked by the War.'[15] Despite, or perhaps because of, extremely high casualty figures the war remained popular in Scotland, which had shown its exceptional contribution to the Empire. When it was planned to establish a war museum in London, the Duke of Atholl 'expressed the emphatic opinion that Scotland ought to have its own National War Museum'.[16] The memorial, located in Edinburgh castle, was financed through public subscription and £144,000 had been raised by 1931.[17] As with much of Scotland, the war had drawn Elliot closer to the Union through the idea of common effort and sacrifice.

Elliot's politics have been seen as rather inchoate, but they complemented the moderate Unionism of the 1920s and the 'new Conservatism' favoured by Stanley Baldwin, leader of the party from 1923 to 1937.[18] Baldwin sought to accommodate the Labour Party within the political system while remaining resolutely anti-socialist. He considered it electorally necessary to win former Liberals to voting Conservative through offering a moderate social policy.[19] Much of the party would have preferred more vigorous anti-socialist and anti-trade union policies with fewer concessions to the perceived materialism of the new working-class electorate.[20] Indeed, there were Unionist class warriors in the Scottish party, such as Sir James Lithgow, John Craig and Sir Robert Horne.[21] Elliot, however, was comfortable with

Baldwin's style of Conservatism. Baldwin presented his Conservatism as associated with Englishness, but this was rarely exclusive of the other national identities within the United Kingdom.[22] Elliot's short book *Toryism and the Twentieth Century* supported the ideas associated with Baldwinite thought, and it is unsurprising that Baldwin endorsed the book with a foreword. Elliot argued that, 'in England the beliefs of the Right are descended from the beliefs of a great mass of people held for hundreds of years, based on the observation of life and not on *a priori* reasoning.'[23] Putting aside the significant elision of England and Britain here, Elliot provided detailed exposition for Baldwin's speeches on the continuity and organic nature of Conservatism, based on experience and not on ideology. In his conclusion Elliot provided substantial support for the 'national' nature of Conservatism with his argument that 'History shows the extraordinary strength and persistence of national characteristics, and the success of policy based upon these.'[24] Baldwin considered his Conservatism to be mainly English. Elliot, however, considered his to be Scottish and Unionist.

Elliot suggested that Scots had distinctive characteristics. In his 1934 rectoral address at Aberdeen University, where his prominence in politics gave him a position in civil society, he described the qualities of Scots in contrast to those of the English: 'We can never be by instinct as tolerant as the English, as fair as the English, as forbearing as the English. We must make our special contribution from our special qualities – industry, fury, romance ... Change and crisis have formed our people.'[25] This can be contrasted with Baldwin's emphasis on continuity and timelessness on the formation of Englishness. Elliot accommodated Scotland's turbulent past to its more stable present inside the Union.

When given the freedom of the City of Edinburgh in 1938, Elliot distilled Scottishness to three essential traditions 'of arms, of learning, of equality.'[26] This was combined with a reading of Scottish history that recognized conflict with England. Elliot was prone to providing a long historical overview for any event he sought to explain. In 1920, when explaining the origins of the Great War he began in AD 9 when Roman Legions had been defeated in Germany, and his account of Toryism in the twentieth century began in 1640.[27] The history of Scotland was his great interest. In speech after speech, he referred to the Border wars of the medieval and early modern periods. In a broadcast to Australia during the Second World War he described a journey northwards through Britain. 'Over by Lancaster and Preston,' he said, 'down to Carlisle and the country of the Border wars. Talk about scorched earth

– Scotland had nothing to learn in those old days. "They crossed Liddel at curfew hour – And burned my lonely little tower."'[28] Graeme Morton's designation of nineteenth-century Scottish civil society as Unionist-nationalism seems appropriate here, for Elliot's next point was that the wars had 'kept Scotland independent.'[29] Elliot was a Unionist through and through, but he believed that it had been Scottish determination in the past that had meant that Scotland had entered the Union as an equal partner rather than as a conquered country.

Indeed, Elliot saw a leading role for Scotland in world affairs, within the United Kingdom, but nonetheless distinctive and unique. He told the House of Common in 1951 that

> Scotland is one of the great power houses of modern society. It is one of the foundation states of Europe, if not the whole western world. It is one of the ancient blocks of which Europe is built. I think that we have a contribution all our own to make both to the United Kingdom and to world politics.[30]

Elliot celebrated Scotland and Scottishness and saw the Union as providing the opportunity for Scotland to play a positive role in world affairs. Elliot's Scottishness was not only compatible with the Union but was enabled by it. Elliot saw the Union and Scottishness not only as reconcilable but also as integral to each other.

Elliot and the United Kingdom

Elliot's desire to serve in government was not solely to serve Scotland but also the Union. He eagerly accepted junior posts in the Scottish Office in the 1920s, which was the nursery for his moderate Scottish Conservatism. He dealt with specifically Scottish issues of housing and children's ill health, in both situations encouraging interventionist action by the state, via the Scottish Office. In housing, he established the Scottish National Housing Company, which erected a record number of pre-fabricated houses.[31] In 1927, as chairman of the Empire Marketing Board's research committee, with John Orr (a fellow graduate of Glasgow and close friend) he oversaw an experiment to give free milk to Scottish schoolchildren. When it was shown that the children in the trial grew taller than the average, Elliot put through permissive legislation to enable local authorities in Scotland to continue the scheme.[32] Such initiatives gave the Scottish Unionists a significant place in British Conservatism. I.G.C. Hutchison has described the 'vitality and *élan* of the Scots Tories between the wars'. Five Scottish MPs held cabinet posts outside the Scottish Office, and Elliot's *Toryism and the Twentieth Century* took its place alongside the Duchess of Atholl's *Women and Politics* and Noel Skelton's coining of the phrase 'property-owning democracy' as major contributions to the formation of coherent Conservative thought.[33] They ensured that Conservatism between the wars was British rather than English.

In the 1930s Elliot moved closer still to the centre of UK politics where he faced the two major political problems of the decade: the economic depression and the foreign policy crisis. He did not lose sight of the interconnected nature of Scottish, British and imperial politics.[34] Elliot was fully aware of the depth of economic crisis. His public letter of support for Oswald Mosley's desire to act 'nationally' to overcome the economic and political crisis had potentially damaged his political career. Baldwin had required an explanation for this disloyalty. Elliot said that he was putting country before party.[35] It is little surprise that he felt happy within the National government formed in August 1931 and confirmed in office by the election of October 1931. He served as Financial Secretary to the Treasury until 1932 when he was promoted to be Minister of Agriculture. Both offices placed him at the forefront of dealing with the economic crisis. Elliot's election address of 1935 did not mention Scotland directly, but considered the issues of foreign policy and economics to concern 'the whole nation'.[36] Nonetheless, Elliot felt the sense of anxiety over the future of Scottish national identity occasioned by depression, population decline, Irish immigration and Scottish emigration.[37]

The Unionists in Scotland were concerned about the emergence of a right-wing version of Scottish nationalism that such anxieties were producing. The secession of the office holders of the Cathcart Unionist Association in 1933 to the Scottish Party encouraged this concern. Previously, nationalism had been associated mainly with the left, and Labour and the Independent Labour Party in Scotland, along with the Liberals, had championed Scottish Home Rule. Elliot considered the complaints of the nationalists as 'whining formulae' but nonetheless felt that the National government needed to take the electoral threat of the nationalists seriously, particularly after the unification of the nationalists into the Scottish National Party in 1934.[38] As Scottish Secretary between 1936 and 1938 Elliot appointed the Gilmour Committee to consider devolution of executive powers to Scotland, and in 1938 St Andrew's House in Edinburgh became the home of the

Scottish Office. Elliot still believed that the Scottish Secretary should be mainly resident in London to ensure that he played a full role in UK government. Scotland's contribution was not to be solely within its own borders but would continue to be part of the management of the whole Union's affairs. While Finlay has argued that the crisis of Scottish national identity was deep and severe, indeed almost terminal, given that it appeared that Scotland could only solve its problems through dependency on its bigger southern neighbour, it might be argued that Elliot continued to perceive the relationship as a partnership.[39] Elliot considered that Unionism had to demonstrate that it could respond to the Scottish sense of national distinctiveness. His solutions for Scotland continued to stress the nation's relationship to the Union not as subordinate but equal. In pursuit of this aim, Scotland was subject to more royal visits in the 1930s and in 1938 a major British Empire exhibition was staged in Glasgow. Without underestimating the depths of the scars caused by the economic depression, it might be argued, given some administrative devolution and Scotland's falling unemployment in the late 1930s as armament contracts had their effect, that there was a sense of optimism that the crisis could be overcome through Scottish initiative within the Union.

The other main issue facing British governments in the 1930s related to foreign policy. The British Empire was confronted by expansionist European and Asian powers which challenged it in continental Europe, the Mediterranean, Africa, and the Far East. All the major indicators of British power seemed to point towards appeasement as the only rational policy for an over-stretched great power. British military capability had been pared back as a result of financial constraints, the dominions supported a policy of appeasement, and there were few domestic opponents of the government's policy in the 1930s. There were few consistently anti-appeasement Conservatives and those that there were remained divided. Winston Churchill had isolated himself on the right of the party in opposition to the government's relatively liberal policy in India and in 1936 over his miscalculated stance on the abdication. While Anthony Eden was to resign in February 1938, he chose not to lead opposition to Neville Chamberlain's continued appeasement. The Labour Party remained divided over foreign policy, with only a few such as Hugh Dalton and Ernest Bevin calling for full scale rearmament and vigorous opposition to the expansionist demands of Hitler and Mussolini.[40]

As the 1930s progressed, like many other Conservatives, Elliot became increasingly uneasy about appeasement. However, he continued to support Chamberlain, the Prime Minister after 1937, in the House of Commons. In 1935 Elliot and others within the cabinet had forced the resignation of Samuel Hoare over appeasement of Italy in Abyssinia, and Elliot had a number of close friends who were solidly against the government's policy.[41] These friends put pressure on Elliot to make a stand, becoming increasingly frustrated as he remained in the government as diplomatic crisis after crisis seemed to reveal British weakness. Such pressures, particularly from Colin Coote and Baffy Dugdale, with whom Elliot was having an intimate relationship, only served to draw attention to Elliot's failure to oppose appeasement publicly.[42] Within the cabinet, Chamberlain contemptuously dismissed the arguments of Elliot, Oliver Stanley and Ormsby-Gore as those of the 'Boy's Brigade'.[43]

On New Year's Day 1938 Elliot hinted at the possibilities of the coming cabinet crisis that would result in Eden's resignation. He wrote to Baffy: 'I wonder what one is to make of Neville taking the F[oreign] O[ffice] himself while Anthony is away. It is what ought to be, of course. But it may portend a grip of policy as well as merely signing letters.'[44] Eden resigned, and it is difficult to disagree with Coote that Elliot's 'failure to follow him was probably the turning point of Walter's career. If he had resigned with Eden, his future would have been very different.'[45] Elliot worked hard to justify his failure to resign despite his claim to be opposed to the appeasement policy. He said that he had to accept responsibility for not having pushed harder for rearmament in the cabinet earlier, and that this failure meant that he had to remain to take collective responsibility for subsequent policy. In both March and October 1938 he said that military weakness, for which he shared responsibility, meant that appeasement was the only option.[46]

Elliot wavered at various points. Dugdale wrote in her diary that on 18 September 1938 Elliot 'had made it plain that if he had to choose between giving in altogether and War, he would choose War.'[47] Two days later, Dugdale resigned from the National Labour Party because it was not opposing the steady surrender to Hitler's demands on Czechoslovakia. She was convinced that Elliot would resign from the government, and he led her to believe that he would. At dinner on 20 September he 'affirm[ed] that he *can* pull himself up somewhere on this slippery slope of concession to Hitler.' On 22 September she wrote, 'I believe now he will resign rather than submit to the next demand.' On 30 September she wrote, 'Came down to breakfast to read that in Munich honour died.'[48] Elliot did not resign.

A year later, when Germany invaded Poland, Elliot and ten other Conservatives went to see Chamberlain to demand that he agree to issue an immediate ultimatum to Germany rather than seeking another compromise. They achieved their aim but it was too late to restore Elliot's reputation. Even Chamberlain considered him 'a weak brother in a crisis'.[49] It is little wonder that Elliot was relieved that he was not named as one of the 'guilty men' in the best-selling pamphlet of that name written by three Beaverbrook journalists in the wake of the withdrawal of the British Expeditionary Force from France at Dunkirk.[50] Elliot had, throughout his life, from his university days in the OTC, through his military service and then into politics, acted according to his sense of both Scottish and British patriotism. In the late 1930s, however, his patriotism, as one of those associated with the guilty men 'who took over a great empire, supreme in arms and secure in liberty ... [and] conducted it to the edge of national annihilation,' had taken a wrong turn.[51]

Winston Churchill did not like Elliot, saying that he talked too much.[52] Elliot's exclusion from government during the Second World War and subsequently, however, rested on more than personal dislike. In September 1938, at a meeting of the Other Club, Churchill had berated Elliot for condoning the cowardly policy of appeasement.[53] 'Chips' Channon noted in his diary that nobody, including Labour, wanted Elliot in the government after 1940.[54] The damage went wider than Elliot alone. Support for Chamberlain's appeasement had been strong in Scottish Unionism. As John Foster has argued, 'it was the depth of this involvement which was ... to cause irreversible damage to the political influence of Scotland's ruling élite.'[55]

As discussed above, Elliot sought to console himself by revived affection for his Scottish home and through his return to the army. Elliot never really found himself a role with which he could feel comfortable during the Second World War. After working at Western Command in Chester, he became the public relations officer for the War Office during 1941. He wrote to Katharine of the advantages of his acceptance of the post, 'that I remain in the King's Coat, that I come to London, that I am in the centre of things,' but the disadvantage was 'that I am accepting a definitely subordinate kind of post'.[56] By the end of the year he resigned from the army, turning his attention to broadcasting and to Tom Johnston's Council of State of the ex-Secretaries of State for Scotland.

In his broadcasting, Elliot recognized the effect that the war had on Scotland, as the war effort drew the Scottish economy out of its prolonged crisis.[57] He argued that the crisis had been one of lack of purpose, but Scotland's distinctive role in the war had filled this vacuum:

> Since the War [he told Australia and New Zealand], Scotland, like everywhere else, has begun to be busy with the hammer, busy with the plough. We have found difficulty in casting off the effects, both spiritual and physical, of the depression and so we go a little uncertainly to work. But our first inspiration is the urgent need for our outstanding product. The demand, nowadays, above everything, is for ships, ships of war, ships of trade. Scotland feels her chief craft honoured again, and rises to it.[58]

Scotland had restored its place in the Empire through its industrial efforts but Elliot clearly felt uncomfortable about his own limited role. In January 1943 he fell as he boarded a train at Hawick and was confined to bed for five months. His accident was widely reported but his absence from government was almost unnoticed.

Elliot's political misfortunes continued when he was not offered a place in Churchill's caretaker government and when he lost his Kelvingrove seat in the July 1945 general election. However, the weakness of British Conservatism in the wake of the election meant that Churchill was prepared to call on all the expertise available to restore the party's position. The party's UK share of the vote was reduced from 47.7 per cent in the election of 1935 to 39.8 per cent in 1945, but in Scotland the collapse was not so drastic, falling from 42 to 40.3 per cent. The Conservatives were demoralized and Elliot's success in the Scottish Universities by-election in 1946 went some small way to rallying the party's spirit.

The war had encouraged the central planning and interventionism associated with Labour's thinking formulated in the 1930s. In 1945 Labour had secured a mandate to implement their manifesto promises of nationalization and the creation of a centralist welfare state. The Conservatives had been dealt a severe bow at the election and needed to restore their confidence through the creation of new policies on the one hand and through effective opposition on the other. Elliot's stance in his by-election gave the Conservatives an ideologically consistent position on which to build such opposition. His election address spelled out his Scottish Unionist opposition to the state-centralizing tendencies of Labour's legislative programme, without rejecting the Britishness which the Conservatives were keen to retain, for Churchill was still seen as a tremendous electoral asset. Elliot explained his politics thus:

> I am a Conservative and Unionist. I believe in the orderly develop-
> ment of this country, but by the consent of all the citizens; the
> more so since Britain has again saved herself by her exertions, and it
> may be her task to save Europe by her example....
>   The legislative Union between Scotland and England was never
> meant to entail, and should not entail, a complete swamping of the
> economic identity of the Northern Kingdom such as is now being
> conducted in the name of nationalisation. The transfer by statute of
> the control of the whole of Scottish industry to Westminster is not
> nationalisation, it is de-nationalisation.[59]

Elliot's moderate Unionism included support for state intervention to deal with social problems. This enabled him to lead opposition to Labour's own interventionism without being branded simply as a reactionary. In the House of Commons, Elliot led the Conservatives' critique of the National Health Service Bill, and in the country he emphasised the centralizing trends of nationalization. Not only did this connect well with the Conservatives' rhetoric of freedom from control but it also restored the dynamic voice of Scottish Unionism in British Conservatism.

Elliot saw his own Scottishness being reaffirmed at a personal and political level. After his by-election victory in 1946, the *Observer* printed a profile of Elliot. It combined the benign stereotypes held by many of the English about the Scottish with an accurate interpretation of the way in which Elliot liked to see himself. 'At the end,' it decided

> Walter Elliot is a Scotsman, with that mysterious blend of race
> which so often disturbs the simpler English. The hard, humorous
> and sentimental Lowlander, the storied ardour of the Border, the
> quick temper of the Highlander 'whose wars are merry and whose
> songs are sad' all go to the making of many modern Scotsmen.[60]

With its clear role in revitalizing British Conservatism, and the sincerity of its nationalist critique of Labour's centralized control, Scottish Unionism sought to politically solidify its Scottishness. A committee was established to consider the party's attitude to Scottish government to which Elliot explained the basis of Unionism in a memorandum on 'Scottish Administration' in 1949. He reiterated the argument that the

Union was one of equals and was not 'a policy of amalgamation'. 'This is proved,' he wrote, 'by the careful provision for the preservation of the Church of Scotland, of the legal system of Scotland, and the fostering and strengthening of the Scottish Regiments.'[61] The need now, he argued, was 'the arrest and reversal' of the centralizing threat. His influence on Conservative policy for Scotland was apparent when the party issued 'Scottish Control of Scottish Affairs,' which declared that

> Union is not amalgamation. Scotland is a nation … It is only since 1945, under the first socialist majority, that we have seen the policy of amalgamation superseding that of Union. This must inevitably result from the fulfilment of the socialist creed, which is basically one of amalgamation and centralisation. To this policy we are fundamentally opposed.[62]

The Conservatives playing of the Scottish card worked very well. Their share of the vote increased in 1950, 1951 and 1955, as they rallied the collapsing Liberal vote around opposition to British socialism and centralization. In political terms, when the party was elected back into government in 1951 it provided the Scottish Office with a third Under-Secretary and a Minister of State who would reside mainly in Edinburgh. This had been one of Elliot's suggestions in his memorandum. It seemed that Elliot was again in the ascendant, his Scottish patriotism and its beneficial effect on Conservative electoral success finally overcoming his failure of patriotism in the appeasement years.

Elliot, however, was to be bitterly disappointed once more. There was the brief possibility that Elliot might have been offered the Ministry of Education because he had not answered his telephone Churchill offered the post instead to Florence Horsbrugh, whose gender and Scottishness allowed Churchill to emphasise the inclusive nature of his government.[63]

Elliot was not discarded completely. He turned down posts which he believed were beneath his status but his loyalty continued and he was given political roles that indicated the strength of the Union. He spoke on behalf of Scotland and backbench MPs when George VI died in 1952, paying tribute to Queen Elizabeth, 'a countrywoman of some of us', for her role in blitzed London.[64] He provided valuable Scottish support for the government in the debate over the Royal Titles Bill when there was much Scottish criticism over the designation of the new queen as Elizabeth II despite the first Elizabeth not having ruled Scotland.[65]

His final political role amply signified his life within the Union as he was appointed the Lord High Commissioner to the General Assembly of the Church of Scotland. He had been offered the post during the Second World War but had refused it, but now, in 1956, it seemed to provide the culmination to his Unionism. The Presbyterian Church of Scotland had retained its established position after the Act of Union. The existence of a separate 'state' church enabled Scotland to assert its difference from England, while shared Protestantism had a role in constructing a sense of commonality against Catholicism. Linda Colley has emphasised the importance of this joint religious identity in the eighteenth and early nineteenth centuries. In Scotland, Conservatives maintained the claims of the Church against the Free Church which emerged from the Disruption of 1843. The links were strengthened further in the 1920s and 1930s in hostility to Catholic Irish immigration. As Michael Fry has noted, 'by dint of condemning all things Irish [the Church, which had reunited with the Free Church in 1929] celebrated all things British, underwrote the Union and incidentally rejected Scottish Nationalism'.[66] Elliot had long considered the General Assembly as 'the characteristic gathering' of 'the political heritage of Scotland.' He had defended its 'fierce egalitarianism … respect for intellectual pre-eminence, and … lust for argument on abstract issues' as 'the traditions of Scotland to-day.'[67] The Lord High Commissioner represented the Crown to the state church of Scotland. In symbolic form, Elliot represented the Union between Scotland and England. He was always Scottish, but this was but one identity among the concentric circles of being British and imperial, but in each case his Scottishness shaped his attitude to the other identities. It was only very rarely that he saw these identities coming into conflict, as when he became frustrated at seeming government slowness in its actions for Scotland.

Elliot and Empire

As a middle-class Briton in the early and mid-twentieth century, Elliot's was a life lived within the Empire. All Britons were accustomed to imperial symbolism in their daily lives. Education, advertising, literature, street names and statuary brought the empire to the metropolis. The signifiers in Scotland were no fewer than in England, and Glasgow, where Elliot attended university and where he had his Kelvingrove parliamentary constituency, was proud to consider itself as the 'second city of Empire'.[68]

Almost as soon as he had been elected, Elliot had taken advantage of the privileges bestowed by being an MP. Coote outlines the position of a Member of the Imperial Parliament:

> In the years following the First World War, it still counted to be a British MP. Foreigners ... on the whole ... had a greater respect for us than at any other time before or since. There was a British battalion at most key points in the world.... Walter used this situation to explore Europe and its neighbourhood.[69]

In the early 1920s, armed with this moral power, Elliot made extensive excursions into southern and south-eastern Europe and north Africa. Coote's style of describing Elliot's travels is that of the Buchanesque adventure story. Having motored through Spain, Elliot went on to Spanish North Africa, where he met a young Spanish officer called Franco. In Albania, having been robbed, he secured a loan from the Albanian Chancellor of the Exchequer, and unwittingly he aided the smuggling of the Hungarian revolutionary Bela Kun's chief lieutenant across east European borders.[70]

The tragic side of the amateurish nature of the British gentleman manifested itself on Elliot's honeymoon in 1919. Elliot married Helen Hamilton, the daughter of a fellow officer in the RAMC. They took their honeymoon on Skye; where they walked on the hills unprepared for changing weather. Trapped overnight by mist, Elliot's new wife died of exposure. Coote could not resist sensationalising this tragedy in his biography. 'The superstitious,' he wrote, 'will not be surprised to learn that the sleeping berth on the train was numbered 13, so was their room at the hotel; and the tragedy took place on the 13th day after their wedding.'[71]

Elliot's life, therefore, was shaped by the global nature of British citizenship, which rested on its domination of a worldwide empire. The place of the Empire as the nexus between Britishness and Scottishness has been the subject of much historiographical discussion. The Union, it is argued, provided the opportunity for Scotland's economic and spiritual exploitation of the Empire and its demise, therefore, entailed a decline of belief in the Union.[72]

However, the beginnings of the decline of imperial sentiment are often seen as preceding the decline of Empire. Hence, Richard Finlay has argued that the popularity of imperialism in Scotland waned after 1918 as the First World War dislocated the Scottish economy and society at the same time as concern turned inwards towards the appalling social conditions of urban Scotland. Finlay argues that Britishness survived the end of popular imperialism because the UK-wide welfare state dealt successfully with much Scottish poverty, providing an alternative focus of loyalty to Britain.[73] The welfare state did much to buttress the Union. It acted as additional support for a stable structure rather than as a substitute for imperialism. In Scotland, there was an adjustment to the changing circumstances of Britain's global position as Scots like Elliot (and Tweedsmuir) considered the challenges facing post-war Britain.

Elliot had no direct material interest in the Empire. Whereas many of his contemporaries at Glasgow University found employment throughout the Empire, and many of his constituents manufactured for imperial export, his own financial interests were relatively local. His connection to the Empire came through his politics and his scientific background. He had worked at the Rowett Research Institute at Aberdeen in the early 1920s, investigating the nutritional value of grasses for animal consumption. Combined with his successful undertaking of government posts, this scientific background resulted in his appointment as chairman of the research committee of the Empire Marketing Board, described by Stephen Constantine as 'an official government department formally charged with impressing aspects of an imperial ideology on the general public'.[74]

Elliot explained his imperialist thought in a series of four articles in *The Times* in May 1929. He outlined with a sense of wonder the extent and diversity of the British Empire in the 1920s:

It is at once sparse and gigantic, streaming across the map like a constellation – the West Indies, the Central and South American footholds (we are the only Power in the world which is at once a North American, a Central, and a South American Power), Africa East and Africa West, Ceylon, Malaya, Singapore, and so to Hong-kong.[75]

In line with a change in the culture of imperialism from military to administrative heroism (expressed cinematically in *Sanders of the River* in 1936), Elliot argued that the domination of the colonial Empire rested on the civil service and its filing system. He used this point to strengthen his own argument that science and reason needed to be applied to imperial problems. The diversity of Empire, he concluded in his first article, had 'to be fitted upon the shelves of Downing-street.'[76] He saw the strength of the British Empire as lying in 'indirect rule' and in allowing diversity to continue within the Empire.

Elliot extended his argument to include black Africa. He did not believe that Africans should be Anglicized, arguing instead that 'An African should be a good African and not a European.'[77] He argued that the response to 'an Empire of diversity almost to madness' was devolution, not to the colonial peoples, but to the men on the spot who should be equipped with the latest scientific research.[78] This then was Elliot's Empire, it was 'a matter of pay sheets and order-books, of factories and workshops – literally, of bread and butter,' but these belonged to the 'Home Country' as a whole rather than to himself as an individual.[79] The 'Home Country' was the United Kingdom, of which Scotland was part.

Elliot certainly utilized Scottish imperial myths. Not only was he president of the Robert Louis Stevenson Club,[80] but he also drew on the Livingstone myth when he addressed the federal assembly in Northern Rhodesia in 1954.[81] David Livingstone had been widely invoked to draw out Scotland's contribution to the Empire. As a lad o'pairts, his imperial mobility was portrayed as peculiarly Scottish, especially given his relationship to the Kirk.[82]

The distinctiveness of Scottishness within imperialism was the central theme of the 1938 Glasgow Empire Exhibition over which Elliot presided as Scottish Secretary of State. It was staged in an attempt to show that the National government was at least doing something economic for Scotland to match the devolution of the executive to Edinburgh. Colin McArthur has argued that the Exhibition revealed 'the dialectic of Scottish identity,' juxtaposing the Clachan's thatched cottages and rural backdrop to the modernity of the Tower of Empire. He argues that these 'polar points of the dialectic' threatened 'to render individual Scots schizoid' and illustrate 'the generality of the ideological struggle between cores and peripheries.'[83] Like the Exhibition, Elliot too depicted this dialectic. On the one hand, he championed rural Scotland, not only through his political representation of farming, but also in his descriptions of the Scotland he visited as Scottish Secretary. From one trip he wrote to Baffy Dugdale that 'The Far North of Scotland is a very lovely place. Sutherland is full of great mountains and Cheviot sheep.'[84] On the other hand, Elliot was a sponsor of modernity, through his scientific research, the application of which he encouraged in imperial and Scottish agriculture. His EMB committee provided grants to investigate and implement the chilling of meat and the gas storage of fruit. It also established research stations throughout the Empire.[85] Elliot did not recognise a contradiction between the rural and the modern, and saw the overwhelmingly rural Empire as the site of scientific modernity. He reconciled the dialectic.

An example was Elliot's encouragement of the documentary film movement under the auspices of the EMB. John Grierson, founder of the movement in Britain, described Elliot's role in a memorandum for Colin Coote:

> [H]e got the E.M.B into the first nutritional films (on milk in schools), the first films on agricultural research at home and in the Empire (grass development at Aberystwyth, experiments at the Rowett & Torry Institutes and at West Malling and in the West Indies). He also got films into the description and appreciation of the fast changing pattern of international communications.[86]

Elliot encouraged his colleagues in government to view innovative foreign films, including those by Sergei Eisenstein, and backed the early classic documentary film, *Drifters*, about the Scottish herring industry. Indeed, *O'er Hill and Dale*, which Grierson described as 'the second film of note' to come from the EMB was filmed at Harwood, Elliot's farm in Roxburghshire.[87]

If Elliot overcame the dialectic of the rural with the modern, then the dialectic of core and periphery rarely occurred to him. Certainly he saw Scotland as different from England, and in the late 1940s published and broadcast on the characteristics of 'The English', from a position which he described as 'although near ... certainly outside.'[88] He also saw London as the centre of power in the United Kingdom and strongly advised against the Scottish Secretary spending too much time in Edinburgh rather than London. Yet, he saw Scotland's role in the Empire as both significant and integral and considered the Scottish people as imperial partners with England, not part of the periphery.

Elliot was aware that the Empire was a process rather than a fixed event. His *Times* articles had referred to 'the new Empire' because as he explained, 'It may be called the Third British Empire, reckoning the secession of the United States as the end of the first, and the statutory recognition of the Dominions as the transformation of the second.'[89] He expanded on this in his essay on 'The English' in the *Times Literary Supplement*, asserting that

> The most important political and economic fact of the day is the break-up of the British Empire.... The question is whether and, if so, in what shape, it will reform ... Very few societies have done this

trick twice.... The English have to do it a third time, or perish. *Or Perish*. There is no middle way.[90]

Elliot believed that consolidation of imperialism was possible, and saw the process of decolonization as the method of revitalising British imperial influence. In December 1943 he went as leader of an inquiry into higher education in the British West African colonies of Sierra Leone, the Gambia, the Gold Coast and Nigeria. Again, he was fascinated by the variety of the Empire, referring to Nigeria as 'a demi-continent rather than a country, with the Sahara just over the edge to the North, and the forests and the swamps and the original Black-amoors to the South.'[91] He saw universities as providing the training for Africans to run their own affairs, but within continuing British influence, which he saw as a necessary civilizing force.[92]

He returned twice again to Africa in the 1950s, once to head a parliamentary delegation into the Mau Mau rebellion in Kenya. He had applied his scientific version of imperialism to Kenya in the late 1920s, when he had provided a pseudo-nutritional explanation for the divisions between the Kikuyu and the Masai peoples. The latter's diet of 'milk, meat and blood,' he argued, enabled them to 'lord it among the starch-eating Kikuyu like wolves amongst sheep, fifty thousand of them amongst some two and a half million.'[93] Elliot was convinced that the Mau Mau rebellion had to be 'exterminated' and that a multiracial society was necessary.[94] 'Multiracialism' in the Kenyan context meant continued white control, for it enabled at least parity for the 60,000 whites with the overwhelming black majority.[95]

Elliot's report had expressed concern about some of the British methods being used to defeat the Mau Mau rebellion. This provoked a letter that revealed some of the continuing post-war bonds of Empire in Scotland, when the mother of a Kenya policeman from Aberdeen wrote to Elliot criticizing his report. He replied that while the delegation had drawn attention to malpractice they had also 'paid tribute to the excellent work being done by the Police Force in Kenya.'[96]

Elliot saw his work in the 1950s as contributing to the development of the Empire rather than its destruction.[97] In 1954, he headed a further delegation, this time to the newly formed Central African Federation assembly, to which he took a replica of the mace of the House of Commons. The federation was a compromise aimed at accommodating white settler nationalism in Southern Rhodesia with the desires of the British government to maintain control without provoking black nationalism. It was not a move towards decolonization so much as an effort to retain British influence, and Elliot's speech to the assembly, carrying the mace as a symbolic gift of British democracy, stressed the Scottish role in 'the teaching of ideals and the practice of development.'[98] Elliot shared the general view of British policymakers that they were redeveloping the Empire rather than presiding over its demise.

Elliot's life within the Union reflected the mutually reinforcing nature of his Scottishness, Unionism and, to a lesser extent, imperialism. He was a Scottish patriot, firmly committed to Lowland Scotland, and believing that the Union had accommodated Scottish partnership in a larger enterprise. In the 1920s, he contributed to the strength of British Conservatism as a diverse force. Baldwin's emphasis on Englishness was tempered by the attention Elliot gave to Scottish character and history. In the 1930s, when Scotland faced severe economic problems and a crisis of identity, Elliot devolved Scottish administration to Edinburgh. Unionism was able to express the demands of Scottish nationality. Elliot was always deeply concerned to be involved in British issues. He was interested in the Empire, though from a position on the sidelines. In the 1930s, he opposed appeasement, but his opposition remained private. He did not make a stand against Chamberlain until too late. The cost was exclusion from government in 1940. There was the potential for return to the centres of power in British Conservatism in the late 1940s. Again, his Scottish Unionism seemed to offer the potential to strengthen a weakened British Conservatism as he developed the idea of opposition to the nationalization of socialism as a centralizing force. His personal hopes were dashed when Churchill left him out of government when the Conservatives won the 1951 election. He was appointed Lord High Commissioner to the General Assembly of the Church of Scotland, representing the Crown to this most characteristic element of Scotland's special position within the Union. The Conservatives reaped the rewards of the recognition of Scottish nationality in the 1950s. Elliot's contribution was to ensure that Scottish Unionists considered themselves full and equal partners in the Union, even as the Empire was being dismantled.

3
Our Good and Faithful Friend: Tom Johnston (1881–1965)

It is axiomatic that a party officially adopting the label 'Unionist' for half a century between 1912 and 1965 and adhering primarily to the concept of the Union since 1886 should be the site of constant and firm allegiance to the Acts of Union that held the United Kingdom together in the twentieth century. However, the Labour movement too, despite its adherence to the principles of Scottish Home Rule from the 1880s to the mid-1920s, and a continuing paper commitment to devolution until the 1950s, was as much a unionist movement as its main rival in Scotland.

Despite the myths of Scottish radicalism, Labour's advance came slower in Scotland than in the rest of Britain. In 1914 it had only two MPs, but by the end of the First World War it had secured 28 per cent of the vote and seven seats. Yet its real breakthrough came in 1922, when Labour MPs were elected in ten of Glasgow's fifteen seats. They held these seats in 1923 and lost only two in 1924. In large part, this advance was made possible by the shift of the Catholic vote to Labour. The unusual circumstances of the 1930s allowed the Unionists to stem the Labour advance, but between 1945 and 1966 the lowest share of the vote achieved by Labour in Scotland was 46.2 per cent, and in 1966 it had come within a whisker of securing a majority of the votes cast.[1]

Tom Johnston was of the same generation as Walter Elliot. He was born in Kirkintilloch in Dunbartonshire in 1881, the son of a provision merchant, and remained attached to this locality all his life, serving on the council and writing a history of the area. Like Elliot, Johnston's life was lived within the circles of Scotland, Union and Empire, though his connection to the Union was almost one of convenience rather than commitment. There was a further circle within which Johnston operated, not geographical but sociological. Johnston maintained a

41

commitment to the politics of labour. Johnston treated the Union as an expedient constitutional device for the social progress of the working class in Scotland. The effect was to strengthen the hold of Labour, a unionist party, over urban Scotland.

Johnston and the Scottish people

Johnston emerged into Scottish politics simultaneously at a local and national level through membership of the Independent Labour Party and his ownership, through inheritance, of a printing works that enabled him to become editor of *Forward*, which he founded in 1906.[2] At a local level, Johnston was elected to the Kirkintilloch school board, and served on the Town Council for eight years after 1913. His political activity was combined with a cultural interest in his locality. As Graham Walker has said,

> He certainly immersed himself in the history and folklore of his home town, and the proximity of the surrounding countryside encouraged in him a love of leisure pursuits such as fishing. Small-town life in such an inspiriting rural setting defined for Johnson a life-long aversion to urban conglomerations.[3]

Johnston sought a dynamic role for municipal politics and was responsible for many local initiatives including the first municipal cinema, municipal fire insurance, municipal jam manufacture, and most importantly, Scotland's first municipal bank.[4] Despite subsequent moves into national politics, Johnston always maintained his links with what he considered as his community. In the 1930s, when the political crisis of 1931 resulted in his exclusion from Westminster politics, he turned his attention to writing a detailed and scholarly history of Kirkintilloch, which appeared in 1937. While he returned to parliament in 1935, it was his intention to retire from national politics at the next election (due in 1940) to devote himself further to research and writing.

The early Labour movement, of which Johnston was part, inhabited a radical world that combined a desire for social reform with demands for some greater autonomy for Scotland within the United Kingdom. The multinational nature of the United Kingdom was clear to labour activists in Scotland, with its proximity to north-east Ireland and the existence of numerous Irish immigrants in Scottish cities. With its links to Liberalism, Scottish labour supported the Irish Home Rule cause.

This combined with a sense of difference from England, expressed through the separate existence of the Scottish Trades Union Congress, the formation of the Scottish Labour Party in 1888 (which merged with the ILP in 1893), and the Scottish Workers' Representation Committee in 1900. In addition, many labour activists were also supporters of 'nationalist' bodies, such as the Scottish Home Rule Association. Keir Hardie and Robert Smillie, the miners' leader, were vice-presidents and James Ramsay MacDonald was its London secretary.[5] Johnston's politics, therefore, entailed a combination of class, local and national identities. All socialists operated within the confines of the nation-state yet most held that there was a pure form of internationalist socialism that rejected the ties of nationality completely. Because the *Communist Manifesto* had suggested that the working man had no country, purists had been able to maintain that engagement with the nation was a betrayal of the class politics of socialism.[6] Johnston confronted this tension in *Forward* in what amounted to a retrospect of his socialist thought since his first engagement with politics:

> It may be true that if I were properly internationalised I should not have any preference at any international football match. It may even be true, for aught I know to the contrary, that on some subliminal plane, I ought to be a citizen of the world and desire my sister to marry a Negro or a Chinaman. But rightly, or wrongly, and I agree with the late James Connolly that you may as well bay at the moon as seek to construct your socialist scaffolding without taking account of the facts of nationality and race – rightly or wrongly, these prejudices are strong in most of us.[7]

In Edwardian Britain, Johnston operated not only within the tension of class and nation, but also with the tension between the Scottish nation and the United Kingdom state. He provided a Scottish perspective on politics shaped by the interplay of outer and inner Britain. Anti-aristocratic politics had been a growing feature of radicalism since the 1870s, driven on from Ireland, Scotland and Wales. The culmination came when Lloyd George launched his 'people's budget' as Chancellor of the Exchequer of the Liberal government. Johnston provided a class version of anti-landlord politics through the publication of *Our Scots Noble Families*, first in *Forward* in 1908 and then as a book in 1909, which condemned the Scottish aristocracy for its 'successful crime,' 'legal trickery,' and 'underhand dodgery.' '[T]hese few families of tax-gatherers,' it argued, 'have sucked the life-blood of our nation.'[8]

As Walker has drawn out, Johnston was concerned as much with rural Scotland as he was with the urban working class and he saw land reform as the way in which Scotland could be revitalized. To achieve this, Johnston was involved in founding the Highland Land League in August 1909, with the former crofters' MP, G.B. Clark as its president.[9] While the League's success proved transient, it signified not only Johnston's perspective of politics which drew on rural Scotland as the essence of Scottishness but also the way in which such issues were drawn into Union politics. Land and nationalism had been driven forward by the Irish question, but in turn had resulted in demands for Scottish land reform and Home Rule as two sides of the same coin. The radical cry of 'the people to the land' was transformed into a nationalist demand.

Johnston was for the urban working class but not of it. He was born into the small town middle class and his entry into labour politics had come through the 'new journalism' when a newspaper press had fallen fortuitously into his ownership.[10] Politics that combined land and town in hostility to the aristocracy might be described as 'populist', if that is taken to mean 'a belief in the basic goodness of the people who are perceived as threatened by sinister elites'.[11] Without taking on all the historiographical baggage that accompanies the use of the term, Johnston might usefully be described as a populist in the sense that he combined the politics of class and nation.[12] His political objective was to secure an improvement in the condition of the Scottish people, of urban Clydeside *and* small town Kirkintilloch. In such circumstances, the rhetoric of nation could resonate more effectively than the rhetoric of class.

The outbreak of European war in 1914 drew attention away from Scottish Home Rule. More than 320,000 Scottish men enlisted voluntarily in the British Army between August 1914 and the introduction of conscription in January 1916, the highest proportion of men in the United Kingdom.[13] However, the proportion of the labour movement taking an anti-war stance seems also to have been higher in Scotland than in England. *Forward* under Johnston's editorship generally opposed the war without actively campaigning against it.

Johnston saw opposition to the war falling within a Scottish tradition. He took inspiration from Keir Hardie's resistance to the surrender of the European working class to chauvinist nationalism. Hardie's anguish was widely seen as having contributed to his early death in September 1915. Johnston's obituary called Hardie 'Scots to the marrow ... introspective, logical-minded, but effusively kind, generously sympathetic and magnanimously charitable.'[14] This was the line that Johnston tried to take. He blamed the war on secret diplomacy and campaigned against its effects on the Scottish working class. Unaware that the government had banned reporting of the response to Lloyd George's speech to the Clyde workers on Christmas day 1915, when the Minister of Munitions was given a rough ride by the shop stewards, *Forward* was suppressed.[15] Johnston secured an audience with Lloyd George where he negotiated the conditions for the re-opening of the paper. Subsequently Johnston took a line of neutrality in relation to the war effort, or as he explained, *Forward* would 'retreat to the next line of defence,' for example opposing conscription until it was imposed. He tried to rally his readers with Scottishness, reminding them that they were 'the children of the covenanters, in our veins beat the blood of Thomas Muir and the Chartist weavers and James Keir Hardie: our national anthem is "Scots Wha Hae."'[16]

The war increased political class consciousness in industrial Scotland, offering opportunities for the ILP and Labour Party to make significant electoral gains. In the December 1910 general election, Labour had returned only two MPs and the Liberals remained the hegemonic party with 53.6 per cent of the vote and fifty-eight of Scotland's seventy-two seats. With the rent strike of 1915 and the campaigns against dilution of skilled work on the Clyde, Labourism was strengthened, so that in the December 1918 election, while Labour was disappointed with its seven MPs, its share of the vote had reached 22.9 per cent. Labour's momentum was continued by the events of early 1919 when strikes and demonstrations in Glasgow were seen by the government in London as a Bolshevist rising.[17] 'Red Clydeside' might not have been the political eruption of a revolutionary working class but it was nonetheless symbolic of a heightened class consciousness, even if was built in defence of the privileges of craft and skill.[18] It would not do, however, to underplay the distinctively Scottish consciousness that accompanied the class militancy. That Scotland's leading communist, John Maclean, resisted absorption into the Communist Party of Great Britain, formed in 1920–1, is representative of the impact of the war on the Scottish labour movement. Johnston was much more moderate than Maclean both in his socialism and his nationalism, but he too revived his interest in Home Rule through the reformed Scottish Home Rule Association. Supported by the Scottish TUC as well as the ILP, with James Maxton and Johnston prominent, the restoration of the Scottish Home Rule Association symbolised the continuing Scottish orientation of Labour.[19]

In 1920, Johnston made a significant intellectual contribution to the association of the working class to the Scottish nation with the publication of *The History of the Working Classes in Scotland*. His *History* attacked Scottish feudalism, assigned the working class a role in the Wars of Independence, saw the Covenants as the work of a scheming nobility and condemned the subsequent witch hunts as anti-working class. Above all else, Johnston privileged the role of the working class within the nation, though he used that phrase interchangeably with 'the people'. 'The history of a country,' he wrote, 'is the history of the masses of its people, not the history, legendary or otherwise, of a few selected stocks.'[20] Johnston provided a democratic national history, which took a whiggish approach as history moved towards the development and success of the labour movement in Scotland.

While Johnston demythologized the Protestant-Presbyterian national history of Scotland, he remained concerned to be able to appeal to the Protestant working-class vote in urban Scotland. Labour was beginning to find a ready audience among the Catholic working class, whose previous allegiance had been to the Liberals for their support for Irish Home Rule. Labour, with Catholic Socialist figures like John Wheatley, was happy to take up the demand for separate Catholic education after the Education Act of 1918 had moved towards secular education. Given the continuing strength of Protestantism in Scotland's towns and cities, Johnston remained concerned to maintain Labour's appeal. These were sensitive issues of nationality. In 1923 the General Assembly of the Church of Scotland had warned that Irish immigrants were 'subverting' Scottish national identity, and in Glasgow and Edinburgh a populist Protestantism had substantial electoral impact.[21] However, with the direct questioning of the Union with Ireland removed from United Kingdom politics by the establishment of the Irish Free State and the founding of a separate parliament in Belfast, Labour was able to become Janus-faced, appealing to both Protestant and Catholic workers through their class identities. There was certainly a continuing place for the appeal to religion and Johnston's instinctive attraction to the supposedly radical spirit of Scottish Presbyterianism gave him an affinity to the forms of Scottishness adopted in Protestant Scotland.[22]

The collapse of the Liberals in the cities and increased belief that class mattered in politics above other identities had enabled Labour in Scotland to make the electoral breakthrough that had eluded it in 1918. The result of the 1922 general election contributed significantly, though somewhat erroneously, to two myths: the conviction that

Scottishness was hegemonically attached to the left in its politics and that this was combined with a fundamental opposition to the English and Anglicized establishment who saw Westminster rather than the Scottish towns and cities as central to political life. Labour had increased its number of seats from seven in 1918 to twenty-nine in 1922, with an increase in its share of vote from 23 per cent to 32 per cent. Unionists and Liberal Coalitionists, who in Scotland had rarely opposed each other, had secured nearly 43 per cent of the vote but only twenty-seven seats (fifteen Unionist and twelve Liberal).

Johnston had fought and lost West Stirlingshire, a seat near to Kirkintilloch, in 1918. In 1922 he won the seat. He was one of the Scottish MPs who departed for London from St Enoch Station in Glasgow on 20 November 1922. He was a 'Clydesider' as editor of *Forward* rather than for his territorial representation. In the midst of a crowd of tens of thousands, the new MPs declared that they would soon return to a Scotland with a parliament of its own.[23] The MPs represented their journey as a national crusade, to restore dignity and to improve the conditions of the Scottish working class, not as a favour from London but as the result of the demands of a militant and Scottish working class. Johnston shared in the building of this image, and instinctively he felt that he was going to an alien parliament. He never settled in London, and being among the English confirmed his sense of Scottishness as distinct and different. In the 1950s he wrote 'Upon soul and conscious I never wanted the life Parliamentary, and most assuredly not in London.'[24] He, like the other Clydesiders, disdained the social aspects of parliamentary life, verifying their sense of difference from many of the English MPs. Beatrice Webb, keen to make the Parliamentary Labour Party in the image of the bourgeois parties, described Johnston as a 'dour Scot'.[25]

This was an image the Clydeside MPs were content to accept. They characterized their radical Labourist politics as particularly Scottish and staged scenes in the House of Commons to draw attention to the poverty of the people of Scotland. Johnston's role was far less prominent than those of James Maxton and David Kirkwood. This resulted from the essentially moderate nature of Johnston's politics, which sat uncomfortably within the radicalism of many of the Clydesiders. The Scottish MPs had been decisive in securing Ramsay MacDonald's leadership of the parliamentary party in 1922, because he was Scottish and a member of the ILP. Johnston, on the other hand, had supported MacDonald because he shared an affinity to the gradualist politics of Labour that MacDonald represented.

MacDonald was, however, much more 'British' than Johnston. He had moved to Bristol from Scotland in the 1880s, and then on to London. He had been involved in the all-British debates over the direction of socialism, which had become particularly significant after the Bolshevik Revolution of 1917. MacDonald and others on Labour's moderate wing had formulated a strengthened 'British socialism' that located itself firmly within a reading of British history that privileged, indeed celebrated, the parliamentary nature of politics.[26]

Johnston fundamentally shared this evolutionary approach to social progress, though he more often utilized the rhetoric of Scottishness to amplify his gradualism. In the early 1920s, while he expressed support for Maxton's scene of 27 June 1923 in which Maxton had declared that the neglect of Glasgow's slum children by the Conservative government amounted to murder, Johnston had in fact moved much closer towards MacDonald. However, Johnston was not offered a place in the first Labour government because he had been associated with the 'murderers' scene and, in addition, Johnston had accused the Conservative government of corruption when it had loaned money to a failing imperial company. Johnston had argued that it had done so only because Liberal leader Asquith's son was a director.[27]

Empire socialism

Johnston had a wider interest in the Empire. He wrote that

> the assumption that all colonial development was imperialist and anti-Socialist, and liable to embroil us in international strife, seemed to me to be as irrational and absurd as that we should endeavour to arrange nothing more in trade priorities, or in co-operation for security with our cousins, the five Labour governments in Australia (out of six possibles there) than we arranged with the Tibetans or the Argentinos.[28]

In 1922 he helped to form the Commonwealth Labour Group, which he hoped could build on the ties of kinship within the Empire for socialist ends.[29] The CLG wanted a 'Commonwealth of Nations ... coming together as free and equal partners in a Commonwealth representative of all peoples at present living under the British flag.'[30] Johnston recognised the Empire in the same way he recognised nationality: as 'a fact'. Hence while the CLG called for India's 'full and complete political and economic freedom,'[31] Johnston saw the potential break-up of the Empire as damaging to the future of socialism. Labour, it was clear, was not immune to the claims of imperial Scotland. Indeed, Empire moved close to the centre of the thought of Scottish (though not British) socialism in the 1920s.

Johnston's imperial thought tried to reconcile the interests of the Scottish working class with those of the colonial peoples. However, his interest in imperial matters was primarily metropolitan. He looked for ways in which the Empire could be used to the benefit of the Scottish working class before considering the needs and desires of the colonial peoples. Having lost his Stirling seat when the 1924 Labour government fell, he had been elected for Dundee in December. Dundee's economy was reliant on the export of jute, for which the markets had collapsed in the 1920s. In response, Johnston and a local trade union leader undertook a three-month tour of India to enquire into the nature of the competition, which was seen as undercutting Dundee's workers through substantially lower labour costs.[32] Johnston drew the labourist conclusion that unionization of the Bengal textile workers would prevent 'sweating' and raise wages, and indeed on his return he set out to raise £100 for the union.[33] He seemed to have sympathy for the Indian working class, but it was very much a paternalist concern that grew from a sense of charitable benevolence echoing that of nineteenth-century feminists for their Indian sisters.[34] Johnston was driven forward in his imperial reformism by concern for Scottish rather than Indian workers. He identified India's economic and social problems as emerging from the class system within India rather than Britain's imperialism. He viewed the Indian Civil Service with admiration and the Indian capitalist and land-owning classes with suspicion. In a sketch in his autobiography, he at once criticized Indian religions as superstitious and depicted the importance of the role he attached to the Scottish in the Raj. He described a scene at Nagpur railway station in which a single 'stocky Glasgow keelie soldier in a Highland regiment' kept order over thousands of Hindus and Muslims who drank from separate water taps. The Glaswegian kept order by constant urgings to 'Move along, Whiskers' and 'Come on, Granpaw', telling Johnston that 'it's a' the same watter onywey'.[35] This fitted closely with a view of the state as a neutral body over which it was possible for British Labour to gain power through parliamentary democracy. A visit to Canada in late 1928 brought Johnston into contact with nationalized hydroelectric power and wheat marketing schemes.[36] He linked Labour's electoral advance in Britain with the ability to initiate such schemes.

Johnston came to view a reformed Empire as the 'greatest lever for human emancipation the world has ever known'.[37] This potentiality emerged from a combination of racial and democratic factors. He argued that

> We have to face the fact that every second household in this country has a brother or a son or a cousin in some British colony beyond the seas, and that these British Colonies are going Labour and Socialist, and only on the assumption that we are politically and economically daft can we be expected to regard our kindred beyond the seas as no more to us than Bornean Headhunters or Esquimeaux.[38]

Given that his political outlook now rested so heavily on Empire, Johnston felt the need to mobilize imperial sentiment among the working class, to politicize this sentiment and to point it in the direction of Labour rather than the Conservatives. The thrust of this strategy was to emphasize the economic benefits of Empire to the working class.[39] For example, he favoured bulk purchasing of food from within the Empire to bring down prices, and with the other Clydeside ILPers came out in support of Imperial Preference in 1925. As Douds has noted, however, there was significant opposition to Johnston's Empire Socialism from within British Labour. At the 1925 Labour conference, Arthur Greenwood condemned 'protectionist economic imperialism' as 'anti-socialist and not helpful to the metropolitan people generally'.[40]

Johnston did not abandon his sense of Scottishness in his quest for an imperial socialism. His sense of Scottish nationalism was not incompatible with his British imperialism; indeed he argued that each supported the other. In May 1924, with Labour in office, George Buchanan, supported by Johnston, presented a Scottish Home Rule bill to the House of Commons. Johnston argued that allowing national distinctions within an imperial framework would strengthen the British Empire.[41] In 1927 Johnston seconded another Bill which would have given Scotland dominion status. This would have put Scotland on a level with the Irish Free State, but it was the loyal dominions of Canada and Australia that the supporters of the Bill considered to be their example rather than the radical anti-British nationalism of Sinn Fein.[42] The failure of the 1927 Bill led to the secession of some Labour Home Rulers, including Roland Muirhead, ILP member, financier of *Forward* and a close associate of Johnston, and the formation of the National Party of Scotland. The new party performed badly in its few electoral contests, which encouraged Labour to distance itself from nationalism.[43] This was especially the case because Labour's British forward march resulted in its election as the largest single party in the House of Commons in 1929.

Devolution and planning

Whereas in 1924 Johnston had been omitted from the government, his support for MacDonald and gradualism in the intervening years made him a safer appointment in 1929. He was appointed Parliamentary Under-Secretary for Scotland. His experience in the post had two seemingly contradictory effects upon him. First, through his admiration for nationalization in Canada he came to see the UK state as an appropriate means to institute social reform, and he believed that Labour was the only means by which the state could be captured. Secondly, though, the persistence of mass unemployment in Scotland convinced him that action above party was necessary to tackle major problems. His chairmanship of the EMB marketing committee and his friendship with moderate Conservatives like Elliot had already suggested that non-partisan politics was possible. As Under-Secretary he held 'weekly conferences of MPs from all parties to discuss Scottish issues'.[44] Johnston was propelled towards all-British solutions to social problems, while also being encouraged in his sense that Scotland was a more manageable arena for consensus-seeking politics.

Labour's experience in office was fundamentally affected by the global economic crisis. Unemployment in the United Kingdom rose from 1.3 million to 1929 to 2.5 million in December 1930. Johnston was appointed to represent Scottish interests on J.H. Thomas's subcommittee to tackle employment. Given that the fundamental crisis was in export industries, Scotland's unemployment was higher than that in the United Kingdom as a whole. Johnston had suggested Scottish public works such as building a road around Loch Lomond to encourage tourism but the Treasury, confined by its economic orthodoxy, refused to contemplate high government spending. The outcome of Labour's failure to endure the economic crisis was the fall of the government in 1931 when MacDonald formed the National government with the other major parties.

Johnston's immediate response was a flurry of socialist conspiracy theory, as he became prominent in expanding the view that there had been 'bankers' ramp' against the government.[45] Briefly, it looked as if Johnston might be a contender for the leadership of the party, but the loss of his seat in the 1931 election combined with his attachment to Scotland and his distaste for London kept him within the bounds of Scottish rather than British politics. Throughout the 1930s, he explored the configuration of his politics and identity of place. The outcome was a combination of planning and devolution, in conjunction with a belief in the possibilities of a national consensual politics, built from above.

Johnston was deeply impressed by the emphasis that the centre left and left placed on planning in the 1930s.[46] He, like many other political figures, visited the Soviet Union,[47] but equally with most of those from the British left who made the pilgrimage, he returned committed to a British path to socialist planning. Johnston's commitment remained to Scotland and his efforts towards rational planning included the founding of the Saltire Society in 1935 to encourage Scottish self-confidence. He was also engaged in writing a history of Kirkintilloch, which appeared in 1937. Johnston, therefore, remained deeply engaged with the minutiae of Scottish history and yet this did not lead him to embrace a separatist or romantic nationalism. He retained a desire for devolution. In 1937, having returned to the House of Commons in 1935, he established the London Scots Self-Government Committee.[48] This was a consciously socialist body and Johnston carefully spelled out his attitude towards nationalism and social progress. He rejected the 'form of Scots nationalism which had lost itself in Jacobite mists,' explaining that he and 'all London Scots Labourmen [were] vastly more disturbed that Scotland's unemployment relative to her population was $68\frac{1}{2}$ per cent worse than England's ... that our maternal mortality was 50 per cent higher than it was south of the border.' The solution, he said, 'lay not in heraldic restoration but in social ownership of soil, industry, and finance, and there was one political route and one only to social ownership: it was through the British Labour Party.'[49] Devolution was necessary, he suggested, because business in the Commons had become congested. He wanted the Scots Grand Committee of MPs to meet in Edinburgh and to be given greater authority over estimates for agriculture, education and health. Following this, legislative power could be expanded from these to other services.[50] By the end of the 1930s, therefore, Johnston was looking for moderate devolutionist measures that hinted at a cooperation of Scottish MPs of all parties.

That is not to say that Johnston did not denounce Conservatism, and particularly that of the National government. However, Johnston's pragmatic belief in the need to act in the immediate interests of the

Scottish people meant that he supported the plans for civil defence in the late 1930s, against the opposition of the majority of the Labour Party.[51] When he was offered the post of Regional Commissioner for Civil Defence in Scotland he nearly refused it because of his distrust of Neville Chamberlain's government.[52]

A Scottish 'People's War'

Whereas the outbreak of the Second World War led to the questioning of Elliot's British patriotism, Johnston's acceptance of the civil defence post signified the compatibility of his desire to do well for Scotland without jeopardy to wider British interests. With the fall of Chamberlain and Churchill's succession in May 1940, Johnston's power was enhanced. Labour had played a major part in the fall of Chamberlain, but in addition, Churchill was concerned to keep the organized working class firmly behind the war effort. At a national level Ernest Bevin, the transport workers' leader, became Minister of Labour to oversee the co-option of the unions, and in 1941 Johnston was appointed as Secretary of State for Scotland to encourage the industrial co-operation of the Scottish working class.[53] Johnston could be trusted and Churchill described him as 'our good and faithful friend'.[54]

The social democratic tendency of the 'people's war' suited Johnston's socialism very well when combined with his 'dictatorship' over Scotland.[55] He was able to forge instruments of consensus to consider Scotland's future, but in an atmosphere in which the working class was seen as central to the nation's sense of itself. Johnston saw the potential for using the Secretaryship to build 'Scotia Resurgent'. Yet when he made this statement he referred also to 'our finest hour'.[56] The Second World War encouraged Johnston in his Scottishness but simultaneously drew his attention to the importance of the Union in creating and sustaining the conditions for his administrative devolution.

Johnston showed that he believed that Scottish national unity was possible by insisting on his authority to shape the institutions of the Scottish Office. He established a Council of State of the former Scottish Secretaries to form the manpower for a series of committees on Scottish problems. Between the wars there had been only two periods of Labour government during both of which Willie Adamson had served as Scottish Secretary. Adamson's death meant that the Council was a decidedly un-Labour body.[57] The committees addressed Scotland's 'crisis of national identity' through consideration of the economy. Johnston has been widely proclaimed as the most successful

Scottish Secretary because he drew so much devolved power to Edinburgh, in part by scaring his government colleagues with the potential for the growth of Scottish nationalism as a 'sort of Sinn Fein movement'.[58] His warnings were boosted by the improved fortunes of the SNP in by-elections, culminating in victory at Motherwell in April 1945. But the increased nationalist vote was almost entirely due to the electoral truce between the major parties. The nationalists provided anti-government candidates who were supplied by independent and Common Wealth candidates in the rest of the UK.

It is certain that war once more encouraged and enabled the Scottish people to assert their distinctiveness. There was agitation over the conscription of Scottish women to English munitions factories, for example, and stress was placed on the particular role that the Scottish were playing in the war effort. An article written in 1943, in Johnston's papers, listed Scotland's contribution to the war. These included a Clyde paddle-steamer at Dunkirk, two Scottish RAF squadrons 'in the thick of' the Battle of Britain, four Scottish VCs, the role of Scottish merchant seamen, of Highland regiments in North Africa, and the Scottishness of the generals Sir Bernard Montgomery and Wingate.[59] However, this distinctiveness was being affirmed within the context of the Union. In late 1943 Johnston submitted a memorandum to the Ministerial Machinery of Government Committee. Johnston argued that 'today Scotland expects that the central administration of her domestic matters will be based on Edinburgh rather than on Whitehall unless there are overriding reasons to the contrary.'[60] The committee endorsed the 'intense local patriotism and "sense of difference"' in Scotland but also 'at the same time (with insignificant exceptions) by an entire devotion to the Union and "sense of oneness" with its other constituent parts, [which] is probably unique in the history of modern government'.[61]

While Johnston always remained detached from London politics, he also saw Scotland in the context of the wider Union because his power depended on British Labour as well as his position in Scotland. Hence he played a role in UK-wide reconstruction in relation to town planning and national health schemes.[62] Walker argues that Johnston wanted a fair share for Scotland within a partnership with England in the Union.[63] He wanted de-centralization of power to Scotland but its retention by the Scottish Office in Edinburgh. While he did not give up the idea of Home Rule, supporting the covenant movement of the late 1940s, the experience of state-sponsored reform during the war led him firmly towards a de-politicized devolution, in which democratic participation was subordinated.[64]

The war had established that it was possible to set up separate Scottish bodies within the context of the advance of British socialism. Whereas John Taylor, secretary of the Scottish Labour Party, declared in 1947 that 'I, myself, ceased to desire self-government as soon as we secured a Socialist Government for Britain,'[65] Johnston continued to defend separate institutions for Scotland against the centralizing tendency of British Labour in power. He had developed a particular interest in the North of Scotland Hydro-Electric Board of which he was chairman and which he saw as potentially instrumental in re-establishing the Highlands as self-supporting and as the heart of 'Scotia'.[66] With the nationalization of the electricity industry, Johnston successfully defended his Board's independence. In the post-war years, he also chaired or sat on the boards of the Scottish Tourist Board, the Scottish National Forestry Commission and the Broadcasting Council for Scotland. He saw the Tourist Board as 'tighten[ing] the bands of racial fraternity' within the Commonwealth. Tourism was an important contributor to the Scottish economy but Johnston maintained a cultural pride in 'The greater Scotland beyond the seas with its nostalgia for the old-birth place'. He saw it as 'a fact of some importance in the world, and who having experienced it, can ever forget the overpowering intensity of the Scottishness in the gatherings of our folk from Calcutta to Chicago?'[67]

Johnston's Scottishness after 1941 was increasingly pronounced, but it was also beholden to Westminster. He was stressing the distinctive nature of Scotland and Scottishness within the United Kingdom, so in 1951 he was on the committee that organized the Scottish elements of the Festival of Britain. His vision celebrated the working-class nature of Scotland in an 'Exhibition of Industrial Power'.[68] While this involved a successful appropriation of Scottishness for the working class, the ability to achieve this rested on appointment from London. T.C. Smout has judged that Johnston 'moved from democratic socialist to quango-man'.[69]

Tom Johnston contributed to the development of the Labour Party in Scotland. He adopted a community-based municipal politics in Kirkintilloch that reflected the growth of labour elsewhere in Britain. At the same time, though, he accepted 'the fact' of nationality, which he associated with the working class and the people rather than with Scotland's elites. The Labour Party in its early pluralist phase could accommodate support for Scottish Home Rule with its desire to win power at a British level. Johnston was associated with the Clydeside MPs. With them, he welcomed Labour's British advance while attempting to maintain a distinctive Scottish style of politics. Johnston, however, held aloof from their radicalism. As Ramsay MacDonald constructed 'British socialism' to be moderate, constitutional and gradual, so Johnston presented similar moderation but with a Scottish flavour. It included support for the Empire as a vehicle for the improvement of the condition of the Scottish people, which would also allow Scotland to distinguish itself from England within the Union. He continued to support Home Rule as a complement to his Empire Socialism.

Another aspect of Johnston's regard for the Scottish people was through his belief in planning. This encouraged the centralization of power. In the late 1930s Johnston reiterated his commitment to the devolution of power to Scotland, but in the context of strengthening the British Labour Party to enable the diffusion of planning to Scotland. The Second World War provided the opportunity. Johnston was appointed Secretary of State and set about creating 'Scotia Resurgent'. He restored the idea of national consensus that he had used at the Scottish Office in the early 1930s. This did not mean that Johnston ever lost the awareness that Scotland operated inside the Union. He was little interested in British politics as a whole, and Attlee rightly considered that Johnston was 'too wedded to Scotland' to want a government post concerned with British issues.[70] Johnston was, however, fully aware that Labour's British power was the prerequisite for the fulfilment of his own brand of Scottish Labourism. Given the moderate nature of much Scottish Unionism, Johnston believed that with a Labour government in power in London and a national consensus in Scotland, the Union would work very well. Hence, he told the *Daily Record* in 1944 that his policy was 'the equivalent of saying: "We will do this by agreement, and then we will go to London and say, 'This is the voice of Scotland. We are agreed on such-and-such a scheme".'[71]

4
Empire, Europe and the Union: Lady Priscilla Tweedsmuir (1915–1978)

Like Walter Elliot and Thomas Johnston, Lady Priscilla Tweedsmuir held to an outward-looking version of Scottishness that operated within the framework of the Union. She told the House of Commons in 1955 that 'Scotland is a voluntary partner in the Union with England and Wales. We must take our share – and a large share – of responsibility in the great issues of foreign and Commonwealth affairs, defence and the wider matters of Government.'[1] Tweedsmuir differed from Elliot and Johnston in two fundamental ways. Firstly, and most obviously, she was a woman, and secondly, born in 1915, she was of a subsequent political generation to them. Whereas Elliot and Johnston's political careers were conducted against the backdrop of Empire, hers coincided with the end of Empire and the United Kingdom's turn towards Europe. She was compelled to re-negotiate unionist identity to take such developments into account. Another way in which she differed was that while Elliot and Johnston were subordinate figures in UK politics, it is fair to say that they were the two most eminent figures of their day in Scottish politics. Tweedsmuir was far less prominent. Her highest political position in Scotland was as Minister of State in the Scottish Office (1970–1972), and in the UK government it was as Minister of State in the Foreign and Commonwealth Office (1972–1974), where she was the first woman to serve. This chapter examines Tweedsmuir's political identity in relation to her gender, her political ideas about the connections between Scotland and the rest of Britain, and the emphasis she placed on Scotland's international role. Her political life in the second half of the twentieth century, a period of re-adjustment for the United Kingdom, required her to re-evaluate her identity.

Women, unionism and Scottishness

The position of women within Scottish national identity and Unionism was complicated. Women were left out of most representations of
Scottishness. They found little place, for example, in the democratic
and meritocratic aspects of education seen as central to Scottish
national identity.[2] The Unionist Party shared this gendered conservatism. Although the party emphasized the importance of women's
role within the family and home, it also took special measures to
ensure that women were represented within the structure of the organization. Between the wars, the Unionists stood sixteen women as candidates compared to twelve for Labour and six for the Liberals. Of
these, three women were elected as Unionists, compared to two for
Labour and none for the Liberals.[3] In addition, the party concentrated
on the political education of its women members.

After the disastrous election defeat of 1945 the party reaffirmed its
recognition of women's importance to its electoral fortunes. Lady
Priscilla Grant had stood unsuccessfully for North Aberdeen in the
1945 election and was elected for South Aberdeen in a by-election in
November 1946. Born on 25 January 1915, she was from the Scottish
(aristocratic) military family of the Thomsons.[4] After education in
England, Germany and France, she married in 1934. Her husband,
Sir Arthur Lindsay Grant, a major in the Grenadier Guards, was killed
in action in 1944. Her own war service was as commandant of an
auxiliary hospital in her family home, and as an assistant welfare
officer at an Aberdeen munitions factory. In 1948 she married John
Buchan, the second Lord Tweedsmuir, who she had met in the Houses
of Parliament.

The Conservatives in the late 1940s attacked the Labour government's rationing and austerity policies and Lady Tweedsmuir provided
the party with an effective symbol to oppose the impact of socialism
on housewives. As well as serving on a party committee on 'women's
affairs', Tweedsmuir also appeared in Conservative propaganda films
and election broadcasts.[5] The emphasis on domesticity was carried
into the propaganda aimed at women. Their stress on the impact of
rationing and controls on food seems to have paid off in the 1951 election, when the Conservatives returned to power with a majority of
sixteen.[6] However, the party had secured fewer votes than Labour and
Churchill was keen to continue his emphasis on the 'national' nature
of the Conservatives. As well as appointing moderate Conservatives
and National Liberals to government posts, he gave the Ministry of

Education to Florence Horsbrugh to reward the female electorate.[7] This was one of the 'domestic' posts within the government, considered suitable for a woman. Churchill emphasized his disdain for Horsbrugh by excluding her from the cabinet until 1953. Even then, he ensured that she knew how he felt about having a woman in the cabinet. If she contributed to cabinet discussions on foreign policy, Churchill is said to have commented sarcastically: 'Fancy the Minister of *Education* taking an interest in foreign affairs.'[8] Such thinking had a direct impact on Tweedsmuir's political career. Churchill considered appointing her as Under-Secretary at the Scottish Office, but the minister, James Stuart, objected because he disliked the idea of women as ministers.[9]

Tweedsmuir was assigned to women's roles within the party. She was appointed as a delegate to the Council of Europe between 1950 and 1953, but the most comment upon her performance came from Harold Macmillan who noted in his diary on 8 May 1951 that she had 'scored a great success by her charms. *"Mais elle est épatante!"* ... French senators seemed particularly susceptible.'[10] In 1959, Tweedsmuir's gender and nationality were brought together again in the service of the party. Oliver Poole, the party chairman, wrote to her explaining that 'the Prime Minister is anxious that you, as a lady Member and representing Scotland' should make one of the party's four election broadcasts on the BBC Light Programme.[11]

This is not to say that Tweedsmuir had no agency of her own. She shared many tenets of the Conservative ideology of feminine domesticity. In her private notes for use in the election of 1945, she said that the position of women MPs should be one of '*Partnership* with men in Reconstruction – not equal but different outlook – not specialists – but deep knowledge of problems of living – a woman's difficulties. Represent all round – leave specialisation in foreign affairs etc. to others.'[12] Such ideas certainly did not preclude her own activism, but in the 1940s she shared the dominant view of Conservatism that women's political activity was more appropriately concerned with the social sphere rather than the traditional realms of the public sphere.

Economic unionism

Tweedsmuir was firmly Unionist and her most common defence of the Union was economic. The Second World War had temporarily overcome inter-war economic dislocation and much of Johnston's work at the Scottish Office had been aimed at encouraging economic improvement, but Tweedsmuir's 1945 campaign showed the importance she attached to the Union as the source of economic strength. Her 1945 political notes stressed the importance of securing Britain's economic future through education of 'trained personnel to ensure utmost efficiency in production'.[13] Her concern with Scotland was as part of the Union that had 'special problems – the chief is our dependence on heavy industry'.[14] She tended to see Scotland's problems as those of a region within a wider British economy. That was not to say that she did not see the Scottish as a distinct people within the United Kingdom, and she emphasised their 'national characteristics', which harmonized with her economic Conservatism: '*Scots* independence, courage, pioneering, hard work, curiosity, initiative, passion & knowledge & adventure, thrifty civil servants.'[15] But as Under-Secretary at the Scottish Office between 1962 and 1964 she implemented the regional economic policy of the Conservative government, which was a response to the loss of five seats in the 1959 general election rather than an effective strategy.[16] In the 1964 general election, which her party lost, Tweedsmuir combated the 'white heat of technology' stance being taken by Harold Wilson. She emphasized the modernizing role of Alec Douglas-Home as new Scottish leader of the party:

> [I] saw him last at [the] opening of the Forth Bridge, which is symbolic of the Scotland now being created. Modernisation [is] not a catch phrase but a fact. The power stations, nuclear and conventional, the new factories and industries coming into the growth areas at an increasing pace, and the miles of new roads, are transforming the face of Scotland and building her economy on a stronger and more varied basis. Seeing that Forth Road Bridge and the Tay Road Bridge in the making, and so much else, makes one wonder where Mr. Wilson spends his time if he feels that the country is rotten and its people are flabby and soft, which is what his manifesto said.[17]

She emphasised the interventionist nature of the Conservative government to her constituents, pointing out that 'Aberdeen now has a modern fishing fleet, largely built with Government grants and loans.'[18] Tweedsmuir was always keen to highlight Scotland's modernity. As Minister of State at the Scottish Office in 1972 she declared that 'despite the Scotland of tourist publicity, the Scotland of heather hills and misty islands, we are a highly industrial society'.[19]

Her focus on the Scottish economy within the United Kingdom economy was linked to her political attitude to the Union. In her first election she explained that 'I support all ideas for bringing industry and employment to the North – therefore I do not support Home Rule, thinking that Scotland derives more benefit for exercising her right to a share of world trade and financial advantages open to Britain as a whole.'

While she wanted de-centralization of administrative power and more Scottish debates in Parliament, she felt 'confident that history has shewn [*sic*] Union is strength'.[20] In the balance between Union and devolution, Tweedsmuir was firmly in favour of the former. Her declarations on the de-centralization of power were not her own initiatives but accompanied the ebb and flow of Conservative central policy. She took up the Scottish Unionist rhetoric against nationalization as a centralizing force, so in 1959 in her eve of poll meeting, she asked, 'Does Mr Gaitskell think that nationalisation is going to help Scotland? Mr Gaitskell's supporters should point out to him, pretty firmly, that Scotland is not just a Region, but a country.'[21] It is perhaps significant that she did not refer to Scotland as a nation, choosing the less political designation of 'country'. In her UK election broadcast in the same year, she declared that 'I support the Tories because their ideas work – and because we are a National Party. Because the class war seems to us not only years out of date but dangerous. We know that if we quarrel among ourselves, we shall be a weak and unhappy country.'[22] Tweedsmuir's 'nation' was the United Kingdom, with Scotland a constituent element that aided the strength of the greater whole.

The 1950s was a decade of minimal Nationalist activity. In the early 1950s, MacCormick's Covenant had failed to bring a legislative body to Scotland. However, the new Conservative government of Churchill did feel that it had to initiate some reform of Scottish administration, not least because senior and junior Conservatives, including Elliot and Tweedsmuir, had campaigned for MacCormick, who was standing as a Liberal, in the December 1947 Paisley by-election in a failed attempt to inflict a defeat on Labour.[23] The Covenant had attracted two million signatures, not for nationalism, but for devolution within the United Kingdom. Its political failure meant that when Churchill set up a Royal Commission on Scottish Affairs, investigation into a devolved legislative body was not included within its remit. There was some transfer of functions to the Scottish Office, but as James Mitchell has argued, 'The Conservatives' interpretation of "Scottish control of Scottish affairs" was merely an unimaginative tidying up operation within the administrative apparatus of the Scottish Office.'[24]

Conservative and Unionist concern in the 1950s was with the weakness of the Scottish economy relative to that of the wider UK economy. This concern was heightened when Scottish politics diverged from British politics in 1959, when the Unionist vote in Scotland faltered. Given that in 1955 the Unionists had achieved more than 50 per cent of the share of the vote, some decrease was unsurprising. Indeed, the Unionists still secured 47.2 per cent of the vote, which was higher than Labour's share. However, the party did lose five seats in Scotland, while in the rest of the UK it won an additional 20 seats including one in Wales and two in Northern Ireland.

In the early 1960s, with Tweedsmuir as a junior minister at the Scottish Office, efforts were made to improve Scotland's economic infrastructure. The modernizing rhetoric failed, to the benefit of Labour in 1964, when the Unionist vote fell to 37.3 per cent. Labour improved its position in 1966, achieving 49.9 per cent to the Unionists' 37.7 per cent. Tweedsmuir was a casualty of the Unionist decline, losing South Aberdeen, which she had held in five elections.[25] The party's response to continuing decline in the mid-1960s was to reorganize the party in Scotland and to change its name.[26] Unionism was seen as being of less importance to the electorate. This was not because of the rise of nationalism but because the issue of the Union came to be seen as outdated. The Conservatives were 'modernizing' – responding to a perception of changed social structures, including the declining significance of Protestant Unionism within the Scottish working class.[27] The party, therefore, subordinated Unionism to Conservatism on the eve of the rise of the Scottish National Party. As the critics of the Union were once more beginning to make the Union the central issue in Scottish politics, the Conservatives had retreated from their symbolic Unionism, believing its relevance was limited in modern Scotland.

The advance of the SNP was dramatic. In 1962 the party had only forty branches and 2,000 members, by 1968 it had five hundred branches and possibly 120,000 members.[28] In November 1966 it won the Hamilton seat from Labour in a by-election. Edward Heath, the new Conservative leader, thought Scottish nationalism to be 'the biggest single factor in our politics today'.[29] The Conservatives' response to nationalism was to surrender to its demands without principle.

Richard Finlay has argued that there was substantial continuity in the Conservatives' rejoinder to the SNP in the 1960s, which built on previous devolutionary responses to demands for national recognition of Scotland within the Union. He argues correctly that 'The

Conservative Party in Scotland had always accepted the principle of a distinctive national dimension in Scottish politics, and as a consequence of this there was always the potential for acknowledging this within the framework of political devolution.'[30] However, when Heath made his speech at the Scottish party conference in 1968, which became known as the 'Declaration of Perth,' it did not seem to be a Scottish Unionist initiative but the startled response of the English leader. The party itself had identified that Conservatism in Scotland was increasingly associated with Anglicizing influences. In 1968 a report for Central Office said that the party in Scotland 'has got an exceedingly bad image. It is thought to be out of touch, a bastion of "foreign" (English) privilege, Westminster oriented, associated with recalcitrant landowners'.[31] The party had already decided that policy for Scotland must look like it was emanating from Scotland.[32] A 'Thistle Group' was established among Scottish MPs and a committee of Scottish Conservatives, meeting in the wake of the Hamilton by-election, suggested a Scottish assembly, partly elected and partly appointed, with powers to initiate legislation but with Westminster retaining a veto. At Perth, Heath announced a further committee that would develop policy in public. He grandly named it the Constitutional Committee, to be chaired by Sir Alec Douglas-Home. He stressed that he was recommending that this new committee accept the idea of an assembly. It appeared, therefore, that Heath had made policy which would be rubber stamped by Home, an aristocratic and Anglicized Unionist.

The Conservatives did win the general election of 1970. Nearly four out of ten Scottish voters supported them. However, Heath's manoeuvres seem to have had no discernible effect on the Conservatives' performance in Scotland.[33] The Conservatives' share of the vote rose by less than half of one percent. The SNP did not, though, make its predicted breakthrough, securing a disappointing average of 12.2 per cent of the votes in the seats it contested. It lost Hamilton, but maintained its presence at Westminster through victory in the Western Isles.[34] It was Labour rather than the Conservatives who had stemmed the SNP rise. The Scottish Office after 1964 had been under the custody of Willie Ross, who fought hard in cabinet to secure economic subsidies for Scotland and who attacked the SNP as a 'phoney' party and as 'narks', but made sure that he quoted Burns in his speeches.[35] Labour, like the Conservatives, feared the potential for Nationalist growth. The Labour government set up a Royal Commission as both concession and delaying tactic. In 1970 Labour's share of the vote fell in Scotland by about five per cent but it only lost two MPs. With the SNP's failure to break through, both the Conservatives in government and Labour in opposition turned away from devolution between 1970 and 1974. The Conservative government implemented none of the recommendations of the Home committee, which included a directly elected assembly that would consider bills declared 'Scottish' by the Speaker of the House of Commons.[36]

Tweedsmuir served on Home's Constitutional Committee but her attentions had already turned elsewhere. Out of parliament, she had become a director of the shipping company Cunard. Her interests were increasingly in foreign policy and she saw policy towards Scotland lying within wider international considerations. For the October 1974 general election she explained the position in which she saw Scotland:

> While all Scots have confidence in their country there is no evidence that the majority want the Union to be broken ... The evidence is that modern industry needs the *interdependence* of the Union ... This is an age of greater interdependence between nations – which is of course the reason why we joined the European Communities. We need as many Allies as possible in this uncertain world.[37]

The crux of Tweedsmuir's politics was the desire to maintain the United Kingdom as a major force of influence in the world. Despite her assertion in 1945 that foreign policy was the business of male politicians, she became increasingly interested in Britain's world role. In 1964 she coupled her preoccupation with the Scottish economy to British foreign policy when she declared that 'The real test for this country is which Party has the ability to keep sound economy at home, and Britain's real influence abroad.'[38] This was against the backdrop of Tweedsmuir's awareness of Britain's declining imperial influence.

The Buchan legacy

Tweedsmuir's ideas fitted into the multinational politics of Unionism. It would be fair to say that through her second marriage, Tweedsmuir entered the Scottish-British-imperial political world exemplified by her (deceased) father-in-law, John Buchan. While he had been born in Scotland and certainly retained intimate political and social links with that nation, his public life had been lived outside Scotland. He had made his main home at Elsfield in Oxfordshire. He represented the

Scottish Universities for the Unionists between 1927 and 1935, a seat without a territorial constituency, and always saw Scotland as residing within the British Empire rather than in isolation. The culmination of his career came in his appointment as Governor-General of Canada, which was to have a significant influence on his son, also John, and his future daughter-in-law.[39] The second Lord Tweedsmuir was, therefore, Scottish by descent rather than by residency. He was educated at Eton and Oxford and then embarked upon an imperial career much like one of the characters in his father's novels. He was in the diplomatic service in Uganda in the mid-1930s and spent a year as a fur trapper for the Hudson Bay Company in Canada in 1938–39. When war broke out, he served in the Canadian army.[40] He saw 'the Scottish race' as imperial and global, and believed that this had enabled Scots to exert great influence for a small nation. He said that 'far from being confined by Cape Wrath to the North West and Berwick-on-Tweed to the South East, they are dispersed between the outposts of North Western Canada to the South Island of New Zealand'.[41] Lady Priscilla had not had the imperial experience of her husband though her family connections had tied her into the institution of the British Army and her Scottishness was firmly associated with Britishness and its imperial service.

In the wake of the Second World War, Lady Tweedsmuir took up the idea of the imperial dispersal of the Scots as part of her political programme. At this time, her Britain was wider than the United Kingdom. 'Surely we cannot think of Britain as just Britain,' she told the Commons in 1950. 'Britain is part of the Commonwealth, and one of our major points of policy should be to allow a greater number of emigrants to spread our ideas and spread our British stock throughout the world.'[42] In 1955, in the debate on the Royal Commission on Scottish Affairs' report, she said that

> We should also recall as a matter of pride that it is one of the greatest personal characteristics of our countrymen that Scotsmen and Scotswomen will try their lot if they are given the chance in young countries or in competitive areas where the challenge is greater than it is at home.[43]

Tweedsmuir of course realised that times were changing. She played a minor role in the decolonization of Africa, through a parliamentary visit to investigate the killings at the Hola detention camp in Kenya. As a delegate to the United Nations, she was fully aware of the emergence of new nations from the disintegration of the British Empire. She argued that the Empire's great role had been its preparation of colonies for self-government. As she told the Empire Club of Canada:

> [S]ince the Second World War, a quarter of the world's population which was formerly administered for Britain, has become independent. We have always tried to carry out one main objective, and that is that the granting of self-government shall, in fact, mean the granting of responsible government; that the economy of the countries concerned shall be stable; that there shall be provision for the respect of minorities; and that there has been some experience in government and in running the civil service.[44]

Many Britons believed that in ending its political dominance of the Empire the United Kingdom was fulfilling a benevolent role. The idea of the end of Empire as the culmination of British destiny enabled Tweedsmuir, and many others, to come to terms with what was a fundamental shift in Britain's global role. She saw Britain's challenge as being to form a coherent and effective block out of Commonwealth members at the UN. Britain, she thought, could maintain its moral leadership through example, even when new nations had emerged. While in geographical terms the Empire was disappearing, in psychological terms it remained a reality.

Tweedsmuir and her husband were products of imperial Britain. Their relationship and domestic life were tied up with imperialism. Hunting trophies were usually associated with male spaces, such as billiard and smoking rooms, but the whole of the Tweedsmuir house at Potterton, near Aberdeen, provided a showcase for their imperial hunting trophies.[45] Lord Tweedsmuir called these the 'reminders of the extent of our wanderings, mostly on duties concerned with Britain's old responsibilities of Empire'.[46] They had a particularly memorable trip to Canada in 1955, which brought back memories of former family and imperial glory. The Tweedsmuirs were invited to take a three-week trip through the Tweedsmuir National Park in British Columbia, and it brought home to Lady Tweedsmuir the expanse of the former Empire. 'I cannot get over the enormity of Canada,' she wrote in her journal of the tour, 'huge lakes, endless bush, range upon range of mountains.'[47] The holiday enabled Lady Tweedsmuir to play out the role of imperial explorer. While she had sponsored a Protection of Birds Act in the House of Commons in 1954, her attitude to wildlife in Canada was distinctly imperial. She recorded a disappointing day in Tweedsmuir Park:

> Al [their guide] was driving, J[ohnnie] and I idling trolling rods and looking at the scenery, when suddenly there was a yell from Al. 'A grizzly swimming the river!' Rifles unloaded somewhere... When at last I had my rifle in my hand, I had one quick view of the bear's head as it neared the bank among the 'swimming trees'. I fired, too hasty, and ill-prepared, and missed. Oh the desolation. I fired once more as grizzly clambered up a steep bank, not more than 30 yards away, but he was off at full gallop. We hurled ourselves ashore, and hunted him in fairly open bush, in sun and the hot smell of pines, but we were on an island, and he had gone, maybe swum across the other river channel. I <u>was</u> sad, for hunting here is difficult, and maybe I'll not see one again.[48]

She was more successful when she saw her first moose, which she shot from 270 yards, and which 'redeemed the muddle over the grizzly!'[49] Her shooting of a bull caribou a few days later provided further sport. This was a post-imperial encounter with Canada and the mounting of the caribou's head in Potterton retained its memory in a domestic setting. Hunting had provided a method of incorporation of European women into the masculine world of imperial India before 1947. Mary Procida has argued that 'sport was an integral and essential component of an imperial femininity that incorporated traditionally masculine attributes without completely eradicating fundamental gender distinctions'.[50] This provides a useful way of considering Tweedsmuir's view of herself, as an essentially Buchanesque heroine, capable, confident and skilful, transgressing normal gender boundaries yet retaining a feminine attractiveness. The companionate nature of her marriage to her second husband enabled her to reconcile the transgression.[51]

A decade later she emphasized her personal regret over the end of Empire as she flew across the Atlantic. 'How Johnnie would love to be G[overnor] G[eneral] & I would love to support him,' she wrote. 'We would do great things together, but times have changed & I doubt if a British person will ever be asked again.'[52]

Tweedsmuir sought to come to terms with Britain's post-imperial role. In 1965 she wound up for the Conservatives in a debate on foreign affairs. Now she considered that it was incumbent upon her 'to establish once & for all that a woman is a[n] MP & should take her place in all branches of political affairs on merit'. She declared that 'foreign affairs is my first love – not only for itself but because it brings me in contact with the whole House of Commons & of the elements in it which are fundamental to an existence in this country'.[53] In the debate she stressed the continuing importance of the Commonwealth, drew attention to the role of Highland regiments in Malaysia and argued that Britain needed 'sound diplomacy backed by strength'. She considered that this was possible through turning towards Europe. 'It is, surely,' she argued, 'a prime British interest to share in shaping Europe.'[54] Despite a dislike of Edward Heath (which was mutual),[55] she was given a life peerage that enabled her to take a seat in the House of Lords. She was appointed Minister of State at the Scottish Office in 1970. Her pro-European stance encouraged Heath to promote her in 1972 to Minister of State at the Foreign and Commonwealth Office (FCO), the first woman to hold office in that ministry.

At the FCO, much of her role was to react to events, such as the dispute with Spain over Gibraltar. However, office did allow her to pursue her long interest in the UK's relations with Europe. In the 1940s and 1950s, she had been concerned that relations with Europe should accord with Britain's imperial role, declaring that 'Europe cannot live without the Commonwealth, or the Commonwealth without Western Europe.'[56] Later, she argued that the relationship with Europe allowed for the maintenance of a distinctive role for Scots in the wake of the end of Empire. At the Scottish Office in the 1970s she explained that

> Without undue pride I can say that Scots have skills and ideas to contribute to the growth of Europe and we still have the Scottish qualities of perseverance, spiced with ambition, which helped to forge the prototype of all Common Markets – the Union of Scotland and England two and a half centuries ago.[57]

Tweedsmuir was again stressing that the Union provided the nexus between Scotland and its wider international role, as it had when that role had been imperial. She was formulating a post-colonial Scottishness in which the Union remained the essential constitutional form that allowed Scotland to remain a global force despite its small size. She combined this view with the construction of a post-colonial Britishness, when she told the Lords that entry into Europe was a challenge: 'My Lords, I think there is no doubt that to begin with the going will be rough and it will be a test of what we in Britain really are: of whether we have the nerve and the character to meet the demands not only on our skill but also on our judgement.'[58]

At the FCO, Tweedsmuir could not be other than fully aware of the diminished world role of the United Kingdom. In the House of Lords she had to respond to questions on the treatment of the remnants of Britain's Empire.[59] Her most prominent moment was when she took the leadership of Britain's position in the 'cod war' with Iceland in 1972. The Icelandic government extended its territorial limits in order to defend its fishing rights. To some it seemed that British opposition, based on its defence of the interests of east coast fishing fleets from Hull to Aberdeen, was the bullying stance of a large power towards a small nation.[60] Tweedsmuir was keen to dispel such myth formation, pointing out that Iceland's per capita GNP, based on hydro-electric and geo-thermal resources as well as fishing, was only seventy five US dollars lower than that of Britain.[61] Britain's position was certainly conciliatory, even when the Icelandic navy fired on British trawlers. Despite international legality resting on the British side, the Royal Navy was ordered not to respond. Tweedsmuir's difficulty lay in asserting British rights without becoming embroiled in a hot war or with establishing Britain's weakness.[62]

Mary Kenny in the *Evening Standard* dubbed Tweedsmuir as 'Lady T'. For the first time in the twentieth century, a British war was being run by a woman, and the novelty of such an occasion was not lost on the press. Kenny continued that 'The Government can be completely confident of Lady Tweedsmuir. She is a sort of gentler version of Barbara Castle: very charming and able. Dead posh and dead tough.'[63] The *Daily Mail* continued such gendered themes at the end of the year, informing its readers that 'Lady Tweedsmuir, our tough and very feminine negotiator over the Icelandic Cod War, is ... quite the mistress of her own kitchen.'[64]

Tweedsmuir battled to establish a role for herself as a woman within the Conservative Party and governments. She was able to transgress the impositions placed on women within the governance of the Union. She was not confined to 'traditional' women's offices of education and health but was eventually appointed to the Foreign and Commonwealth Office. From the late 1950s, she had been concerned to address issues of Scottish economic weakness. She was determined that Scotland needed a programme of modernization that would enable it to continue to play a role in the British foreign policy. She recognized the weakening of Britain's position in the world and re-negotiated her Scottish-British national identity in the light of imperial decline. In the late 1960s, she was involved in the Conservative discussions on devolution but her preferred solution to Britain's loss of power was integration with Europe. She saw the economic and political integration as a necessary readjustment to enable Scotland and Britain to continue to play a benevolent international role.

Tweedsmuir was, however, a casualty of the Conservative Party's decline in Scotland. She died in March 1978 and, therefore, did not see the party's temporary revival in 1979 and 1983 under its most Unionist, and first woman, leader, Margaret Thatcher. The party believed in the mid-1960s that defence of the Union was no longer a fundamental political issue in Scotland. It turned to a programme of economic modernization to restore its fortunes but in the process went some way to abandoning its distinctive form of multi-identity Scottishness. There was a striking irony that the task of convincing the Scottish electorate that modernization was possible under the Conservatives was handed to aristocratic figures like Sir Alec Douglas-Home and Lady Priscilla Tweedsmuir.

Scotland and the Union: epilogue

Between 1918 and 1970s there were episodic, limited and failed Scottish challenges to the Union. The SNP was a very weak force even at the peak of its strength in the 1960s. The weakness of the Scottish economy became more apparent as the 1960s and 1970s progressed. The Labour government, pushed forward by its minority position and its overreaction to nationalism, introduced Bills that would provide differing degrees of devolution for Scotland and Wales. In 1975 Margaret Thatcher became leader of the Conservative Party. She described herself 'an instinctive Unionist'.[65] Her Unionism allowed little space for the recognition that the United Kingdom was constituted from different national and regional identities. Under her the Conservatives opposed the Bills. When they were passed, the Conservatives campaigned for 'No' votes in the referendums on devolution. Some, like Sir Alec Douglas-Home, did so while trying to reiterate the Conservatives' Scottishness by arguing that the Conservatives would introduce 'a better bill'. Many commentators were predicting 'the break-up of Britain' – Tom Nairn's book was published first in 1977. Thatcher and the Conservatives argued that they alone could put a halt to the crisis of the UK state. The long period of Conservative dominance after the 1979 election was possible because substantial numbers in England, Scotland and Wales believed that claim.

In the 1979 Scottish referendum a majority of those who voted did so for devolution. The norms of British democracy had been subverted by an amendment to the Scotland Act requiring more than 40 per cent of the electorate to vote for devolution. In the event, less than one-third of the Scottish electorate (32.85 per cent) voted for devolution, though this was 51.6 per cent of those voting. As Vernon Bogdanor argues: 'The result destroyed the credibility of devolution. It had been pressed in Parliament on the ground that there was a surge of popular demand for it in Scotland, but the outcome of the referendum entirely undermined that claim.'[66] In the short term, the Conservatives were the political beneficiaries. On 28 March 1979, the SNP MPs at Westminster supported a Conservative motion of no confidence in the Labour government, which was passed by one vote. In the election that followed the Conservative vote in Scotland rose by 6.7 per cent to 31.4 per cent. The SNP vote fell by 13.1 per cent. The break-up of Britain, it seemed, had been halted. Thatcher believed that the lesson to be learned was that Scotland should not be treated differently within her programme but should be brought into line. There was no space left within the Conservative Party for the distinctive contribution of Scottish Unionists. The outcome for Unionism in Scotland was catastrophic. In the 1997 general election, not a single Scottish seat sent a Conservative MP to Westminster.[67]

All was not lost for the Union though. The beneficiaries of Unionist decline were not the nationalists but Labour. They learnt the lessons of 1979. In the 1980s and 1990s, Scottish Labour transformed itself from monolithic unionism to sincere support for devolution. In the 1990s, Labour rediscovered the pluralism of its early years and established itself again as an all-British party that could reconcile geographical and national difference within the Union through the establishment of the Scottish Parliament in 1999.

5
Wales and the Union

Wales in the twentieth century was more culturally distinct and yet more politically integrated into the United Kingdom than Scotland. The existence of two languages made dual identities more palpable. The numbers of Welsh speakers fell until the last decades of the twentieth century. In 1901, 50 per cent of the population of Wales could speak Welsh. In 1971, the proportion had fallen to only 21 per cent. Decline was much more to do with the processes of modernization – for example, the rise of towns, the development of industry and immigration from southern England, radio and television broadcasting – than any deliberate policy of English cultural imperialism.[1] Nationalism in Wales rooted itself firmly in defence of the language. Plaid Cymru was formed at the Pwllheli National Eisteddfod in 1925 with only the language within its scope. At its summer school at Machynlleth in 1926, despite the continuing miners' strike, the new party failed to discuss social or economic questions.[2] Welsh and Welsh nationalism have sometimes therefore been seen as synonymous, with the eisteddfodau seemingly symbolizing that relationship. But the eisteddfodau were frequently cultural events that drew out Welsh distinctiveness only within the British context. The full title of the main annual event was the Royal National Eisteddfod, and Sir J. Prichard Jones told the national eisteddfod at Colwyn Bay that

> For generations the Eisteddfod has been the pivot around which Welsh nationalism has catered to us who are of Wales ... that Nationalism is a living thing, by it and for it we strive to attain higher things, not in a mean provincial spirit, but in a spirit that teaches us to do the best we can, not only for Wales, not only for Britain but for that wider British community, all over the world of which we form a part.[3]

In the 1920s and 1930s union jacks were more prevalent at eisteddfodau than red dragons. In the late 1930s it was decided that the official language of the eisteddfod should be Welsh and this rule was implemented in 1950, but in 1953 Queen Elizabeth II, or 'Elisabeth o Windsor', was confirmed as patron of the Royal National Eisteddfod.[4] Defending the Welsh language could have political outcomes other than nationalism and remained compatible with a range of other identities.

Welshness therefore had a complex relationship with Britishness, but it was a more secure relationship than Welshness had with political nationalism. Plaid Cymru could rely on a fairly solid base of support in rural mid and north Wales, but it was a very small base for at least forty years after the party's foundation. There were episodes when the party could rally sympathy, as when three party members, including Saunders Lewis, the party leader, were imprisoned for setting fire to an RAF bombing school in the Lleyn peninsula in 1936.[5] During the Second World War, the party secured 17.9 per cent of the vote in the University of Wales by-election, 24.8 per cent in Caernarfon Boroughs and 16.2 per cent in Neath.[6] But these were wartime elections, in which non-government candidates performed well across the United Kingdom. Hence while D. Hywell Davies is right to argue that 'The formation of the Welsh nationalist Party was an explicit challenge to the growing idea of British nationality,' it was certainly not an effective electoral challenge by the 1940s. The Parliament for Wales Campaign of the 1950s and the agitation over the language in the 1960s did provide fertile soil for Plaid Cymru's growth, resulting in the success of Gwynfor Evans, the party's president, in the by-election following Megan Lloyd George's death in 1966. The party had only secured 4.3 per cent of the total Welsh vote in the general election of that year and Evans' success severely worried the Labour government. In June 1970, the party improved its vote to 11.5 per cent, but this remained based on high votes in particular areas – over 30 per cent in Aberdare, Carmarthen and Caernarfon, and over 25 per cent in four other constituencies. As Kenneth Morgan has argued, 'For Plaid Cymru, 1970 was a turning-point at which Welsh politics obstinately refused to turn.'[7]

Plaid Cymru made claims to be the real heart of Wales, but all the major British parties represented Welshness, as the subsequent two chapters show. Chapter 6 discusses the lives of Gwilym and Megan Lloyd George in order to examine the way in which Liberalism represented Welshness at the beginning of the twentieth century and in the wake of the decline of the Liberal Party, how both Labour and the Conservatives could claim Welshness. The Lloyd George family's political status rested on the strength of the Liberal Party in Wales in the late nineteenth century. This strength was based on a particular and powerful version of Welshness associated with nonconformity, which in turn had resonance in both rural Wales and in the industrial south of mining and metal industries. Nonconformity in Wales considered itself as the democratic representative of the Welsh people or *gwerin* against the established Anglican church of the aristocracy. Class harmony among the productive classes was combined with hostility to landowners and other parasites upon the people. This fitted very well with British Liberalism, which achieved some spectacular electoral results after the extension of the franchise in 1867 and 1884, and especially after the introduction of the secret ballot in 1872. The Liberals won 24 of the 33 Welsh seats in 1868 and 30 of the 34 seats in 1885. Even when Liberalism across Britain showed its weakness in 1900, the Welsh Liberals won 28 seats. Liberal revival in 1906 meant that the party won 33 out of the 34 seats, with the remaining seat going to Labour.

It was in this context that David Lloyd George built his political career. Kenneth Morgan has pointed out that Lloyd George's relationship with Wales was far from straightforward.[8] He did not embrace nonconformity sincerely, neither was he concerned with agriculture. His involvement in the Cymru Fydd movement of the mid-1890s created conflict within Welsh Liberalism, because the Liberals of South Wales would not accept the leadership of the north nor measures for Welsh self-government. This was at a time when the national party could do without yet another weakness. Yet Lloyd George contributed in important ways to Welsh cultural-political identity, particularly in the Edwardian period, when as Chancellor of the Exchequer he rewarded Wales for its almost unanimous support for Liberalism. The National Museum of Wales, the National Library of Wales and the University of Wales all received substantial subventions, and Lloyd George happily observed, 'What's the use of being a Welsh Chancellor if one can do nothing in Wales?'[9] Lloyd George brought Welshness to the core of the United Kingdom, and Downing Street was adorned with the sound of Welsh between 1908 and 1922. After the failure of Cymru Fydd, Lloyd George's Welshness was always connected to a wider Britishness. Lloyd George wanted to do well for Wales, but he also wanted to tackle social problems across the United Kingdom, and to direct a British foreign and imperial policy. Wales was an important component within this Britishness not an identity exclusive of others.

This was shown in the 1911 investiture of the Prince of Wales, which emphasized that the distinctiveness of Wales could be displayed within the plurality of the United Kingdom and Empire. As John Ellis has argued, the Liberal government was keen to show that ethnic diversity was possible within the United Kingdom as a family of distinct nations. Hence, 'the iconography of Welsh nationality saturated the ceremony' as dragons, leeks and daffodils represented difference recognized by the office of the Prince of Wales while references to the King and Empire represented unity.[10] In the 1960s it was the Labour government's turn to use the monarchy to display their recognition of Welsh distinctiveness by staging another investiture. George Thomas, the Welsh Secretary, organized the event with the Duke of Norfolk on 1 July 1969. Thomas recalled the 'latent hostility' to the event, including 50 bomb blasts in the preceding year.[11] As in 1911, the event was a success. The bombs had been the work of a tiny minority and while nationalists derided the investiture, opinion polls suggested that three-quarters of the Welsh people favoured its staging.

The hegemonic hold of Liberalism was loosened during the First World War. Wales was proud of the Welsh Prime Minister, but the tensions evident in the party before 1914 were exacerbated by the divisions encouraged by personal conflict between Lloyd George and Asquith over the direction of the war effort. In 1918 Lloyd George triumphed in Wales. Fighting as part of the coalition that had won the war, Lloyd George Liberals won twenty Welsh seats, while Unionist and labour coalition candidates won an additional five seats. Asquith could muster only one supporter, elected unopposed in Merioneth.[12] After the fall of the coalition in 1922, Liberalism mounted a brief recovery in 1923 when the issue of free trade reunited the party and it was able to win 159 seats across the United Kingdom. In Wales, the position was not as optimistic. The Liberals won only twelve seats. The devastating result of 1924, when the Liberals collapsed to 40 seats across the United Kingdom, strengthened the position of Wales within the party because ten of those elected held seats in the principality. Lloyd George contributed to a sense of Liberal vibrancy in the late 1920s with his championing of dynamic measures to revive industry, agriculture and employment. In 1929, the party won nearly a quarter of the UK vote but elected only 59 MPs. Of these, nine were from Wales.

Lloyd George had harmed his standing with the Welsh working class as leader of the coalition government after 1918. The mines had not been nationalized despite a mass strike in support of that demand, and troops had been widely deployed in the strike of 1921.[13] The fragmentation of Welsh Liberalism was delayed by personal loyalty to the Lloyd George family. Both Gwilym and Megan were elected as Liberal MPs in the 1920s, and Goronwy Owen, Gwilym's brother-in-law, added to the Lloyd George family group. Frank Owen, another adherent, lost his seat in the 1931 election. The weakness of the politics of family were shown by rumours as early as the 1930s that Megan would join the Labour Party. With the death of his father in 1945, Gwilym stood and won as National Liberal and Conservative in the general election of that year. Despite this clear adherence to a party unconnected to the Liberals he was offered the chairmanship of the Liberal Party. The Liberals appeared to be a spent force. In 1955 only three Liberals were elected and in 1966 the once dominant party had only a single MP in Wales.[14]

Liberalism was pushed back into the Welsh periphery; its claims to Welshness were increasingly limited as Labour inherited the Liberal hegemony. This was both an electoral and cultural takeover. Chapter 7 shows that much of Labour's claim to Welshness was built in opposition to Liberalism. Labour's forward march in Wales was rapid after 1918. In that year the party won 30.8 per cent of the Welsh vote and in 1922 40.8 per cent. Even in 1931, when the party's share of the vote fell across the UK, it rose in Wales, from 43.9 to 44.1 per cent. Huw T. Edwards was symbolic of Labour's rise. Labour was able to capture the leadership of a new class-based Welshness that could be linked to the democratic and nonconformist traditions of the *gwerin*. In north Wales, Labour activists like Edwards developed an assertive Welshness based on the use of the Welsh language and the membership of trade unions.

Many activists in the Welsh labour movement at the turn of the century had been Liberals, and had commanded the respect and support of the growing Welsh industrial working class in the coal and metal industries of South Wales and the slate industry of the north. William Abraham, known as Mabon, was emblematic of Lib-Labism and its demise in late Victorian and Edwardian Wales. He combined Methodist lay preaching and conducting eisteddfodic choirs with a moderate and consensual Liberalism which fell victim to bitter industrial relations in the coalfields and slate quarries.[15] Edwards was one of the younger generation, whose early work experiences were of strikes and lock-outs. He was never a Liberal, joining the Independent Labour Party before the First World War. Like Mabon, he was a Welsh speaker and a nonconformist, but absorbed a class identity that was far less compatible with harmonious relations with employers. Labour in Wales was able to take in Welshness, so ILP members such as Silyn Roberts and Thomas Gwynn Jones were also prominent bards.[16]

In the rest of the United Kingdom it tended to be those Welsh Labour figures who were against political expressions of Welsh national distinctiveness who were best known. Aneurin Bevan caustically asked how Welsh sheep differed from English sheep on the first 'Welsh Day' in the House of Commons in 1944, and in the 1960s George Thomas as Secretary of State for Wales battled the nationalists within and without his party.[17] The paradox was that such figures were seen externally as archetypically Welsh. Both represented the big battalions of South Wales trade unions. The Anglicized nature and connections to London politics of the big trade unions were indicated in a variety of ways. In 1954 the South Wales National Union of Mineworkers voted 121 to 34 against Home Rule for Wales.[18] Voting against Home Rule did not mean giving up Welshness but the development of a variety linked to the British labour movement through a range of contacts such as union conferences and the Central Labour College.

J. Graham Jones has described a schism in Welsh Labour in the 1950s between those who supported and those who opposed demands for a parliament for Wales.[19] The opponents were in the majority and included Bevan, Thomas and others such as Ness Edwards, MP for Caerphilly, and Morgan Phillips, secretary of the Labour Party from 1944 to 1962. Phillips acted to symbolize the UK party's opposition to devolution. There was nothing determinist about the relationship between Welshness and the desire for devolution and opposition to it was not a product of English domination of the party. Phillips, 'the dominant apparatchik of British socialism' according to Morgan, was a Welsh-speaking miner from Aberdare.[20] In 1947 the Welsh party had gained a separate council for the party in Wales, but the UK party, including Phillips, had insisted that the council was 'regional' and not 'national'.[21]

Ranged against the opponents of devolution and active in the campaign for a Welsh parliament were a number of MPs: Cledwyn Hughes (Anglesey), Goronwy Roberts (Caernarvon), T.W. Jones (Merioneth), Tudor Watkins (Brecon and Radnor) and S.O. Davies (Merthyr).[22] But the schism was neither clear cut nor fixed. James Griffiths, deputy leader of the Labour Party in the late 1950s, had always had a deep Welsh patriotism, based on 'a village and valley and a town ... in which my life has been rooted all the seventy-odd years of my journey'.[23] He opposed the parliament for

Wales campaign but was converted to support for the establishment of a Secretaryship of State for Wales in the late 1950s, effectively ensuring that the measure became part of Labour's official policy. In 1964, the new government of Harold Wilson created the post and Griffiths became its first holder.[24] Edwards, as will be discussed below, provides a further example of the fluidity of the politics of Welshness in the Labour Party.

The configuration of Welsh to British national identity was affected by the lack of Welsh institutions. Whereas Scotland retained a separate legal, religious and educational system after Union, Wales had been absorbed into English institutions. In Scotland the existence of vested Scottish interests provided fertile ground for the development of an organic Scottish Conservatism. It was not very strong until its reinforcement by Liberal Unionism, but nonetheless provided a solid base of personnel and electoral support, strengthened by Protestant hostility to Irish Catholic immigration. In Wales, in contrast, the Conservatives remained very much a minority party. Their fortunes improved only fleetingly in favourable circumstances such Liberal demoralization in 1895, when eight Conservatives were elected. In 1924, again because of Liberal disarray, the Conservatives won nine seats. In Wales, unionism existed mainly outside of the Unionist Party. Gwilym Lloyd-George, however, moved readily into the Unionist Party in the 1940s and 1950s, pushed by his opposition to socialism and the collapse of Liberalism. His move did not mean he had to give up on Welshness, rather he worked hard to accommodate the politics of the Union to the distinctive representation of Wales without devolution.

Wales did not gain a cabinet minister responsible for its affairs until the 1950s, when the Home Secretary was made Minister for Welsh Affairs, but British governments made many other concessions to Welsh difference. In 1893 the University of Wales was established and in 1907 a Welsh Board was set up in the Department of Education.[25] In 1905 Balfour's Unionists allowed the establishment of the National Library of Wales at Aberystwyth and a national museum at Cardiff. Often Welsh politicians felt that reforms were only reluctantly and belatedly given, as disestablishment of the Anglican Church in Wales was only passed in 1914 and achieved in 1920. Nonetheless, the Welsh MPs showed evidence of the plurality of parliamentary politics when they sang the Welsh national anthem as the Bill was passed in 1914. The First World War also confirmed Wales' distinctive place within the United Kingdom, not least because after 1916 Lloyd George was Prime Minister. He called on Wales to support the war effort in support of other 'five foot five' nations in Europe, bullied by more aggressive powers. He told Wales that

> I would like to see a Welsh Army in the field. I should like to see the race that faced the Normans for hundreds of years in a struggle for freedom, the race that helped win Crecy, the race that fought for a generation under Glyndwr against the greatest Captain in Europe – I should like to see that race give a good taste of their quality in this struggle in Europe, and they are going to do it.[26]

His support was undoubtedly crucial in the establishment of a Welsh Division of the British Army, where the Irish Parliamentary Party failed to secure such recognition of national difference. Lloyd George's wife Margaret was made a Dame of the British Empire for her efforts in raising money for comforts for Welsh soldiers.[27] She used three rooms in 11 Downing Street and raised £200,000, providing a feminine symbol of patriotism to Welsh women as the two sons of the Lloyd George family, Gwilym and Richard, provided masculine symbols in their enlistment into the army. The experience of the Second World War and the establishment of the welfare state afterwards further confirmed the benefits of Britishness for Wales. The 'people's war' rhetoric complemented the democratic vision of the *gwerin* and Labour's social reforms had a decisive impact on poverty in Wales.[28]

Unionism (with a small 'u') was therefore being confirmed across the early and middle years of the twentieth century. An additional factor encouraging the integration of Wales into the United Kingdom was the Welsh role in British imperialism. The relationships between Scottishness and imperialism have been well explored in recent years, but those between Welshness and imperialism remain understudied. The Welsh migration to Patagonia in the mid-nineteenth century is seen as representing a rejection of English domination and its extension overseas, but it was only one example of the export of Welshness. It has been argued that imperialism was a method by which an imperial ruling class strove 'to control the cultural expression of a subordinate nationality' through encouraging 'an acceptable, docile Welshness' that was loyal to Empire.[29] Yet the associations between Wales and the Empire were wide ranging, and included the assertion of Welsh distinctiveness in the British imperial project through the use of the Welsh language as a language of domination. In 1891, the Reverend John P. Jones, who ran the Madura mission in southern India, asserted that 'Our nation is almost as ubiquitous as the Irish.' Like other

Britons, Welsh emigrants were attracted to the colonies of white settlement.[30]

Within the United Kingdom, on one occasion at least, Wales asserted its imperial distinctiveness through rugby. In 1905 the unbeaten New Zealand All-Blacks were defeated by Wales in Cardiff. The victory was celebrated as a triumph of Welshness avowing distinctiveness and skill within the British and imperial context. The victory of Wales when England had failed was seen as confirming the Britishness of Wales rather than contesting it. Andrews and Howell argue that 'The path to an Imperial Wales was reached through the promotion of a Welsh cultural nationalism'.[31]

In political terms, James Griffiths served as Colonial Secretary for eighteen significant months in the early 1950s. Labour had begun the dismantling of the Empire with Indian independence and the withdrawal from Palestine, but the government was seeking to refurbish the international relationships entailed in imperialism rather than to bring Britain's global role to an end. Griffiths shared this vision. He told the Fabian Colonial Research Bureau that 'We have undertaken the task of transforming the Empire into a partnership of self-governing nations within a British Commonwealth'.[32] He wanted to maintain British influence and saw the development of political institutions in the Empire/Commonwealth as the fulfillment of the imperial mission, not as its repudiation. He saw himself as 'being in at the making of history', presiding over the granting of new constitutions to eleven colonies during his twenty-month tenure of the office of colonial secretary. These constitutions, he was proud to say, took Westminster as their model.[33] This was the application of British standards to the Empire.

Megan Lloyd George spent a year in India, socializing with the viceregal elite. As the daughter of her father she was welcomed into the world of imperial rule. While in the 1950s, she began to champion African nationalism, before the Second World War she was more concerned to explain the Welsh contribution to the formation of the British Empire and she expressed faith in the version of imperialism formulated by Edwardian Liberalism and expounded by her father. The Empire could be strengthened by the application of political pluralism, allowing the expression of difference within the unity of the Empire.

Richard Finlay has examined the way in which even Scottish nationalism was in part imbued with imperialist ideas.[34] Likewise, Welsh nationalism in the 1930s did not fully reject Empire. Saunders Lewis said there was an issue as to whether 'the recognition of political

Welsh nationhood [can] be reconciled with the political arrangements of the British Empire without serious disturbance.' He concluded 'I believe it can.'[35] This was not embracing imperialism, but was certainly an accommodation to it. Certainly, Plaid Cymru contained many opponents of British imperialism and in the 1950s and 1960s, and some nationalists saw colonial liberation movements as a model for Wales to follow.[36] A distinction must be made between an adherence to the values of British imperialism and a concern with the effects of British imperialism. However, both indicate the impact of Empire on political discourses within the United Kingdom.

In the mid-twentieth century, all parties operating in Wales sought to make political advantage from their claims to Welshness. The subsequent chapters argue that the Liberal decline in Wales forced Gwilym and Megan Lloyd George to re-think their politics. Both held to the Welsh identity that their father had done so much to construct. It was also a British identity and in the disarray of the Liberal collapse, the Lloyd George children found that their British-Welsh identities could find a place in competing parties. Huw T. Edwards deliberated continually on the nature of his Welsh identity and its place within politics. In the late 1950s, he turned away from Labour when he believed that its unionist sentiment had reached the point at which Welsh interests could no longer be delivered adequately. However, I argue in chapter 7 that Edwards' return to Labour demonstrates the continuing ability of Labour to recognize the need for diversity to be represented inside the Union.

6
The First Family of Wales: The Lloyd George Children in British Politics

Gwilym and Megan Lloyd George were brought up in a family in which by virtue of their father's successful political career their multiple national identities were fully apparent to them. David Lloyd George had utilized his Welshness to strengthen his position in British Liberalism, and then as Prime Minister during the First World War and its aftermath had established himself as a world statesman, although one who represented British interests. The Lloyd George name was Welsh and instantly recognizable. Lloyd George was celebrated as the 'Welsh wizard' and criticized as the 'Welsh goat'.[1] Politics was seen as a natural occupation for the Lloyd George children. Megan remarked in a speech in 1928 that 'I've had politics for breakfast, lunch, tea and dinner all my life.'[2] With their father being appointed Chancellor of the Exchequer in 1908, the children found the family home coincided exactly with the centre of power of the United Kingdom and its Empire in Downing Street. Despite this British context, the Lloyd George family did retain its Welshness, not least through the deliberate and conscious actions of Margaret Lloyd George, the children's mother. Richard, the oldest son of the Lloyd Georges, wrote of his mother that 'her love of Wales and everything Welsh was so great as to have left an indelible imprint on all her children'.[3] When the first three Lloyd George children were born between 1889 and 1892, David Lloyd George was establishing his political reputation in North Wales.[4] During 1894 when Gwilym was born, his father's political concerns were still founded in Wales as he led the Cymru Fydd movement in an effort to convert Welsh Liberalism to more nationalist aims. When Megan was born in 1902 his attentions had turned much more firmly to the centre of British Liberalism in London. Margaret felt rooted in Criccieth, spending much of her time there, and she returned to give birth to Megan. When Lloyd George's ministerial salary allowed it, the family built a new home in Criccieth called 'Brynawelon', which was passed on to Megan after her parents' deaths. Except for Richard, all the children were given Welsh names and Megan's middle name, Arfon, was the Welsh name for the area around Snowdonia.[5] The family spoke Welsh at home in Criccieth and Downing Street. The family backgrounds of both David and Margaret Lloyd George placed them in the social stratum that desired to take the leadership of the democratic Welsh people or *gwerin*. Margaret's father had been a substantial farmer and, as G.R. Searle has said, David Lloyd George's 'background can be best described as "petty-bourgeois"'.[6] The conscious and sincere maintenance of a Welsh identity was linked to their politics as well as their personal lives.

The environment of the family was changed by the involvement of David Lloyd George in British politics. With the formation of the Liberal government in December 1905 and its electoral landslide in 1906, Lloyd George became President of the Board of Trade, being promoted to Chancellor of the Exchequer in 1908 when Asquith became Prime Minister. Now based for much of the year in London, Gwilym and Megan continued to speak Welsh within the family but as they undertook the traditional education of the British upper middle class according to their gender their lives began to diverge. After a period at a London County Council school, Gwilym was educated privately at Eastbourne College, meeting some hostility during the Liberal campaign against the House of Lords initiated by his father's budget of 1909.[7] Despite this, Gwilym recalled in his unpublished autobiography, written in the late 1950s or early 1960s, that 'I must confess that I cannot claim the much sought-after distinction of having been utterly miserable at school. On the contrary, I loved every minute of Eastbourne.'[8] In 1913 Gwilym went to university at Jesus College, Cambridge, where he read history.

Being the youngest child, Megan was doted on by her father. In some ways, she was a consolation for the loss of his daughter Mair, who died from appendicitis. The decision was taken to educate Megan at home.[9] This gave her more prolonged exposure to the Welsh world of her parents in London and Criccieth, while also drawing her into the orbit of British high politics. Some people saw Megan as managing this dichotomous situation with ease: Emlyn Williams described 'the twofoldedness of her personality ... a London dazzler at home with the cottagers under Snowdon' who was also 'a Welsh girl holding her own in Claridge's with Margot Asquith'.[10] In 1912 Frances Stevenson was appointed as Megan's tutor. Subsequently Frances became David Lloyd George's lover, and given Megan's closeness to her mother this created long-standing tensions after Megan became aware of the relationship in the early 1920s. Despite this, Megan remained devoted to her father.

After the fall of Lloyd George as Prime Minister in 1922 Gwilym and Megan became more important in his political life.[11] Gwilym was elected Liberal MP for Pembrokeshire, holding the seat in 1923 but losing it when the Liberals collapsed to 40 seats after first putting the Labour government into power in January 1923 and then removing it in October. With help from her parents, Megan was adopted as Liberal candidate for Anglesey in 1928 and won the seat in the general election of 1929 to become the first Welsh woman MP.[12] From David Lloyd George's point of view, Megan and Gwilym (who won Pembrokeshire again in 1929) provided firm and loyal support as the Liberal Party fragmented. After the 1931 election, with Goronwy Owen, who married into the Lloyd George family, they formed a group of four MPs facing two other wings of the Liberal Party – the Simonites, who supported the National government, and the Samuelites, who had withdrawn support from the National government when it introduced protective tariffs. In addition, they provided valuable sources of intelligence gathering as Lloyd George grew older. The benefits accruing to Gwilym and Megan included the proximity it gave them to the central events of post-war Britain and Europe. In 1919 they had both accompanied their father to the peace conference in Paris, and in 1936 they went with him on a tour of Germany culminating in a meeting with Hitler.[13]

This chapter examines the nature of Gwilym and Megan's politics in relation to the Union. They were brought up at the centre of British power yet maintained close ties to their Welshness. This was despite the divergence of their politics, as Megan moved steadily to the left, eventually joining the Labour Party and Gwilym moved to the right, becoming Home Secretary in the Conservative governments of the 1950s.[14] This chapter examines their political ideas, the impact of gender on their relationships to the nations of Wales and Britain, and it finally considers their ideas about the British Empire in order to show that the Union acted as a central force in their political lives.

Gwilym Lloyd-George (1894–1967): Welsh nation and British state

In the 1960s Gwilym said 'I was never keen on politics. My ambition had always been the sea[,] either the Royal Navy or the mercantile navy.'[15] His relationship with his father had constrained him towards a political future.[16] His past, again a result of his father's position, had determined that his politics would take on a 'British' aspect. Brought up and educated in England, Gwilym built a Welsh territorial base in politics, as had his father and later Megan. He was adopted as Liberal candidate for Pembrokeshire, which was a convenient constituency at a convenient time. He held the seat from 1922 to 1924 and from 1929 to 1950. The longevity of his representation led him to form a close attachment to the constituency. However, his relationship to the seat remained that of a Liberal Member of Parliament with national concerns rather than as local representative. Indeed the nature of the constituency was such that it encouraged consideration of British and Welsh diversity. According to *The Times*, 'Politically and ethnographically the county resolves itself into two separate entities, the northern half being predominantly Welsh and Radical and the southern portion English and Conservative.'[17] In addition, the elections of the 1920s were fought over the issue of unemployment because of the running down and closure of Pembroke naval dockyards. In the 1923 election, the Conservative candidate Major C.W.M. Price promised that a Conservative government would build light cruisers at Pembroke. In 1924, David Lloyd George claimed that he had personally intervened to keep the dockyard open against the Conservative cries of anti-waste while he was Prime Minister, with the clear implication that Gwilym should be the recipient of the voters' gratitude.[18] This was a dockyard seat in which patriotism was an issue, confirmed by the continuing use of military ranks by both the Conservative and Liberal candidates. Gwilym's electoral politics therefore occurred in a Welsh seat but within the context of British issues. After defeat in 1950 he moved readily to an English seat.

Gwilym's attitude to religion similarly showed a relaxed outlook towards the nature of his Welshness. His father had been a Baptist and his mother a Presbyterian. Gwilym considered Baptism 'a religion of fear' so he chose his mother's religion. While going to church himself, he considered 'the relaxation of religious discipline for the young [as] one of the modern developments of which I wholeheartedly approve'. At Eastbourne he had, he wrote, 'acquired an abiding love of the Anglican liturgy' and later in life he went 'contentedly to the parish church'.[19] Gwilym's sense of religion reinforced his belief in the easy accommodation of his Welsh and British identities.

In the House of Commons, Gwilym continued to be drawn into the British character of politics. He enjoyed the clubbability of the House of Commons, in its easy sociability between members of different parties. Mrinalini Sinha has examined the club in imperial India as a 'peculiarly British' institution and as 'a cultural site for the distribution and mediation of elite power'.[20] Such a perspective is useful for considering the way in which the Houses of Parliament distributed power to the sub-nations of the United Kingdom and also to understand the way in which Gwilym sought to overcome the outsider status bestowed by his family connection and membership of a minority party.

Neither the Conservatives nor the Liberals impressed him in the 1930s. He considered the Conservatives 'a spectacle of mediocrity' while 'the Liberals were the pathetic remnants of a party which had ceased to stand for anything distinctive and retained only a rather oppressive conviction of its own superiority'.[21] He saw Labour as having MacDonald's 'Celtic eloquence' and Lansbury's 'sincerity and kindness' when 'toughness and realism' were needed.[22] Nevertheless, he got on very well with individuals of all parties, and in return was very well liked. As almost a non-party figure, he was to be suggested as a potential Speaker on three occasions in the 1930s, 1940s and 1950s.[23] This was not, however, just a product of his affability but of his deep interest in the history and conventions of the Commons, which he considered to be essential components of the British political system. 'It is almost impossible to exaggerate the importance of these conventions,' he wrote, 'It is no easy task to give an assembly as varied as the Commons, perpetually divided into warring bodies a sense of unity. At Westminster this has been achieved with singular success.'[24] Indeed, he became increasingly conservative in regard to parliament, arguing that 'As a revising Chamber and as a repository of the wisdom of elder statesmanship the House of Lords has an indispensable function with which no scheme of reform must be allowed to meddle.'[25] His father's hostility to the Lords in the Edwardian period makes this ironic, but in 1944 David Lloyd George's acceptance of an earldom probably went far towards Gwilym being able to reconcile his own new constitutional conservatism.

This affectionate attitude towards the parliamentary system was not combined with any great sense of ideological commitment. He thought in terms of a common sense approach to politics, so frequently seen as a British tradition. Gwilym differentiated between those who saw politics as about implementing grand strategic designs and those like himself who saw it as 'a method of managing affairs'.[26] Yet he was not without political principle. He held firm to free trade ideas. In 1931 he accepted a junior post as Parliamentary Secretary at the Board of Trade in the National government formed by MacDonald, but resigned after five weeks when the 'doctor's mandate' election was called because he believed that the outcome would be protectionism, as indeed it was. He then watched as the Simonite Liberals 'became indistinguishable from the rank and file of the Conservative party'.[27] The other aspect of his political ideas that developed, and to which he remained committed, was anti-socialism. It was certainly the case that after 1945 his hostility to the state interventionist measures of the Labour government eased his transition into the Conservative governments of the 1950s.

He had already embarked on a course away from his father and towards the Conservatives through his return to government office under the wartime coalition. Again, the context of his service was that of putting the (British) nation ahead of political considerations. Gwilym rejoined the government as Parliamentary Secretary at the Board of Trade. He did so under Neville Chamberlain's leadership in September 1939 – that is before the major political transformation of Churchill's accession to the premiership and Labour's entry into the coalition.[28] This did not damage Gwilym's advance under Churchill. In February 1941 he was appointed Parliamentary Secretary at the Ministry of Food.[29] It is likely that his inclusion in both governments was an attempt to conciliate his father, who was seen as providing an asset to the coalition government.[30] However, Gwilym's success at the Ministry of Food saw his appointment to the important post of Minister of Fuel and Power, with responsibility for ensuring increased production from Britain's coal mines. He generally sought voluntary restraint in the use of fuel but having failed to secure volunteers to work in the mines he introduced conscription by ballot, in a scheme devised by the Minister of Labour, Ernest Bevin. By the end of the war in Europe, 21,800 men had been compelled to work in the industry. He also endeavoured to increase state control of the mines but failed in the face of Conservative opposition.[31] He was offered a number of other equal government posts, but considered it necessary to remain in a difficult job and see it through. Through his ministerial service during the war, Gwilym continued his detachment from the Liberal Party and when the war in Europe was over he showed his allegiance to Churchill by remaining in the caretaker government when the Liberal and Labour parties withdrew from the coalition.

In the general election of 1945, Gwilym again stood for Pembrokeshire.[32] He stood as 'National Liberal and Conservative', marking an important stage in the transformation of his politics. It is noteworthy that the 'National' epithet referred to the United Kingdom, stressing again the Britishness of his political outlook. In a straight fight with the Labour candidate, Major Fienburgh, Gwilym won by 168 votes. In the aftermath of the election, Gwilym was considered for the chairmanship of the two branches of Liberalism – those led by Sir Archibald Sinclair and Sir John Simon – but he declined both. Instead he accepted a place on the Conservative front bench, though he insisted to Churchill that he would sit there as a 'Liberal', to which Churchill replied 'And what the hell else should you sit as?'[33]

Gwilym was defeated at Pembrokeshire in the 1950 election. His adherence to the Conservative Party brought him the seat of Newcastle upon Tyne North. Wales was unlikely to prove fruitful for him in the future. The Liberals were faring badly and besides they had already repudiated him for campaigning for Conservatives in seats where Liberals were standing. His candidacy at Newcastle had the advantage of appealing to Churchill's continuing desire to maintain the 'National' rather than party mantle. Churchill spoke for Violet Bonham-Carter in Colne Valley, despite her standing as a straight Liberal. He also endorsed Gwilym in a public letter of support as 'the bearer of a famous Liberal name, and ... the candidate of the Conservative Party'.[34] This unity with the Conservatives was forged over Gwilym's opposition to socialism. Gwilym's election address declared that 'Socialism is bankrupt,' and branded the Labour government as 'Squandermaniacs'. He told Liberals that 'The old antagonism between Liberals and Conservatives has lost its meaning today. I can find no essential difference between them in policy and outlook, while both are fundamentally opposed to Socialism, the deadly enemy of Liberalism and freedom.'[35] Churchill linked this opposition to socialism directly to the fate of the nation, telling Gwilym that 'You are best qualified for uniting in this important constituency the forces opposed to Socialism and making for the revival of the greatness of Britain and the Empire.'[36]

The Conservatives were successful, both nationally and in Newcastle, winning a slender parliamentary majority. In Wales, their share of the vote had risen from 23.8 per cent in 1945 to 27.4 per cent in 1950 and 30.8 per cent in 1951. Gwilym was rewarded with the Ministry of Food, a difficult position to take given the Conservatives desire to 'set the people free' by removing the remaining restrictions on consumption.[37] The post certainly fitted well with Gwilym's hostility to state intervention and his competence at the Ministry saw him promoted to cabinet rank. In a reshuffle in 1954 he became Home Secretary and Minister for Welsh Affairs.

This post had come about because of pressure from Wales for greater control of Welsh affairs by the Welsh. The Conservatives in opposition had published their *Charter for Wales*, which had called for an 'ambassador for Wales' within the cabinet. Labour in response had established the Council for Wales and Monmouthshire in 1948.[38] The episode did, however, show that the Conservatives could take the lead in initiatives to accommodate national pluralism within the United Kingdom. In Scotland, this had been accompanied by a great measure of electoral success. The situation in Wales was different.

The historian of the Conservatives in Wales has remarked upon the 'often abysmal Tory election performance' in Wales in the five decades after 1880.[39] Between 1885 and 1935 the Conservatives best performances were in 1895 and 1924 when they won nine out of thirty-three seats. Their average share of the vote across the period from 1880 to 1910 was 37.7 per cent but between 1918 and 1935 it was 21.4 per cent. Aubel has pointed out that their support was concentrated in the borough constituencies, which had been more affected by Anglicizing influences. The Conservatives could win and hold seats in Cardiff, Monmouth Boroughs (which became Newport), and Pembroke, the 'Little England Beyond Wales' but were very weak elsewhere.[40] In local politics too the Conservatives tended to be confined to the Anglicized areas, particularly those adjoining England, such as Flintshire, Radnorshire and Monmouthshire. The Conservatives were, therefore, seen as divorced from Welsh society. Aubel argues that 'One of the greatest obstacles faced by the Conservative Party in Wales was its perceived identification with "Englishness" and "English interests", a factor undoubtedly accentuated by the anglicised nature of its leadership.'[41] Hence of the fifteen Conservative MPs elected in Wales between 1918 and 1935 only one, Gwilym Rowlands (Flint 1935–1945), could speak Welsh.[42] Despite this, Conservatives and Conservative governments did seek to make claims to Welshness and respond to calls for recognition of Welsh distinctiveness. The Balfour government had proved responsive to the demands for national cultural institutions, establishing the national library and museum. The Conservatives could also sometimes field strong Welsh candidates. Megan Lloyd George faced a local, Welsh-speaking Conservative opponent, O.M. Roberts, in Anglesey in 1951, who secured a respectable 6,300 votes.[43]

While the Conservatives in the 1950s were to face the anger of Huw T. Edwards, who resigned from the Council of Wales in 1958, they had instituted a range of political and social reforms for Wales. In 1951 David Maxwell-Fyfe as Home Secretary was given responsibility for

Welsh affairs, and David Llewelyn, Conservative MP for Cardiff North, was appointed Minister of State at the Home Office to assist him.[44] Gwilym's promotion to the Home Office coincided with the intensification of the Parliament for Wales Campaign. In 1955 S.O. Davies, a Labour MP and leading figure in the campaign, introduced a private member's bill calling for Home Rule for Wales.[45] This enabled Gwilym to explain his own position regarding the place of Wales and Welshness within the United Kingdom. His was not a distinctively Conservative position, probably even representing many Welsh Labour MPs in its stance. What it was, though, was a clear exposition of Welsh unionism. Gwilym expressed his sympathy for Welsh aspirations and outlined his position: 'I cannot help feeling that the issue which confronts us today can be very simply stated in two words, "nation" and "State". What we have to consider is whether, in the conduct of domestic affairs, the Welsh nation should become the Welsh State'. He felt that it should not, and linked this to a belief that Welsh nationality did not need a political body for its maintenance; indeed he argued that 'the vitality of the Welsh nation can be better preserved if the Welsh people remain within the framework of Great Britain'.[46] Gwilym did not see the Union between England and Wales as smothering difference but saw its continuation as being beneficial to both sides. He remained proud of his Welshness, which he expressed in a variety of ways. He firmly held on to his pride in his father's name, even though he had hyphenated it to assert his own distinctiveness. He explained his Welshness in his speech accepting the freedom of the city of Cardiff, telling his audience that his first visit to Cardiff City Hall had been as a child with his father. He continued that 'I have been privileged to hold one office which he never held and which I think he would have envied, that of being Minister for Welsh Affairs; and what is more being the first Welshman to hold that post.'[47]

Gwilym therefore balanced his Welshness and Britishness. His Welshness was encompassed by his Britishness, while it remained distinctive. Yet his chief concern was with the wider issues of British rather than Welsh politics.

In a final display of his political gentlemanliness, Gwilym agreed to his elevation to the House of Lords as Viscount Tenby of Bulford in 1957. Harold Macmillan had succeeded to the premiership and leadership of the Conservative Party. To console R.A. Butler, Macmillan wanted to make him Home Secretary. Gwilym readily stepped aside and showed that his family tradition of hostility to the aristocracy did not prevent him from taking a title.[48]

Megan Lloyd George (1902–1966): Welsh radical

The equation of Megan Lloyd George's Welshness and Britishness was different from that of her brother. This certainly reflected their differences in politics. Megan, closer to her father, took up his politics more vigorously, and adopted a more ideological approach than Gwilym. She was interested in developing the political ideas of Radicalism, which she saw as a Welsh tradition. As her father revitalized Liberalism in the 1920s, enhancing the role of the state in the management of society's affairs, she formulated her own complementary political outlook. She was the MP for Anglesey for two decades, which provided the emotional and geographical scenery for her political ideas. She developed her Radicalism with Welsh nationalism, yet never adopted a position that would entail an irrevocable break with the Union.

Megan grew up in greater proximity to her father than the other Lloyd George children. She was educated at home in Downing Street, with only brief periods at school. Even her time at finishing school in Paris was during the negotiations towards the Versailles Treaty in 1919. Being so close to her father in her childhood and young adult years brought Megan fully within the political influence of Lloyd George. As one of Megan's biographers, Mervyn Jones argues that 'For Megan, he was ... her adored Tada [Daddy]. He would be her model and her inspiration throughout her political career, and her life-story can only be understood in relation to his.'[49] Dingle Foot, a close friend and fellow Liberal MP, remarked about Megan's resemblance to her father that 'At times it seemed almost uncanny. There were the same eyes, the same gestures, the same inflections of the voice and, in large degree, the same mastery of the spoken word. Often her speeches were sheer enchantment.'[50] Megan did not seek to imitate her father directly but his genetic and familial shadow fell on her, as it had not on Gwilym, of whom Stanley Baldwin, no admirer of David Lloyd George, observed 'I like Gwilym; he takes after his mother.'[51] This is not to say that Megan did not formulate her own political outlook, but she chose to pay tribute to her father's ideas and name across her political career. She continued to stand on the Lloyd George platform, and not only by virtue of her name, through to the end of her political life. She often said that 'I am a Radical, as my father was.'[52] During the Second World War she played a role in Radical Action, a group of Liberals determined to prevent the drift of the party to the right.[53] In the late 1940s she again opposed the more conservative Liberals on the basis of her

Radicalism and when she joined the Labour Party in 1956, she claimed that it was to remain 'true to the Radical tradition'.[54]

Such adherence to the politics of her father was encouraged because her entry into parliamentary politics came through a very similar constituency to Caernarvon Boroughs, which he held. In 1928 the Equal Franchise Act made it possible for Megan to fight a parliamentary seat. Her parents played a decisive role in securing her the Liberal nomination for Anglesey in a hard fought contest.[55] Anglesey was a rural constituency in which 87 per cent of the population spoke Welsh and to which Welshness was central.[56] In the 1929 election she won the seat with nearly half the vote.[57] Megan spent some parliamentary time seeking to deconstruct the myth of the Welsh rural idyll to reveal the extent of poverty and ill-health, as in her widely praised maiden speech on 7 April 1931. She warned those who would see in the countryside a bucolic Eden:

> You never know that that very quaint attractive cottage which you admire is not a house fit for human beings to live in.... Damp, narrow, littered-up cottages, with only an earth floor, the roofs old and defective and the slates loose, so that sometimes water comes pouring in.... You need not look through your window to see the stars and you need not go outside to get wet.[58]

This did not, however, prevent her from seeing Wales as it was represented in rural and small town Anglesey, as a nation, and one that was culturally distinct from the other British nations. At Anglesey Eisteddfod in 1947 she said that 'The people of Wales had their own way of life ... It found expression in institutions such as the Eisteddfod, Sunday Schools, preaching festivals, and singing festivals.'[59] David Lloyd George had regularly attended on the Thursday of each annual national eisteddfod to make a speech and when he was no longer able to attend Megan took over this tradition confirming the status of the Lloyd Georges as the first family of Welsh Wales.

The Lloyd Georges were not alone in their ability to appeal to the political loyalty of Welshness. It has already been noted that the Conservative candidate opposing Megan in 1951 was a Welsh-speaker from the area. When Megan lost the seat in that year, the loyal *Holyhead Mail* offered an alibi by commenting that 'It would be interesting to know how many English families have in recent years come to live in Anglesey.... The number is sufficient to alter the whole tenor of life.... We venture to say that these newcomers to Anglesey tipped the scales against Lady Megan.'[60] However, the seat was lost to the Labour candidate Cledwyn Hughes, himself the son of a prominent local Liberal, a Welsh-speaker who became active (with Megan) in the Parliament for Wales campaign. The Anglesey seat reveals the fluidity and complexity of the politics of Welshness across the second half of the twentieth century. Labour held the seat from 1951 to 1979. Following the failure of the devolution referendum in 1979, the Conservatives advanced their position in Wales and they won Anglesey with 39 per cent of the vote. In 1983, they once again held the seat now known as Ynys Môn. In 1987, the seat fell to Plaid Cymru. What was noticeable in the 1987 contest, however, was the fall of the Labour vote. In 1979, Labour had won 31.7 per cent but in 1983 and 1987 they received less than 17 per cent. The Conservative vote in 1987 remained strong at 33.2 per cent. The anti-Conservatism of Welsh Wales was far from hegemonic.

In the 1930s, Megan, like Gwilym, formed part of the Lloyd George family group of MPs, loyal to their father. There were rumours of her intentions to join the Labour Party, but she remained faithful to him and his Radical Liberalism, which had been revitalized by the Liberal 'coloured' books of the late 1920s. Most of the major political issues of the inter-war years encouraged a pan-British outlook. The effects of unemployment and depression may have been felt acutely at regional and local levels, but the response of the Liberals had been to construct national plans to tackle the severity of these problems. While in electoral terms the Liberals had begun their long retreat into the 'Celtic fringe', in psychological terms they still considered themselves a party of national government.[61] After the reconciliation of Asquith and Lloyd George over opposition to Baldwin's protectionism in 1923, the Liberals elected 159 MPs, and even if this number collapsed to only forty in 1924, it was still possible to be optimistic about Liberal fortunes. Certainly the other parties remained concerned about the possible effects of Lloyd George's intervention in politics. In 1929, the Liberals secured 5.3 million votes, their highest number ever (in an enlarged electorate). The elections of 1931, however, fought on the 'National' issue, put paid to any hopes of Liberal revival.

Developments in international relations also drew Megan's attention to political rather than cultural nations. With the expansionist threat of Germany and Italy, David Lloyd George sought to re-establish his position in British politics by embarking on a diplomatic mission to Hitler in 1936. He believed that Hitler's foreign policy objectives were limited and certainly did not threaten Britain. In an article for the *Daily Express*, he decided that 'the Germans have definitely made up their minds never to quarrel with us again'.[62] According to Thomas Jones, part of Lloyd George's 'Welsh Mafia' since the First World War, Megan certainly considered the visit to Hitler 'thrilling', but she had severe reservations about her father's judgements in this case. However, in foreign policy her stance was often obscured behind that of her father. This was revealed again through her role in the Norway debate of 8 May 1940 that brought down Neville Chamberlain. Lloyd George was apparently undecided whether to intervene in the debate and was absent from the chamber when Chamberlain remarked that he had 'friends in this House'. At this point, Megan went rapidly in search of her father, and as Dingle Foot explained, 'A little while later he came in to destroy Chamberlain in a speech which lasted only 10 minutes but which contained all the accumulated dislike and contempt of 25 years.'[63] While Megan's role was dramatic, it was also subordinate.

Such deference to her father was also enhanced by her affair with Philip Noel-Baker. Megan had known about her father's affair with his secretary Frances Stevenson since the early 1920s and had been the most hostile member of the family to what was inevitably an awkward situation. Megan's affair with Noel-Baker, a married Labour MP, began in 1936 or 1937, lasting until late 1940. After an interval of four years, it was resumed until the death of Noel-Baker's wife in 1956, when he brought the affair to an end. Only a very few of Megan's friends, and her sister Olwen, knew about it.[64] The need for secrecy could be considered a debilitating factor in Megan's life – she was guilty of the transgression for which she condemned Stevenson.

Megan's politics were, therefore, bound up with her father's and were also shaped by the relationship between Anglesey and Westminster. She saw representation of Anglesey as more effectively possible through the national representation of Wales. In 1938 and again in 1944 she was part of a deputation to Downing Street to call for the establishment of the cabinet post of Secretary of State for Wales, and as Chairman of the Welsh Parliamentary Party she secured the 'Welsh Day' in the House of Commons in 1944.[65] She made Welsh self-rule an issue in the 1945 election, though in an indistinct manner, and in the late 1940s as deputy leader she managed to secure the Liberal Party's support for federal Home Rule. She concluded her 1950 election broadcast for the party with the words '*Nos da. Hunan llywodraeth I Gymru*', or 'Goodnight. Self government for Wales.'[66] Spoken in Welsh, this was not aimed at all listeners or even at the British government, but at her own constituents as a symbolic declaration of her Welshness.

In the late 1940s, the Scottish Covenant movement led by John MacCormick seemed to provide a pattern for Welsh nationalists to follow and the Parliament for Wales campaign was established by a coalition of political and cultural groups including Plaid Cymru, the Communist Party and *Undeb Cymru Fydd*, a language pressure group.[67] The campaign attracted support from some parts of both the Labour and Liberal parties, though others within each were opposed. It had the support of only six Welsh MPs out of thirty-six. When S.O. Davies introduced his Home Rule Bill in 1955 17 Welsh MPs voted against it.[68] The campaign was a minority movement, not the voice of the united Welsh people. The campaign reflected the limited demand for devolution in Wales.

Megan was appointed president of the campaign and when Cledwyn Hughes defeated her in the 1951 general election most of her subsequent political activity occurred under the campaign's auspices. The campaign called for a 'Parliament with adequate legislative authority in Welsh affairs', however, its residence within the tradition of pluralism within the Union was confirmed by its call for 'self-government within the framework of the United Kingdom'.[69] The campaign had flurries of activity while it sought to build a petition to present to the House of Commons. It eventually gathered 240,652 names, which constituted 14 per cent of the Welsh electorate. The organizers sought to add greater moral authority to this number through their claim that more than three quarters asked to sign had done so.[70] As Home Secretary, Gwilym Lloyd-George responded to the petition in his usual affable fashion remarking that 'There are people who will sign petitions for anything. They do not like to disappoint.'[71] As Minister of Welsh Affairs, he accepted the petition but opposed its demands. He told the campaign's organizers that the Council for Wales was currently considering devolution and the government would consider its actions in the light of its forthcoming report.[72]

The 1950s campaign for a Welsh parliament has been judged by historians to have been a 'relative failure'.[73] Its many weaknesses emerged from a number of causes.[74] The first and most important was the continuing difference in political culture between north and west Wales and south and east Wales. The campaign was led from North Wales and its business was conducted in Welsh, yet people in North Wales were lukewarm about a parliament in which the much larger population of South Wales would inevitably have control. In addition, powerful forces within the Labour Party actively opposed the campaign, to the extent that the 1954 conference was aggressively hostile. Such hostility could not be overcome when prominent Welsh political figures were, if not active opponents, then certainly not supporters. The Welshness of James Griffiths, Aneurin Bevan and Gwilym Lloyd-George could not be questioned, and they balanced the support for the campaign from Megan Lloyd George and Huw T. Edwards. Finally, not only were petitions problematic as political strategy – Gwilym's comment had a large element of truth behind it – but the campaign was also poorly organized. Megan could not escape criticism in this respect. As J. Graham Jones has argued, 'Lady Megan Lloyd George ... although an eloquent and persuasive public speaker, a popular, charismatic personality, and a formidable political antagonist, alternately displayed taints of indolence and rashness.'[75]

Megan cannot be blamed for the failure of the campaign, but only for adding to its ineffectiveness. Towards the end of the campaign, Megan joined the Labour Party. Despite Labour's rejection of Home Rule for Wales, it did contain nationalists with whom Megan considered she could ally herself. Besides, her choices were limited. She had left the Liberal Party because of its rightward drift, but it had been equally divided over the Parliament for Wales campaign, with only Clement Davies of its three MPs offering support. Megan, however, went over to Labour on British issues. She had supported Labour's measures creating the welfare state, and joined the party when the Prime Minister Anthony Eden called an election to secure his position as leader of the Conservative Party.[76] Plaid Cymru had made overtures towards Megan urging her to join. She readily described herself as a nationalist, but her Welsh nationalism had, like her father's, been formulated within the context of Westminster politics. For Megan, Welshness was about distinctiveness *within* the United Kingdom not about detachment from the Union. This was one example of how she differed from Gwilym. She did not share his view that Welsh distinctiveness was possible without legislative devolution for Wales.

Gender, Welshness and the Lloyd Georges

'I am not ashamed to be called a nationalist. I am first and foremost a Welshwoman,' Megan Lloyd George declared in a speech at Brecon during the campaign for a parliament for Wales.[77] Both Megan and Gwilym's political national identities were affected by their genders and the expectations that arose from them. Neither figure sits particularly comfortably with the dominant images of gender in Wales. Deirdre Beddoe has argued that 'Welsh women are culturally invisible.

Wales, land of my fathers, is a land of coalminers, rugby players and male voice choirs. Welsh cultural identity is based almost entirely on these three male groups.'[78]

Gwilym's position as a male member of the British upper-middle class, educated at an English public school and university, could never be quite at home in the world of Welsh working-class masculinity. Masculinity has been left understudied because of its pervasiveness in society and politics. It was taken for granted as having no impact on men's conduct in public life. The growth of women's history encouraged the historical study of femininity because of its difference from the normative expectations of behaviour in a masculine world.[79] Consideration of Gwilym's masculinity provides valuable insights into his integration into Britishness. Gwilym was not out of the ordinary as a male product of a British middle class family. He largely conformed to the conventions of manly behaviour current in the first half of the twentieth century. His conformity throws light further on his sense of national identity. His father, even when Prime Minister, had been considered an outsider among Britain's political class, but Gwilym was more readily accepted. His masculinity was essential to his acceptance. As a parliamentarian, Gwilym enjoyed the sociability of the House of Commons. His obituary in *The Times* described him as 'one of the best-liked men in the House ... full of bonhomie and a good companion in any company' and one gets the sense here of Gwilym's ease among the middle and upper class MPs.[80] However, this was an exclusive club. Thelma Cazalet-Keir, a Conservative MP and close friend of the Lloyd Georges, explained how 'The House [of Commons] has often been labelled "the best club in the world," but it was nothing of the sort to women. Not one of the dozen or so women M.P.s ever entered the smoking room where, so the rumour has it, as much constructive business is transacted as on the floor of the House.'[81] However, his acceptance into the chamber, lobbies and bars of Westminster on the basis of his gentlemanly clubbability meant that Gwilym could not take up the leadership of the Welsh *gwerin* as his father had done. David Lloyd George was repeatedly represented as the 'Welsh wizard', un-English but leader of his people through his passion and emotion. Lloyd George played upon a story of his life that portrayed a rise from humble beginnings to Downing Street, in which he rode democratic Welsh society to a path of respectability and self-discipline. This linked in with the Welsh democratic culture of the eisteddfod, when on 'Lloyd George's Day' he would regale the audience with tales of a Welsh boyhood leading to Westminster.[82] These were tales of manly independence that connected to the main threads of Liberalism as a creed encouraging self-reliance and freedom from the vested interests of landlordism and the Anglican Church. Lloyd George's social radicalism in Edwardian Britain developed his leadership of working-class industrial masculinity, although his hold was lessened substantially by his failure to nationalize the coal mines after the First World War.[83]

Gwilym could not draw upon this Welsh fund of manliness. He suffered from the disability that he would never be head of the Lloyd George political family while his father was alive, and in Pembroke he was sometimes mocked by the application of the nickname 'Ask my Dad'.[84] In addition, he could not draw on Welsh passion, which would have fitted uncomfortably with his public school education. Eastbourne College, Gwilym noted, was concerned with 'the production of gentlemen'.[85] There was of course much emphasis on physicality in the public school curriculum. Sport was widely encouraged and Gwilym indeed became (and became known as) a keen sportsman. He played rugby but it was public school 'rugger' rather than Welsh Rugby Union. Later, he did later go some way towards combining the two variants through being president of the London Welsh Rugby Club, but this was through his political prominence rather than his sporting prowess. He enjoyed cricket and shooting, and was known as a 'sturdy and long-hitting golfer'.[86] His contribution to sporting civil society culminated in the 1960s when he became president of the Welsh Football Association. Gwilym's public school education, therefore, mixed sport with gentlemanly restraint. It allowed him a place in Welsh civil society but he retained a certain detachment.

At university Gwilym combined sport with patriotism by joining the Territorial Army. In August 1914, therefore, he was 'preparing to embark on that great adventure' of the First World War.[87] His father initially took great measures to try to prevent Richard, his oldest son, and Gwilym from serving overseas. He wrote to Margaret about Gwilym on 11 August 1914 that 'I am not going to sacrifice my nice boy', and he used his influence to have both boys appointed as ADCs to generals.[88] Nevertheless, both sons did see active service. Richard served in the Royal Engineers and Gwilym became a major in the Royal Artillery. He was mentioned in despatches during Passchendaele. Morgan and Jones both comment that his letters home to his family during 1917 and 1918 show that 'he shared to the full the "patriotic" emotions of the time'.[89] Gwilym could not, however, hide his well-meaning nature, writing in one, 'We got a Boche prisoner today. Looked quite a decent fellow.'[90]

His first action on the outbreak of the Second World War was to turn again to manly patriotism, by joining the London Welsh Regiment. Furthermore, he accepted Chamberlain's offer of a junior post in the mainly unreconstructed government as a measure of his patriotism rather than of his adherence to party and was seen, as his obituary in *The Times* recorded, as making 'an outstanding contribution to the nation's war effort'.[91]

Gwilym, therefore, held to a 'conventional' manliness of sport, military and political service, which stressed the idea of gentlemanliness and decency. He became, as Morgan describes, 'almost squirearchical'.[92] In some aspects of his masculinity, Gwilym expressed his Welshness, though it was always within the context of the Britishness of the Union. He served in the Welsh division during the First World War, but this was a division of the British Army. His political service was mainly as a representative of the Welsh seat of Pembroke but he stood after 1945 as a 'National' candidate and he was Minister of Welsh Affairs as a by-product of being British Home Secretary. Gwilym's masculine identity was interconnected with his national identities.

Gwilym's conventionalism was increased by his long marriage to Edna Gwenfron in 1921 and their production of two sons. Megan Lloyd George did not, however, conform to expectations of marriage and reproduction. As previously mentioned, she did have a long-term intimate relationship with Philip Noel-Baker, but his marriage ensured that theirs would be a discreet relationship. Megan cannot therefore be fitted into the most used version of Welsh womanhood, that of the Welsh Mam.[93] As an independent and self-supporting MP, Megan could not be placed easily within domestic settings. In addition, in the 1920s, as she came of age Megan lived the life of a Society girl, 'a London dazzler' according to Emlyn Williams, educated at finishing school, attendant at parties and balls.[94] In 1924 she went to India for 'the best six months of my life'.[95] Lord Reading, the viceroy of India, with whom she was staying, reassured her mother that 'She is having the most wonderful time in Simla and seems to enjoy every minute of it.... She has a splendid capacity for enjoyment – it is attractive and refreshing to see her.'[96] This was not a Welsh context but was an extension of Society. As the young and attractive daughter of Lloyd George, Megan was news and was a favourite light-hearted story when she accompanied her father on foreign excursions. In 1923 she became the darling of the American press for calling the United States the 'politest nation on earth', suggesting just one improvement of the introduction of afternoon tea.[97] Megan also never lost a concern for her appearance, and in the 1930s she and Thelma Cazalet-Keir, a very close friend and Conservative MP, were branded as 'the dolly birds of Westminster'.[98] Megan was, therefore, some distance from conventional tropes of Welsh femininity.

In 1928 Megan's image nearly inflicted damage on her fledgling political career. The availability of a parliamentary seat had only come about because of the equalization of the franchise in 1928 and while this had secured an overwhelming parliamentary majority, there was still some hostility towards the 'flappers' – the young single women who were to gain the vote.[99] Megan's candidature was bound to have some appeal nationally to the newly enfranchised women. Indeed, Megan made an election broadcast for the Liberals aimed at the new women voters. She asserted her feminine identity with her listeners, and made a claim for their ownership of the nation. Her argument was that women were now active citizens and had desirable qualities to be used in political life: 'As a sex we have many virtues. One of these is a shrewd common sense. I want to look at unemployment from that point of view.... Think what can be done by one of you in a day. Think what could be done by a *million*, to improve this Britain of ours.'[100] Megan's gendered politics drew her into a British political outlook. In Anglesey she again gendered her political appeal and also referred to the way in which Wales was integrated into British history, calling Queen Elizabeth the wisest politician of all time who 'outwitted every statesman and diplomat she encountered, and of all the Tudor monarchs she was the most liberal-minded – and don't forget her ancestors were from Anglesey'.[101] Anglesey was a socially conservative constituency and during the selection procedure for candidates the *Daily Mail* reported that Megan had attended a 'pyjama bottle party'.[102] The potential was for class, gender and age antagonisms to ruin her chances. Fortunately for Megan, the Lloyd Georges' denials were believed. The family's religious nonconformity counted in their favour. Megan remained a devout Methodist throughout her life.

There was a hint of provincial hostility to London in this potential crisis. Megan had nearly fallen foul of an antipathy to metropolitan life as flippant and shallow. At other times, when in London, Megan was represented as being 'other' to London through her Welshness. This was certainly not always accompanied by hostility. Baldwin referred to Megan's parliamentary attack on Sir Herbert Samuel after he joined the National government by quoting Shakespeare: 'Heaven deliver me from this Welsh fairy.'[103] During the 1935 election, the *Daily Mail*'s reporter Paul Brewsher described one of her meetings in Anglesey, drawing out its exotic and appealing nature. This 'fresh looking Welsh girl' (who was in her thirties), he wrote 'spoke in a strange tongue with one of the most beautiful voices that I have ever been privileged to hear in my life. It was low and musical, with a deep undertone of warm feeling.'[104]

Megan's femininity was therefore a composite of Welshness and Britishness, constructed by her but also by the society in which she lived. During the Second World War she took an increasing interest in the feminist campaigns for equal pay. She was active on the Woman Power Committee along with other women MPs including Irene Ward, Mavis Tate and Edith Summerskill. Megan's argument was that women had contributed fully to the (British) nation, telling the Commons in 1942 that 'Women are very proud to have been able to fill the gap; they are glad to have had every opportunity to serve their country; they are very glad to take equal risks with men.'[105] In 1945 she urged greater political parity for women. 'Women should have an equal share in deciding the policy of the state,' she argued. 'They are still shut out of the Foreign Service and are often ignored when delegations go to international conferences.'[106] Yet such a call for sex equality within the British state imposed a limit upon the demand for Welsh rule that she made in 1945 since she continued to see the United Kingdom as the forum for discussion of foreign policy.

There was a further disjuncture in Megan's wartime politics. She rejected the offer of a government post as Parliamentary Secretary at the Ministry of Pensions because the Minister was opposed to sex equality.[107] Her contribution towards the war effort was as a consequence limited to her chairing of the All-Women Committee of Salvage and Recovery Board, which clearly implied a domestic role for women in the war effort. The Board's propaganda was aimed towards making housewives 'waste conscious' and Megan said that this was 'a vital national service that every household can do in her own home'.[108] There was a certain irony in a single career woman urging greater efforts of domesticity on other women.

The Welshness and Britishness of the Lloyd Georges was gendered. In both Gwilym and Megan's case, gender expectations acted to draw them closer into the Union. Gwilym had been trained into the dominant version of British manliness, through his schooling, political and military service. Megan's concern was with women's politics at the British level.

Imperial Wales

During the South African War, the Lloyd George children experienced jingoistic hostility to their father's pro-Boer stance.[109] The extent of the jingo hostility to Lloyd George has left the impression that he was opposed to imperialism, and indeed Wales has been seen as the part of the United Kingdom least concerned with the Greater Britain. The Welsh colony in Patagonia has been seen as the taking of a different road to the domination of the English-speaking Empire. However, there was also an imperial Wales. Kenneth Morgan has pointed out that Lloyd George and other pro-Boers faced much patriotic aggression within Wales.[110] South Wales had an export-led economy which encouraged it to look outwards to the Empire.[111] Indeed, Lloyd George himself did not oppose imperialism but its perversion during the South African War. He believed that vested sectional interests with corrupt and venal motives had dragged Britain into war. His opposition was to the war and not to the Empire. He offered an alternative to the Conservatives' protectionist and aggressive imperialism. Lloyd George called free trade more representative of true patriotism than imperial bluster. His Britain was 'this little island in the sea ... standing against Continents armed at all points with the most systematically devised tariffs, standing alone armed only with the weapon of freedom, and yet beating them all on land and sea'.[112] With the Liberals in power after 1905 the fruits of this kind of imperialism were apparent in the Union of South Africa which allowed for pluralism within the Empire and 'reinforced Lloyd George's conviction that white colonial freedom could be reconciled with imperial unity'.[113] This mirrored Lloyd George's attitude to the position of Wales within the Empire. As Grigg has explained, 'To him, the British Empire and the United Kingdom did not restrict, but on the contrary enhanced, Welsh nationality.'[114]

Lloyd George's radicalism was therefore no barrier to his espousal of imperialism. Radicals opposed the excesses of imperialism rather than its being.[115] This was the position that Megan took in relation to the British Empire. She inherited her father's liberal imperialism, declaring on a tour of Canada in 1923 that 'Tada's exposition of Empire [was] a masterpiece of clear thinking and a triumph of oratory.'[116] She welcomed the Canadians' 'spontaneous affection for England, & ... great pride in the Empire'.[117] She spent much of the following year among the Anglo-Indian ruling elite in India, meeting few Indians other than those approved by her host, Lord Reading, the viceroy and friend of her father's.

By the late 1930s her imperialism was undiminished. Indeed, the coronation of George VI in May 1937 encouraged her to explain her thoughts on empire to the Anglesey county eisteddfod, in the geographical heart of Welsh culture and language. In her speech she illustrated the interconnected nature of her identity, from Anglesey to Wales to Britain to the Empire. The *North Wales Chronicle* reported the speech in which she began by explaining the impact that the coronation had had upon her:

> Last week she had had the privilege of being present as their representative at the Coronation in Westminster Abbey ... What appealed to her was the fact that people had come together to witness that ceremony from all quarters of the globe, all belonging to the great British Empire. The question which came to her was what part Wales had played in the building up of that wonderful Empire?[118]

She assigned Wales and particularly Anglesey an important role in the imperial edifice. She explained that 'It was founded in the reign of a Welsh Queen who came from an Anglesey family.' She lectured to her audience that 'It is high time you should know something about that part of Welsh history,' and proceeded to explain that:

> When Henry VII came to reign it was to rule over a nation that was poor and was regarded as of no consequence among the countries of the world. When Queen Elizabeth died Great Britain had conquered the greatest nation in the World – Spain – and the foundation of the great British Empire had been laid. Much was heard of the Scottish Kings, and had they done a tithe of what the Tudors had accomplished 'We would never have heard the end of it.' Wales had a noble part in the great work of nation-building.[119]

Megan expressed the duality of identity that the Empire made possible. The Britishness of the Empire did not extinguish Welshness but allowed its assertion. Megan's speech at the eisteddfod built on the broadcasts she had been making on the BBC imperial service during 1936, in which her aim had been 'to "get across"' to India, Burma and Ceylon 'the spirit of Wales'.[120] In addition, she drew on the myth of Queen Elizabeth as a powerful woman who had made a significant contribution to British and imperial history. Here then, Megan drew together historic identities of place and gender to assert Welsh distinction in a British and imperial context.

In the 1950s, Megan's explanation for joining the Labour Party drew on an element of anti-imperialism that was further enhanced by her opposition to the Conservative government's armed intervention in Egypt in the wake of Gamal Abdul Nasser's nationalization of the Suez Canal. In the mid-1950s Megan was critical of Conservative policies in the colonies. She condemned 'the spirit of old colonialism' which was in the blood of the Conservatives blaming 'the lamentable events' in some colonies on 'the failure inherent in their party to understand the new spirit among the coloured races'.[121] In February 1957, when the Carmarthen constituency became vacant as a result of the death of the sitting Liberal MP, Megan was selected to fight the seat for Labour. She chose to fight the campaign on the government's actions during the Suez crisis. As with much of Labour's opposition to Eden's handling of the crisis, Megan's major concern was with the perceived lawlessness of the government's actions rather than with opposition to the defence of perceived British interests in the Middle East. This was the stance that the Labour leader, Hugh Gaitskell took in his broadcast on 4 November 1956. He considered that British actions had 'betrayed all that Great Britain has stood for in world affairs'.[122] Facing a Liberal who supported the government over Suez and a Plaid Cymru candidate, Megan won the seat with a 3,000 majority.[123]

Despite his absorption into a unionist version of Britishness, there is little evidence to suggest that Gwilym was overly concerned with imperial and foreign affairs. In the 1930s he 'never shared the pacifism of large sections of the labour party' and he was a critic of appeasement, using firm language to the Liberal Party assembly in May 1939, when he asked 'when will [the government] learn that the only language [the] bully understands is superior force'.[124] This speech also confirmed that he did not share his father's view of Hitler, and established Gwilym as an anti-appeaser, easing his way into Churchill's government in 1940.

Gwilym was, like most Conservatives, a firm defender of the government's actions over Suez in 1956.[125] He placed those actions in both a historical and personal context, justifying in advance the government's military action.

> I am now nearly <u>62</u> [He said in a speech]. At the age of 19 I joined the Army to fight aggression ... Some 25 years later we again fought aggression. Some ..... of my fellow countrymen died. On both occasions many died to keep Egypt free from Turks, Italians, & Germans. We kept the Canal free. We did not regard it as our Canal. It was an

international waterway. The people we saved on two occasions now wish to make it their own[,] in other words to do what Turks, Italians & Germans were prevented from doing.[126]

By a sleight of speech, Gwilym had branded the Egyptians as invaders of their own country. In December he made another speech defending government actions in which, despite his declaration that 'I thought what we did was right – I still think so', he rationalized the governments actions mainly through Britain's material interests. Nasser's control of the Canal would have disrupted the flow of oil, which in turn would have resulted in unemployment. Therefore, 'strange as it may sound to some, the British people have as much right as any other to maintain their means of livelihood in the world. The free passage of ships through the Suez Canal is vital to that livelihood.'[127]

The existence of the British Empire drew both Megan and Gwilym more firmly into a sense of Britishness. The Empire strengthened the Union, and in Megan's case it enhanced her Welshness. She believed that the distinctive cultural identity of Wales should have a greater role in the Empire. Her Radicalism provided her with an alternative to Conservative imperialism. In the changed circumstances of the 1950s, the emergence of nationalism in the colonies emphasized her critique of the power aspects of imperialism, but echoed the pro-Boerism of her father. Her critique was of imperial actions not imperialism *in toto*. Gwilym also hinted at Wales' distinctive role in the Britain's global policies. During 1956, he was a stern defender of his government's actions, claiming a role for his own countrymen in maintaining freedom of the seas.

Megan and Gwilym followed divergent political paths. They both began as Lloyd George Liberals. They were radical and loyal to their father and also to the expression of Welshness in their politics. Gwilym, however, had never had a particular interest in political ideas, and this suited his movement towards Conservatism. He had a deep affection for the parliamentary forms of politics in the United Kingdom, and he saw those forms as caused by and essential to the consensus and chivalry of Britain. He was deeply impressed during the Boer War by a Conservative MP's offer to loan his father money when his pro-Boerism had affected his legal practice. To Gwilym, this was not only an act of individual decency but was 'an incident characteristic of the chivalry of British political life'.[128] Combined with the traditional upbringing of the British middle class, such beliefs drew Gwilym into a patriotic attachment to the United Kingdom as a political form.

He was typically British in his military and political service. He was, however, different from the majority of the political class to which he chose to belong, for he retained substantial and important elements of his Welshness. He spoke Welsh and he prided himself on his crossing the geographical divide between north and south Wales.[129] He was the first Welsh holder of the post of Minister for Welsh Affairs, yet he held that there was little need for further devolution of powers to Wales. He believed not only in the fundamental compatibility of the Wales and the Union, but the necessity for the continuation of that relationship.

Megan seems at first sight to be very different, but in fact the difference was one only of degree. Megan became more 'Welsh' as her political career developed. Parts of her young life had been played out in the privileged world of the British political elite. She never abandoned that life, remaining a keen traveller, for example, but she became increasingly rooted in North Wales through her political representation of Anglesey. Welsh Wales did encourage support for limited political autonomy. In the 1930s she expressed this through her demand for a Secretary of State for Wales. In the 1950s, she supported the calls for a parliament for Wales. But she never envisaged separation from the United Kingdom, because she remained firmly attached to British political parties. She left the Liberals to join Labour, during its most unionist phase. Fighting over the Suez issue in 1956 was to fight over the most British of issues, the global position of the United Kingdom. She did not criticize the government from a Welsh standpoint but as a Briton. Gwilym and Megan took different political paths but their Welsh and British identities could both be represented inside the Union.

7
The Unofficial Prime Minister of Wales: Huw T. Edwards (1892–1970)

Richard Weight has described Huw T. Edwards as 'a man whose gradual loss of patience with Britain's political elite mirrored that of millions of ordinary people.'[1] It certainly seems that Edwards' political life fits into a narrative of the increasing unravelling of the United Kingdom, as he moved from the position of Labour stalwart to Welsh nationalist when he joined Plaid Cymru in 1959. This narrative suggests a steady dismantling of support for the Union. Edwards agitated for greater autonomy for Wales from Labour and Conservative governments. Without doubt he was frustrated by the unwillingness of governments in London to give undivided consideration to the problems of Wales. However, it is simplistic to see Edwards' stance steadily and irrevocably moving away from identification with the United Kingdom. This chapter discusses the complex and dynamic nature of Edwards' Welshness and his negotiation of that identity within the realms of the United Kingdom. Edwards' last political act was not his break with the Labour Party that had become increasingly centralist, but the rejoining of the party when it seemed to him that it was at last recognizing his aspirations for Wales within the Union.

Welsh and working class

Edwards was born in 1892 in the small rural community of Ro Wen in the Conwy Valley, Caernarfonshire. His father was a quarryman, and the importance of the extractive industries in Huw's own life was represented in his entitling the English translation of his autobiography *Hewn from the Rock*.[2] Edwards' background was firmly Welsh and working class. It was a rural Welshness. He described his inheritance from his forebears as having been 'the fruitful soil of the valley, the bare heights of the uplands, collecting sheep wool from the gorse bushes to clothe the children, and heather for the great oven, preachers, publicans, the band, the cobbler's shop, washing the "Plas" laundry, the Big Seat, the Choir of the Hearth, fisticuffs.'[3] He began full time work aged fourteen in the granite quarry at Penmaenmawr where his father worked, and he was socialized into a communitarian and cultured Welshness.

Edwards was, however, unsettled from this rootedness by the death of his mother and set off south to work in a coal mine in Tonypandy. Here in the years before the First World War the class awareness to which his parents had introduced him through tales of 'the heartlessness of the quarry owners' was honed in the bitter industrial relations of the Edwardian coalfields.[4] In the autumn and winter of 1910, the Cambrian Combine collieries of the Liberal MP D.A. Thomas (later Lord Rhondda) were rocked by a strike of 30,000 miners which resulted in rioting and police and military action, in which Edwards was injured. Conditions in the mines were very dangerous. In 1913, an explosion at Senghennydd killed around 450 men, and Edwards was one of the recovery party.[5] This further developed his sense of class solidarity. Edwards found his way into the rising world of Labour in Wales, through trade unionism and the Independent Labour Party (ILP), both of which were suffused with varieties of Welshness. The South Wales Miners' Federation, 'the Fed', conducted itself so as to assimilate the immigrant status of its many members from south west England and from rural north Wales to provide a fusion into a distinct miners' Welshness. The ILP, while a British party, was built from the rank and file upwards, and was therefore enclosed by the optimistic Welshness of those such as Silyn Roberts, the eisteddfodic bard, who became members, attracted by the party's adherence to Welsh causes and socialism.

Yet this was still British Welshness. Edwards considered the industrial and political struggles to be British in character. The Metropolitan Police and Lancashire Fusiliers who policed the 1910 strike were seen as interlopers into the valleys but as Edwards said the strike 'has a place of its own in the history of the workers of Britain' and Senghennydd was 'the greatest tragedy in the mining history of Britain'.[6] The Britishness of the wider labour movement encouraged the nationalization of Welsh class politics.

After the strike, Edwards joined the militia. In his autobiography he does not explain his motives but maintained that he enjoyed the boxing but not the discipline. His enlistment resulted in his being called up into the army on the first day of the Great War. He recalled that he 'began to worry in case the fighting would be over before we got to France' and that he was 'anxious to get to grips with the enemy'.[7] He did see extensive combat on the Western Front and was seriously wounded. His military service should not be seen as in conflict with his membership of the ILP or his Welsh identity. The majority of Independent Labour Party opposed the war but decided that 'such matters of enlistment and the urging of recruitment are matters for individual conscience'.[8] Between one-fifth and a quarter of the party's male members of military age seem to have joined the armed forces before conscription was introduced.[9] In Wales, the recruiting campaign frequently adopted a discourse of Welshness well suited to the defence of Belgium as a small nation.[10]

On his return from the war, Edwards married and lived with his wife's parents at Rachup, near Bethesda. They welcomed the domesticity enabled by moving into their first home together at Hengae, Llanfairfechan, and Edwards entitled the chapter of his autobiography retailing these moves 'starting to live again'.[11] He had also rejoined the ILP, and his socialism was heightened by the death of his son Gwynfor, aged only two. 'I felt,' he wrote, 'when we lost Gwynfor that we had no right to bring children into the world to live in damp houses where the sun was never given any chance to perform its work of healing.'[12]

His activism for Labour was on both the industrial and political fronts, in the quarrymen's union, which merged with the Transport and General Workers' Union in 1926, and as an urban district councillor from 1927. He therefore contributed to Labour's advance in Wales, which in 1929 resulted in the election of twenty-five Labour MPs in Wales, with 43.9 per cent of the vote. To aid Labour's advance Edwards believed greatly in the importance of a socialist newspaper. When the *Daily Herald* floundered in he late 1920s he worked hard to raise the small subscriptions in his area to support the TUC and Odhams Press bid to rescue the paper. Edwards assured audiences that one page of the paper would be devoted to Wales with a column in Welsh. The promise was broken and Edwards experienced a major disappointment in the control of the Labour movement from England.[13]

There were strains between Wales and Labour in this period, but they were not bipolar tensions, with Edwards and Wales pulling against Labour. These were years of growing Labour strength, and in October as Labour's vote fell elsewhere in the crisis election of 1931, in Wales it increased to 44.1 per cent, even though nine seats were lost. The influences on Edwards' life in the 1930s drew him towards Wales and Britain concurrently. He experienced two years of unemployment around 1931, an experience that characterized that of the Welsh working class. Between 1925 and 1938 unemployment averaged over 20 per cent and in the worst years climbed to more than 50 per cent. More than 400,000 people left Wales in the 1920s and 1930s.[14] Searching for solutions to Wales' economic problems, however, drew the Labour movement further towards a centralized version of planning. Edwards secured a job with the TGWU based in Shotton, with responsibility for increasing membership and maintaining the spirit of the unemployed members. This drew his attention to the British nature of the union, because many of the unemployed members were from South Wales and Staffordshire. One of his solutions to the men's boredom was to provide two lectures a week, which he based on a book called *Heroes of Britain*. The book, he explained, 'dealt with the gallantry and bravery of men on land and sea, in disasters and in prison, and I believe that they helped to keep up the spirits of hundreds of steelworkers along the Dee estuary by showing that, however bad things were, they could have been much worse.'[15] Edwards' homilies, did not counter the claims of the need for national unity in the face of economic crisis made by the National government but he did reject the right of the government to speak for the nation.

In the 1935 election, Edwards worked hard as the agent for the Labour candidate for Flint, Cyril O. Jones. Their campaign questioned the 'national' nature of the government declaring that 'The so-called National Government is a Tory Government.' They pointed to the unfairness of the government in its dealings with different groups within British society. Jones' election leaflet, written by Edwards, claimed that 'landlords and capitalists have received a gift of £140,000,000' through de-rating while the government had reduced payments to the unemployed by £100,000,000. In this Welsh (though not Welsh speaking) seat the leaflet enquired of the electors: 'You are British and you like fair play! Is this fair?'[16] At the same time, Edwards was encouraging an increased sense of Welshness among his union members. During the Second World War he associated the TGWU with the national eisteddfod and Coleg Harlech, and 'lost no opportunity of stressing the fact that we were a Welsh branch'.[17] Edwards was, therefore, in the process of developing coexisting identities of Welshness with Britishness within the framework of his trade union and the Labour Party. The landslide election of Labour in 1945 included a tremendous advance for Labour in Wales, where it secured 58.5 per cent of the poll. With Labour in power, Edwards turned his attention to securing representation for Wales as a distinct entity within Britain's New Jerusalem.

The Council of Wales

Edwards was not defensive in the slightest about pushing forward the claims of Wales. He was proud of the Welshness of North Wales and wanted recognition for its contribution to Labour's victory. The Labour government, however, in the moment of its victory had its sights set elsewhere. Kenneth Morgan has argued that in the post-war period the 'overall verdict must be that the specifically Welsh aspect of Labour politics was a limited one. Labour continued to place its emphasis primarily upon centralization and class solidarity which united the workers of all countries.'[18] Edwards resisted this trend and actively pursued political reform of the relationship between Wales and the United Kingdom. This might be seen as part of his steady disillusion with British Labour and an escalation towards nationalism. However, Edwards' attitude was similar to that of most Welsh Labour voters described by Morgan: 'Broad loyalty to the Attlee government, local pride in the achievements of ministers like Bevan and Griffiths ... matched by a constant dialogue of query, complaint and protest.'[19] This in turn also characterizes the attitude of most British Labour voters, who welcomed Labour's welfare reforms but complained about austerity. Many historians have seen the Attlee years as leading to cynicism and apathy or even a disillusion with Labour in power as it failed to live up to its socialist promise.[20] The elections of 1950 and 1951 stand against such interpretations, for Labour consolidated its vote in 1950 and advanced it in 1951, across the United Kingdom and in Wales in particular.

The election of Labour with its first overall parliamentary majority raised Edwards' expectations of what might be achieved for Wales. He himself had no desire to be a Member of Parliament, seeing his arena of political activity as being primarily Welsh. As well as serving on Flintshire County Council, he was on Welsh national bodies such as the Wales and Monmouthshire Trading Estates, which pursued Labour's regional employment policies, and he was also a Welsh representative on British bodies like the BBC and the British Council. In the 1940s he had become a national (Welsh) voice with an audience in London among the Labour leadership. During the last years of the war, parts of Welsh Labour had called for the establishment of the post of Secretary of State for Wales at party conferences.[21] Edwards had been associated with such calls. He attended the 1943 conference and was disturbed by the lack of time to discuss Welsh affairs.[22] He believed that the party had become more centralist, arguing that previously 'the rights of small nations were an integral part in the policy of the party'.[23] He therefore called for the 're-dedication of the [Labour] Movement to problems that are essentially Welsh' in order to prevent the growth of Welsh nationalism.[24]

The formation of the Labour government certainly increased support for central direction of economy and society in the United Kingdom. Within the cabinet, ministers like Ernest Bevin (a friend of Edwards) and Herbert Morrison were determined not to let Labour's policy be diverted by devolution of powers away from London, and Stafford Cripps argued that the problems of Wales would be solved not by regional or national autonomy but by 'closer integration with the British economy'.[25]

In such circumstances, Edwards was determined to draw attention to the national status of Wales. In September 1946, in his capacity as the President of the North Wales Labour Parties Federation, he submitted a memorandum on 'The Problems of Wales' to the Secretary of the Labour Party, Morgan Phillips.[26] This document attempted to exert moral pressure on the London government by claiming that the political situation in Wales was changing. He asserted that 'Wales is a Country, with its language, culture and tradition' and that national consciousness was strong and increasing because of 'the English encroachment of the last twenty five years, bringing with it a different way of life', the output of Welsh literature, self government for Eire, the growth of the Welsh nationalist party and 'a feeling that Westminster has no sympathy with Welsh aspirations.' He said that there were demands in Wales for action in five areas to build up Welsh civil society and infrastructure to belay Welsh concerns. He argued that people in Wales wanted the creation of a Secretary of State for Wales to place Wales 'on a par with Scotland', a north-south road, a broadcasting corporation for Wales (with the Plaid Cymru leader Gwynfor Evans serving on its committee), for Wales needed to be treated as a single administrative unit rather than being integrated into its nearest English regions, and finally, he said that unemployment was an issue in the public eye. Edwards demurred in two areas. He believed government action in employment was sufficient and he rejected the need for a Welsh Secretary, suggesting instead a commissioner for Wales (who must be able to speak Welsh) with an advisory committee.[27] Phillips was unsympathetic. He was a centralizer and while Labour discussed a White Paper on Wales, Edwards did not consider that his concerns were being taken seriously enough. In December 1946, he made these concerns public in an open letter to Clement Attlee as Prime Minister.[28]

As with the memorandum, Edwards was not staging a nationalist rebellion against Labour. His was an appeal for due consideration of the Welsh interest within the policy of the British Labour government. Edwards stressed his loyalty, and that of the Welsh people, to Labour. Given the solidity of Wales in support of the government, he asserted its entitlement to expect 'sympathetic recognition of her special problems'. He strengthened his argument with an appeal to socialist ideas, by stressing that 'I am a Welshman with the conviction that true Socialism means not only inter-national Brotherhood, but also the right of each Nation to make its own contribution in its own way to the total pool of human happiness.'[29] Edwards now called for Welsh parliamentary secretaries for education, agriculture and health with dedicated permanent secretaries, and he repeated his desire for a Welsh advisory committee.

Edwards' aspirations were moderate and despite the centralist opposition he had some important allies. Within the cabinet, James Griffiths, Minister of National Insurance, was seeking recognition for Wales within the administration of the nationalized industries.[30] The formation of a Welsh regional council of Labour was further recognition that something needed to be done, and in the autumn of 1947 the government decided to establish a Welsh advisory committee. Griffiths wanted it to be given executive powers but Morrison was determined that it would not be chaired by a cabinet minister. The Council for Wales and Monmouthshire, as it was called, was established with twelve representatives from local authorities, four from industry and agriculture, four from the trade unions, one from education, one from the University of Wales, one from the National Eisteddfod, one from the Welsh Tourist Board and three nominated by the Prime Minister.[31] Edwards was appointed its chairman because of his previous support for the idea and because he was recognized as a leader of Welsh opinion. A further advantage of his appointment was that he was not an MP, which removed the potential for the Council to become a pole of attraction for the expression of Welsh demands inside parliament or the government.

Both contemporary and historical opinion of the Council has been contemptuous. Megan Lloyd George called it 'a bone without a marrow' and Edwards remembered its 'cold reception'.[32] Kenneth

Morgan has called it 'little more than a talking shop'.[33] Jones and Jones, however, have pointed out that its formation acknowledged Wales as an administrative, economic and cultural unit.[34] Edwards believed that it provided an important forum for the expression of Welsh opinion. At the first meeting of the Council on 20 May 1949 Edwards said 'We welcome the setting-up of the Council – because it is one further recognition that Wales is a Nation.' He made clear that the ambitions of Wales could be met within Britain, for he continued that 'We are very proud to be a part of the British Commonwealth of Nations. We feel that Wales has a distinctive contribution to make and we further feel that this Council is an instrument through which we can make that contribution.'[35] Modest devolution had therefore enhanced Edwards' support for the British connection. At a conference on National Savings in October 1950, in his home town of Penmaenmawr, he asked 'Is the British way of life worth preserving?' and he described three important aspects of this way of life:

a) We enjoy in this country what I would term essential freedoms built around – 'A BRITISHER'S HOME IS HIS CASTLE'
b) We have the freedom to elect our legislators and administrators.
c) We are free to worship God in our own way....
We have seen built in our time, or at least we have seen the foundations laid, of the Welfare State.

In light of these, he declared 'a very definite YES' in answer to his question. The twin actions of the Labour government in establishing British socialism and in creating the Council of Wales had, therefore, enhanced Edwards' belief in the Union. His was not a journey of ever decreasing Britishness, but instead represents the continuing formulation of a British national identity that could accommodate distinctiveness. The Labour government's response to his demands also suggested that Wales could be represented within the United Kingdom without legislative devolution.

In response to the establishment of the Council for Wales the Conservatives formulated their own Welsh policy and moved ahead of Labour by promising the appointment of a Minister for Welsh Affairs. Edwards considered this 'another great step forward' and continued to serve as Chairman of the Council after the return of the Conservatives to government in October 1951, when they delivered on their promise.[36] He worked well with all the ministers with responsibility for Wales: David Maxwell-Fyfe (known in Wales as 'Dai Bananas'), Gwilym Lloyd-George ('a very lovable person'[37]), and, after the post had been moved from the Home Office to the Ministry of Housing and Local Government, Sir Henry Brooke. In a letter to Maxwell-Fyfe in 1952, Edwards had asserted his own Welsh patriotism and flattered the Minister at the same time. 'I am motivated by three things,' Edwards wrote,

> firstly I passionately love this little Country of ours and feel that what we are asking is something we are entitled to as a Nation, secondly I want the Council to succeed in proving its usefulness, mainly because I sincerely believe that devolution should come about in stages. Thirdly, I do sincerely want Sir David Maxwell-Fyfe, as the first Minister for Welsh Affairs, to carve a niche for himself in the history of my Nation.[38]

Edwards tried to retain good working relations with the ministers, consoling Brooke during the Tryweryn reservoir events (when Liverpool council flooded a Welsh valley to secure its water supplies) that he was still respected in Wales.[39] Edwards did not, however, take to Harold Macmillan, who became Prime Minister in January 1957. 'It was perfectly clear to me that he had not the slightest conception of what our national aspirations were,' Edwards wrote in his autobiography. '[H]e just talked almost incessantly of his connection with the Scottish "croft", of his humble beginnings and his desire to do whatever he could in various directions.'[40]

In the same month as Macmillan's accession, the Council published its *Third Memorandum on Government Administration in Wales*. On the grounds of governmental efficiency, it recommended the establishment of a Secretary of State for Wales and a dedicated Welsh Office.[41] Edwards had been converted to parity with Scotland after examining the Scottish Office and because of the example of Tom Johnston as Scottish Secretary. The report, which had taken two years to prepare, had the unanimous backing of the Council, which Edwards wrote, 'had every reason to be proud of themselves'.[42]

The Conservative government decided that it had gone far enough in its recognition of Welsh distinctiveness within the Union and it rejected the *Third Memorandum* in its entirety. As a result Edwards dramatically resigned as Chairman of the Council for Wales. In his resignation statement he defended the Council because it had 'all-embracing' terms of reference, it was non-party, and because it had done constructive work. The government, he said, had accepted its proposals on unemployment and marginal land, but generally had not given satisfaction to the Council. There had been little action to defend Welsh ports against their larger English competitors, and it had rejected the Council's scheme to deal with rural depopulation. But the major grievance was that such acceptance and rejection of the Council's reports had been undertaken without consultation. The government had kept the Council at 'arm's length' and Edwards said he was resigning because of the 'whole attitude and approach of the Government to the Council and towards Wales.'[43]

Peter Stead has argued that his resignation meant 'the dramatic emergence of Huw T. Edwards as the pivotal figure in Welsh politics'.[44] The impact was not felt less the Conservatives than by Labour. The Parliament for Wales campaign had anti-climaxed in 1956. The debate on devolution afterwards had taken place within the Labour Party.[45] The Council's declaration in support of the creation of a Welsh Secretary gave that demand a tremendous boost inside Labour. The accession of James Griffiths to the deputy leadership of the party further aided the demand. In 1959, it was included in the Labour manifesto, significantly entitled *Britain Belongs To You*, which declared that 'the time has now come for the special identity of Wales to be recognized by the appointment of a Secretary of State'.[46] The Labour Party rejected both Scottish and Welsh Home Rule in the 1950s, yet could still act as the vehicle for the national aspirations of much of the electorate in both nations.

The only path I could in honesty tread

As British Labour was hesitantly rediscovering its pluralism at the behest of some of its Welsh members, Edwards resigned from the party of which he had been a member since before the First World War. He announced his resignation in August 1959, declaring that 'The Labour Party appears to have lost its vision in its treatment of Wales as a nation.'[47] Later he expanded upon what he saw as Labour's failure in relation to Wales, which he called 'its positive neglect to make any definite declaration on a nation's rights'.[48] This certainly represented a 'gradual loss of patience' on Edwards' part.[49] Other Labour activists in mid and north Wales had also left the party, some finding their way into Plaid Cymru.[50]

Edwards' decision was, however, also influenced by wider developments within the British Labour Party. The leadership of Hugh

Gaitskell represented a sharp swing to the right within the party. After losing the 1959 election, Gaitskell had urged the party to jettison Clause IV. Such moves were anathema to Edwards, who rejected 'Gaitskell's unofficial Toryism'.[51] As Edwards explained in his auto-biography, he said 'goodbye to the party but not to socialism'.[52] Edwards journey towards nationalism outside the Union was therefore motivated by a combination of factors. It was not simply an act in the unravelling of the Union.

Plaid Cymru had already made overtures towards Edwards after his resignation from the Council of Wales. Gwynfor Evans had called Edwards 'the national leader of Wales in recent years' and urged him to join the party.[53] Edwards had always had some respect for the national-ists, considering that the 'cream of Welsh youth' had been attracted to them.[54] He described his decision to join the party as 'the only path I could in honesty tread'.[55] Combined with the emergence of a strong, lively and youthful language movement in the early 1960s, this seemed like the dawn of nationalist Wales, with daylight of Welsh revival inevitably following.

The defence of the Welsh language became the central concern of the politics of national awareness in Wales in the 1960s. In 1962 the Welsh Language Society was formed, with Edwards as its president. The proportion of Welsh speakers had fallen to 26 per cent or 656,000 people, and much concern was expressed over the impact of the wider ownership of televisions on which the vast majority of the output was in English. Edwards was a board member of Television Wales and West Ltd (TWW), which had won the franchise to broadcast independent television in Wales in 1958. The board considered that television could play an essential part in preserving and enhancing the Welsh language, which it saw as central to Welsh culture.[56] Most Welsh people, how-ever, had little direct influence in programming. BBC Wales was not formed until 1964 and there was little Welsh language broadcasting.[57] Many frustrated young Welsh people supported methods of direct action and civil disobedience in the campaign to revitalize the lan-guage.[58] Without doubt, many of the activists rejected the Union with England, but the activists were only a very small proportion of the population.

The campaigning only benefited Plaid Cymru marginally. The party remained electorally weak in the 1950s and 1960s. In 1955, with 11 candidates, it had won 45,000 votes. In 1959, with 20 candidates, it won 77,000 votes. In 1964, the party's confidence was expressed in its 23 candidates but its vote fell to 69,000.[59] The average share of votes per candidate had fallen by a quarter in the previous decade. At the same time, Labour's support in Wales peaked. In 1964, Labour achieved 57.8 per cent of the vote and in 1966, 60.7 per cent. Thirteen years of Conservative government and its perceived neglect of Wales as a nation had not resulted in the rise of nationalism. Labour's commitment to creating a Secretary of State and a Welsh Office retained the overwhelmingly loyalty of the Welsh electorate in the 1960s. The establishment of Welsh institutions fitted with the aspirations of Wales. There was increased Welsh national awareness but it did not amount to Welsh nationalism. Labour's unionism with a dose of pluralism seemed to be a successful electoral strategy.

Edwards was politically and personally unhappy in Plaid Cymru. He was unclear about what the party's policies were, 'and to be perfectly candid,' he wrote, 'I was not a great deal wiser after having been a Party member for some years'.[60] He recognized its weakness in elections and argued that it should not contest parliamentary seats, and if it did then it should avoid opposing Labour candidates with nationalist tendencies.[61] He suggested instead a strategy of persuasion and local electoral politics, which may have been based on his experience of successfully building Labour's presence in Wales in the 1920s. He also objected to the personal verbal attacks that were made on Labour figures. Indeed he resigned from the party's executive committee over these issues, including the need for courtesy in public life.[62] With Gaitskell's death and Harold Wilson's election as leader, Edwards edged back towards the Labour Party. In the run-up to the election campaign of 1964, he made financial contributions to the party receiving letters of thanks from both George Brown and Harold Wilson.[63]

Labour won the election and in January 1965 Edwards rejoined because he believed that the party had reconciled socialism, unionism and devolution through the appointment of James Griffiths as Secretary of State for Wales.[64] 'It seemed to me,' Edwards wrote in 1967 'that under the leadership of Harold Wilson the movement to which I had devoted my life was beginning to recapture its early socialist vision and indeed moving towards a progressive and realist policy on Welsh affairs.'[65] In 1968, he wrote to another Labour MP that 'My mistake was to leave the Party before Harold arrived, yet I had at the time ample reason for leaving, because of Gaitskell's complete failure as I saw it, to recognise that there was a Welsh problem.'[66] Edwards journey to nationalism was more a rejection of Gaitskell than of the Union. His re-entry into the party was an acknowledgment of Labour's ability to head off the nationalist challenge through recognition of Welsh difference and aspiration.

Empire games and royal visits

It might seem that Edwards' adherence to Labour and the Union was a flag of convenience, in which he considered that the only realistic way to achieve greater Welsh autonomy was within these British structures. Edwards was, however, embedded in the forms of the Union in some quite surprising directions.

Edwards' expressed pride in the Commonwealth but was generally anti-imperialist in sentiment. In a speech in north Wales, he remarked that 'it is well that we in Prestatyn today, should remember that British Imperialism had kept Pandit Nehru a prisoner for about 16 years of his life'[67] The final pages of the first volume of his autobiography published in Welsh in 1956 called for an end to conscription, 'followed by the immediate recall from the four corners of the globe of all those wearing the signs of Britain's oppression of other countries'.[68] His only interest in exporting Welsh cultural identity was through his chairmanship of the Welsh Tourist Board, in which capacity he visited Soviet Russia, the United States and Patagonia. The latter venture of Welsh imperialism he called a 'glorious failure' and suggested that the colonizers would have served Wales better by concentrating their 'vitality ... in the land of their fathers.'[69]

Edwards' role in emphasizing Welsh cultural distinctiveness brought him into close contact with the idea of the monarchy. In 1958 Wales was due to play host to the Empire and Commonwealth Games. The Welsh Tourist Board decided to stage a Festival of Wales to emphasize Welsh culture. In a radio broadcast Edwards stressed the good relations that could be achieved within the Union as a result of these opportunities:

> 1958 will be a memorable year. The Empire Games will be visiting Wales for the first time. It is hoped that a Festival of Wales will also be held to commemorate the birth of the Tudor dynasty and to proclaim to the world the strong ties that link the Royal Household with Wales. 1958 could be made more memorable still and would open a new chapter in Welsh history if in that year it could be recorded (a) that our young Prince could speak Welsh (b) that a permanent Royal Home had been found in Wales (my preference would be Gregynog) and (c) that Wales had a capital.[70]

Edwards' assertion of Welsh difference and his desire for substantial political autonomy was also a desire to be considered in partnership to

England and Scotland within the Union. He was certainly irritated by the government decision not to fund the Festival of Wales and by the frequent subsuming of references to Wales into a generic 'England and Wales' but he continued to stress the nature of the Union as joint venture. In the programme of the Festival of Wales, Edwards wrote that 'we are England's original partner in the great Commonwealth experiment of living together'.[71] He opposed imperial domination but saw the Commonwealth as a means of expression of common interest and distinct identity.

Richard Weight has argued that 'Welsh discontent grew apace in the second half of the 1950s.'[72] Certainly Edwards' resignation from the Council of Wales and the widespread opposition to the Tryweryn reservoir were evidence of substantial irritation with government insensitivities towards Wales. Making Cardiff the capital city of Wales in 1955 and staging the Empire Games and the Festival, however, made a substantial difference to attitudes towards the Union. The links are not easy to establish, but in 1959 the Conservatives improved their electoral performance in Wales to achieve almost one-third of the vote. The election of 1959 is frequently seen as a turning point for the Conservatives in Scotland, when they lost five seats. In Wales, their performance improved, suggesting that it is unwise to see politics in the sub-nations of the United Kingdom as inevitably following the same course.

In many ways, central government was responding to Welsh aspirations. For years Edwards had sought to secure validation of Welsh cultural contributions through the honours system, while rejecting honours for himself. He had accepted an MBE but returned it in protest at Winston Churchill's Gestapo speech in the 1945 general election.[73] Again and again he asked for honours to be granted to people who had made significant contributions to Welshness. In 1947, for example, he asked for a Civil Pension for T. Rowland Hughes, whom he considered 'the finest novelist [in] Wales in the last fifty years ... He is the son of a Quarryman and is a Chaired Bard of Wales; an award ... would be acclaimed by the whole of the Principality.'[74] There are a string of such letters from Edwards in the 1950s, culminating in one in which he says that he had been told that 'the next Honours list, as it concerned Wales, would be devoted to the Games and the Festival. I think this is an excellent idea.'[75]

Another way in which Edwards had encouraged the validation of Wales was in his advice on the routes to be taken during royal visits. He was keen to ensure that as much of Wales as possible was touched by royalty. Hence in 1952 he suggested a route to include substantial parts of working-class in both south and north Wales:

> If I were linking up a run through the Mining Valleys with Cardiff, I would proceed from Cardiff to Porth via Tylors Town, Ferndale, Maerdy – over the Mountain to Aberdare, from Aberdare to Hirwain and coming over the Mountain to Treherbert, Treochey, Llwyn y Pia, Tonypandy, Pen y Graig, Llantrisant – back to Cardiff....
>
> North Wales – Caernarvon, Bangor, Bethesda – through the Nant Ffrancon Pass and down through the Llanberis Pass, this run would only take roughly $1^1/_2$ hours.[76]

When the route was planned he suggested changes to take account of civic and national pride. Hence he wrote that

> The first [adjustment] is that we feel that the County Borough of Merthyr Tydfil should be visited, we feel this, because all the others are being visited and Merthyr might feel slighted.... The only other slight adjustment that I would like to suggest is that in view of the fact that Her Majesty intends to take in the Eisteddfod at Llangollen – which is a very good idea, then I think she should have a look at the National Eisteddfod of Wales Pavilion at Rhyl and might possibly receive the Arch Druid for a minute or two, that would I think do away with any suggestion that preference was shown.[77]

In the 1960s governments became increasingly aware of the need to take Welsh national feeling into account. There was a further royal visit to Wales in 1960, and the establishment of the Welsh Office in 1964 with its steady accumulation of powers. Griffiths as Secretary of State accepted the recommendations of the Hughes-Parry Report which resulted in the acceptance of the equal status of the Welsh language.[78] Such concessions to plurality were partly based on a continuing misconception about the strength of nationalism in Wales. In July 1966, Plaid Cymru won its first parliamentary seat in a by-election at Carmarthen, made vacant by the death of Megan Lloyd George. The victory was certainly representative of some advance in support for nationalism. However, there were special factors that aided the victory, which few took into account. Megan Lloyd George certainly had a substantial personal vote in Carmarthen, much of which had come from Liberals. Her death set these voters adrift. In addition, others felt betrayed by her standing at the general election only three months previously when subsequently it became clear that she had already been terminally ill. Also, Gwynfor Evans was a strong candidate, living within the constituency. Finally, the British, Welsh and local economic situation made a substantial protest vote against the government likely.[79] Evans won the seat with 39 per cent of the vote. Again, it must be stressed that the result did signify Plaid Cymru's advance, but the Labour Party over-reacted. After poor Labour showings in by-elections in Rhondda West and Caerphilly, one miners' leader warned Griffiths that 'all your seats are marginal now'.[80] Yet these were not signs of nationalist apocalypse but protest votes with Welsh flavour.

There was nothing natural about Labour's support in Wales between the 1940s and 1960s, when it never fell below 56 per cent of the vote. The party had constructed a platform of support based on a combination of working class and Welsh identities linked into a programme that undertook to deliver substantial social reforms through the vehicle of the British state. It was to this political identity that Edwards returned in 1965. He, like many other Labour voters in Wales, was disturbed by the centralizing tendencies within the party. But his was not the only, nor the dominant, variety of Welshness in the party. The first three Labour Secretaries of State in the 1960s embodied alternatives to Edwards. The differences between them were not stark and fixed, but they represented the spectrum of views on the place of Wales in the United Kingdom. James Griffiths certainly symbolized a substantial demand for Welsh distinctiveness, which could be accommodated by the establishment of the Welsh Office. He combined such concerns with a deep pride in the British welfare state, for which he could accept much credit.[81] Cledwyn Hughes, who succeeded Griffiths, was a leading figure in the Parliament for Wales campaign in the 1950s and as Welsh Secretary between 1966 and 1968 argued for an elected Welsh council.[82] Hughes did not seek to take Wales out of the Union, but only to enable it to legislate on domestic matters within it. He was a nationalist, within the Labour Party with its fundamental commitment to the Union. His plans for an elected council were defeated. Strictly unionist south Walian MPs were opposed but so too was Scottish Labour. Some Scots in the party did not consider that Wales should run ahead of their own claims, while others like Willie Ross, the Scottish Secretary, saw Hughes' scheme as likely to increase demands for Scottish devolution to which they were opposed.[83] Griffiths and Hughes represented varieties of the desire to see recognition of Wales expressed through the structure of government. The third Welsh Secretary, George Thomas rejected the need for devolution at all. As a Methodist and teetotaller,

Thomas had a strong claim to traditional Welshness, but it was the English-speaking Welshness of the south east that he embraced. He played a major role in the organization of the Investiture of the Prince of Wales in 1969 held at Caernarfon Castle. Prince Charles was sent to the University of Wales at Aberystwyth for a term to learn Welsh (as Edwards had suggested in the 1950s). Thomas considered that Charles should have been sent to Swansea or Cardiff for 'a more rounded picture of what I see as the real Wales, a place proud of its heritage and independence but nevertheless firmly part of a United Kingdom.'[84] Thomas' version of Welshness had as equally strong support in Welsh Labour as that of Griffiths, Hughes and Edwards.

The end of the 1960s saw the Welsh and Scottish Offices headed by consciously unionist ministers. In the Welsh case, the Parliament for Wales campaign, through moving more firmly back inside the Labour Party, had succeeded in seeing the formation of a Welsh Office and the appointment of a Welsh Secretary. Such demands were far in advance of what Edwards had asked for as recently as the mid-1950s. Success, however, revealed the divisions within Welsh Labour and it was ironic that under Thomas the Welsh Office became a bastion of opposition to further devolution. The Labour manifesto in 1970 contained no reference to an elected council for Wales because Thomas did not want to be seen to be making concessions to the nationalists.[85] The Labour Party lost 80,000 votes in Wales but still won 51.6 per cent of the vote. Plaid Cymru gained 115,000 votes but this represented only 11.5 per cent of the electorate. Labour's hold on Wales was being challenged but not threatened.

Edwards was known in the 1950s as 'the unofficial Prime Minister of Wales'. He represented the fluidity of the political expression of national identity in Wales. His Welshness was combined with a sense of class identity which encouraged links to the rest of the United Kingdom through his activities for his trade union and within the Labour Party. In 1959 his resignation from the party revealed the connected nature of his political and national identities, when he declared that he was leaving because of the combination of Labour's centralism with the right-wing leadership of Gaitskell. That this was no confirmation of an uncomplicated tale of the unravelling of the Union was shown when he rejoined Labour. Without doubt, Edwards saw Welsh society as different from those in the rest of the United Kingdom. He played a part in many aspects of political and civil society constructing and defending that sense of difference in relation to language and culture. Yet, he firmly believed that such difference did not lead to antagonism against England, writing that 'if I were allowed to choose our nearest neighbours, my choice would be England every time.'[86] Edwards' Welshness was the central part of his political identity, yet its expression came through partnership of the Welsh with the English and Scottish working class inside the Union.

Wales and the Union: epilogue

Across the twentieth century, Welsh people held simultaneous and multiple identities. There was not a single Welsh identity that was then attached to a single British identity. There were immense varieties and equations in the relationship between them. The small size of Wales certainly discouraged the growth of separatist nationalism, as did divisions within Wales, with many in the south believing that devolution would hand power to the Welsh-speaking north and many in the north, as well as some Liberals and all Conservatives, believing that devolution would grant power in perpetuity to the Labour Party, which retained the loyalty of South Wales. Others, like Nye Bevan in the 1940s and Neil Kinnock in the 1970s, argued that devolution would sever the Welsh working class from the British Labour movement, that class, not nation, was the central identity. That Wales did not seek to break up Britain was shown in the referendum on 1 March 1979, St David's Day. Amongst those who voted (and 42 per cent of the electorate did not), one in five voted for the limited devolution entailed in the Wales Act. Just fewer than 80 per cent rejected devolution. Even in the counties of Welsh-speaking Wales the majority voted no. The majority of the Welsh in 1979 felt that their distinct national identity could be expressed without substantial reform to the terms of the Union. The years of Conservative government between 1979 and 1997 emphasized an intransigent Unionism and saw substantial damage to the party's already limited support in Wales. The Thatcher and Major governments reduced Conservative support from one-third of the electorate to one-fifth. Labour was the beneficiary. Plaid Cymru maintained a solid base of support among about 10 per cent of the electorate, but Labour regained its dominance in Wales. In 1983, with the party divided and the Liberal/SDP Alliance performing well, the Labour vote in Wales fell below 40 per cent for the first time since 1918. In 1997 Labour gained its highest share of the vote since 1964, with 54.7 per cent. Limited devolution in 1998 (on a marginal majority) confirmed the success of Labour's variety of pluralism: recognition of Welsh distinctiveness with continued support for, and a desire to strengthen, the Union.

8
Northern Ireland: The Union and Devolution

There is a certain irony in the fact that the most devout supporters of the Union between 1921 and 1972 inhabited the one part of the United Kingdom that had legislative devolution. In Northern Ireland, as elsewhere in the United Kingdom, the construction of distinctive political and cultural identities was compatible with the existence of the Union. Northern Ireland had been created in the British government's attempt to disengage from Irish politics after the First World War and Ulster Unionists, who had not asked for a separate parliament, came to see its establishment as enabling them to defend their Britishness in a potentially hostile political situation in Britain. Captain Charles Craig, brother of James, the first Northern Irish Prime Minister, gave the House of Commons at Westminster a clear explanation of how the Ulster Unionists saw their position:

> We would much prefer to remain part and parcel of the United Kingdom. We have prospered, we have made our province prosperous under the union ... We do not in any way desire to recede from a position which has been in every way satisfactory to us, but we have many enemies in this country, and we feel that an Ulster without a parliament of its own would not be in nearly as strong a position as one in which a parliament had been set up ... We profoundly distrust the labour party and we profoundly distrust the right hon. gentleman the Member for Paisley (Mr Asquith) ... We see our safety, therefore, in having a parliament of our own.[1]

Precariousness made the Ulster Unionists keen to assert their British identity at almost every conceivable opportunity. Unionists before

125

1921 engaged in elaborate 'performances' to maintain their British national identity. Gillian McIntosh has shown how

> This theatricality and rich symbolism continued to find expression in the new Northern Irish state, particularly in the ceremonies surrounding the erection of the statue to the state's founding father, Edward Carson, in the Festival of Britain in Northern Ireland in 1951, and in the numerous royal visits which culminated in the triumphal coronation visit of Elizabeth II in 1953.[2]

The design of the new parliament at Stormont was another aspect of this assertion. Completed in 1932, it served to verify the Britishness of the new statelet.[3] As Hugh Pollock remarked, the parliament was 'the outward and visible proof of the permanence of our institutions; that for all time we are bound indissolubly to the British Crown.'[4]

The visible display of British nationality was not only carried out at state level. Support for the Union was not imposed from above. From the 1920s the streets of Northern Ireland's loyalist estates, villages, towns and cities became arenas for the exhibition of Britishness in parades, murals and rituals of death and politics.[5] Such everyday displays were necessary because, while the Union was firmly supported by the Protestant majority, it was 'a Union that was always under inspection, one that could not be taken for granted but must be defended repeatedly'.[6]

This was unsurprising because the original Union between Britain and Ireland, which came into effect in 1801, had lasted only twelve decades, and had been disputed for most of those. In the two decades before the partition of Ireland, nationalism had been transformed.[7] The Irish Parliamentary Party, which elected about eighty MPs between the 1880s and 1918, dominated nationalist politics and relied on constitutional methods, with some of its leaders, such as John Redmond, keen to continue a close association with Britain and its Empire. He saw Home Rule as allowing Ireland to offer its own contribution to the imperial mission.[8] When the Home Rule Act was passed in September 1914, Redmond felt it possible to declare that 'Ireland has been admitted by the democracy of England upon equal terms to her proper place in the Empire, which she had as much to do in the building of as England or Scotland (loud applause); and already as a result she has taken her proper place with perfect and absolute good faith and loyalty.'[9] The experience of the First World War, the Easter Rising of 1916 and the British government's attempt to impose conscription in

April 1918 shattered constitutional nationalism. The general election of 1918 resulted in the election of 73 Sinn Fein MPs and only six constitutional nationalists. The Sinn Fein MPs refused to take their seats at Westminster and formed the Dáil Éireann in Dublin, incontrovertibly disputing the sovereignty of the United Kingdom over Ireland. During 1919 the political rebellion became fused with military insurgency, led by republican separatist nationalists. The response of the British government under David Lloyd George was a combination of political manoeuvring and military repression. The formation of the Irish Free State in 1921 had entailed a fundamental re-negotiation of the Union brought about by the force of arms of Irish nationalists, after the failure of 35 years of constitutional pressure. The 1920 Government of Ireland Act, while it did not answer the demands of Irish nationalism, allowed six counties of Ulster to exclude themselves from Irish Home Rule, and largely released the Unionists from the control of Westminster. The process of securing the permanence of the Northern Ireland state took until the repudiation of the Boundary Commission in 1925.

Ulster Unionists had not wanted this parliament but were determined to make use of it in order to defend their British identity. However, the parties that would contest elections in Ulster were not all-British parties. This made Northern Ireland 'a place apart' from the British political contest.[10] Unionists saw the main focus of their political activity as being in the maintenance of their state power in Northern Ireland. They could usually expect to elect around a dozen MPs to the Westminster parliament but the Unionist leadership saw these MPs as acting as representatives of Northern Ireland's interests rather than as contributing to Conservative governments or opposition.

Many nationalists in Northern Ireland stood aloof from Westminster politics, seeing it as an alien institution. This further established Northern Ireland as a political place apart. The third important political force in Northern Ireland was labour. Northern Irish labour, as will be seen in the chapter on Harry Midgley below, would dearly have liked to have been more closely associated with British Labour. Rejected, they had to operate separately from the British party. The Northern Ireland Labour Party was not able to contribute to British Labour governments. As Patrick Buckland has argued, this meant that 'The major battles on behalf of the working classes were fought out in Britain, and the fruits of the Labour movement's victories in Britain were simply transferred to Northern Ireland by the Unionist government.'[11] Parties in Northern Ireland were, therefore, detached from those in the rest of Britain. Claims for resources were not channeled within the broad church British parties but in the narrow sectarianism of Protestant Unionism and Catholic nationalism.[12]

The population of the six counties was two-thirds Protestant Unionist and one-third Catholic nationalist. While the identities of these two ethno-religious-political groups were dichotomous and their lives were largely separated by residence, marriage and education, neither side was a monolithic bloc. There had been an historic divide between constitutional and physical force Irish nationalism, which continued inside Northern Ireland after partition. The constitutionalists fared better in the north after 1918 than in the south. Their figurehead was Joseph Devlin, whose politics were often Catholic as much as nationalist. He had co-opted the Ancient Order of Hibernians for political nationalism but with inevitable consequences.[13] The nationalists moved between abstention and participation in the Northern Ireland parliament, but found themselves ignored, indeed often treated with contempt, by the Unionist government. The inability to represent the Catholic community at parliamentary level meant that nationalist councils, where they survived gerrymandering, ensured that they exclusively served the Catholic population. Another consequence of the inability of constitutional nationalism to represent its political constituency was the continuing support for physical force nationalism in the north.

The support for each group among the Catholic community was fluid. In the 1950s, republicans mobilized their highest vote since partition on the basis of responding to the Unionist government's sectarian legislation. At other times, support for republicanism declined almost to nothing.

Unionism too had been divided. The major division had been geographical. Unionists outside the north-east of Ireland had been a minority of the population. While there were pockets of working class Unionism in Dublin and 'a Pooteresque world of clerks and shopkeepers who lived in the primly respectable townships south of the capital', southern Unionism was dominated by the Anglo-Irish landed class.[14] Southern Unionism, cut adrift from Ulster Unionism, accommodated itself to the new constitutional situation of an Irish national state.[15] In Ulster, Unionists formed a majority in four counties and a substantial minority in two more. Here was a cross-class alliance united in defence of the benefits its members derived from the Union with Great Britain. These benefits were religious, economic, cultural and imperial and combined to produce an extremely strong sense of Ulster Unionist identity. Under Home Rule, the Protestants of the north east would move from forming part of a permanent Protestant majority within the United Kingdom to becoming a permanent minority in a Catholic and nationalist Ireland.[16] The Union also had economic advantages. The north east was industrialized and urban in contrast to the agricultural and rural south and west. Ulster was part of the hinterland of the British industrial revolution, exporting linen and flax and building ships to carry Britain's imperial and foreign trade. Ulster also emulated the cities of northern England in their civic pride associated with the idea of 'progress'. This combined readily with the sense of imperial mission held by many in Britain.[17] As the Belfast Chamber of Commerce told Gladstone in 1893:

> All our progress has been made under the union. We were a small, insignificant town at the end of the last century, deeply disaffected and hostile to the British Empire. Since the union and under equal laws, we have been wedded to the empire and made a progress second to none.... Why should we be driven by force to abandon the conditions which have led to that success?[18]

The success of Irish nationalism in the late nineteenth and early twentieth centuries added significant new aspects to the Ulster political identity. First, the adoption of Gaelic culture by Irish nationalism emphasized the perception of racial difference between Ulster Protestants and Irish Catholics, which led to Ulster Unionism's withdrawal from a sense of its own Irishness.[19] Second, while this withdrawal meant that Britishness became more firmly fixed in the mentalities of Ulster Unionists, the conversion of the Liberal and Labour parties to support for Irish nationalism created a substantial sense of disaffection with English politics. Even the Conservatives could not entirely be trusted. The Ulster Unionist Council was formed in 1905 to enhance the political solidarity of Ulster Unionism in the face of the devolutionist ideas of George Wyndham, the Conservative Irish Secretary.[20]

The campaign against Home Rule added further important themes to Ulster Unionist identity. Alvin Jackson has shown how 'The events of 1912–14 in Ireland have served as a creation myth for Unionism in the twentieth century – as a kind of Orange Genesis.'[21] The apparent unanimity of the Ulster Protestant people in opposition to Home Rule and successful leadership by Edward Carson and James Craig provided subsequent Unionists with martyrs, models and methods to bolster their sense of historic identity. The accusations of out-datedness and atavism, because Unionist popular history seemed to rest so firmly in the seventeenth century, could be countered by reference to the recent past, in which history had been made from below by the mobilization of tens of thousands of Ulster men and women.[22] Ulster's experience of the First World War added a further episode of patriotic sacrifice to Unionist historiography.[23] The Ulster Volunteer Force had been enlisted en masse in the 36th (Ulster) Division of the British Army and their moment came with the opening of the Battle of the Somme on 1 July 1916. The date had already been invested with immense Protestant meaning, as it marked the anniversary of the Battle of the Boyne in 1690. While in Easter week of 1916, nationalist Ireland had seemingly confirmed its disloyalty through military rebellion, in the first week of July, Unionist Ulster again proved its loyalty to King and country as 5,500 Ulstermen fell dead, wounded and missing. James Loughlin has argued that 'It was an impressive, but militarily useless offensive, nevertheless, the process of mythologizing the event began immediately.'[24]

The nature of the Ulster identity created by these historical circumstances has been keenly debated. Some commentators have seen Ulster Unionism as little more than Protestantism. Others have assigned it a class function, suggesting that Unionism emerged from the industrial bourgeoisie in north-east Ireland in the late nineteenth century. Certainly, the association of Unionism with the idea of liberal progress accompanying industrialization serves well to confirm the 'British' nature of Ulster society in the late nineteenth and early twentieth centuries. David Miller, though, has argued that the Unionists' identity was not modern but backward-looking and atavistic, based on a conditional loyalty common in the early modern world built around the idea of a contract with the Protestant monarch.[25] Again, there is an advantage in such an interpretation because it dissociates Unionism from forming a separate nationalism inside the United Kingdom. However, conditional loyalty to the monarch has been a feature of British politics since the 'glorious revolution' of the late seventeenth century. Constitutional monarchies are built on the condition that the monarch acts constitutionally. As Loughlin has pointed out, loyalty to the monarchy in the United Kingdom is vertical and does not need 'a horizontal bond of common national identity across the whole kingdom'.[26] Again, such circumstances made for the integration of Ulster Unionism into the British experience. Loyalty to the Union was also vertical. It enabled the expression of variety of identities. Cohesion was possible without the need for uniformity.

Graham Walker has argued that Unionist identity constituted 'a form of nationalism'.[27] However, before the founding of the Northern Ireland parliament, which Ulster Unionists did not want, there had been little resemblance of Unionism to nationalism. Unionists had argued that as Ireland was a region within the United Kingdom, Ulster formed a region within Ireland. The establishment of what looked like a state in Northern Ireland made the province appear more like a nation than a region. Nonetheless, Unionists still did not make claims to nationhood. As Arthur Aughey has pointed out, they asserted their equivalence with others within the United Kingdom on the basis of citizenship.[28] They emphasized their difference but not a sense of national difference. Ulster was more than a region but less than a nation.

The association of Unionism with Britishness was further complicated by the problematic nature of national identity in the United Kingdom. The relationship could not be one between two developed and coherent bodies of ideas and beliefs, because neither Ulster Unionism nor Britishness were fully formed and fixed. They were in constant development.[29] Far from creating tension, this eased the relationship because Britishness was able to accommodate a variety of forms of identity because of the constitutional device of the Union.

Historians have recently emphasized this fissiparous nature of Unionism. The idea of strength developing from diversity is reversed to accentuate the potential problems emerging from such a variety of interests. As Buckland has recently argued:

> It is often forgotten that Ulster unionism was an alliance of disparate social, economic and religious groups who found coherence only in opposition to nationalism and Catholicism. Landowners and tenant farmers, businessmen and artisans and labourers, town and country, all had different and competing interests. The term 'Protestant' included the three major denominations – Church of Ireland, Methodist and Presbyterian – separated by considerable theological and historical differences, and also numerous small, fiercely independent sects. Thus, the conflict in Northern Ireland was the more intense not just because Protestant distrusted Catholic but because Protestant distrusted Protestant. The unity of Ulster unionism had constantly to be managed.[30]

The cohesion of disparate elements supporting the Union could alternatively be seen as a great source of strength. Jack Sayers, liberal Unionist editor of the *Belfast Telegraph* explained in 1959:

> The unity and strength of the Ulster Unionist Party is one of the most remarkable political phenomenon of the century. Over a span of more than fifty years no other party in the English-speaking world has had such unwavering popular support.... There are in the wide embrace of Unionism men and women of Conservative, Liberal, and even Labour opinions, employers and workers, rich and poor, townsmen and countrymen, Orangemen and non-Orangemen.[31]

Ulster Unionists united around features of religion, economy, culture, empire and history giving them common purpose. Often there was little unity in how that common purpose might be achieved. Some, like Sayers, were liberal and moderate. Andrew Gailey has called these 'constructive Unionists' and has argued that their prominence in the 1890s and 1960s rested on the success of the United Kingdom in empire building in the late nineteenth century and winning the Second World War.[32] Constructive unionism was prepared to go a long way to meet the aspirations of the Catholic population, as it seemed Terence O'Neill was prepared to do as Prime Minister between 1963 and 1969. Gailey argues that 'Under O'Neill Ulster was ... transformed with new housing, motorways, businesses and a university. Moreover, with the help of Sayers and the *Belfast Telegraph*, he established a new, popular, moderate consensus. However fragile this proved to be in the end, it remains a unique achievement in twentieth-century Ulster.'[33]

Others preferred coercion to defend the state. In the 1920s the Unionist state created two levers of power upon which it could rely in times of crisis. The Special Powers Act (1922) gave the security forces powers of arrest and search without warrant and detention without trial, as well as allowing for the banning of political meetings and marches, and capital and corporal punishment. The B Specials were an auxiliary force of part-time and voluntary police, almost entirely Protestant and unanimously unionist by their very nature. This was the Protestant people in arms, prepared to defend the state and Union against the internal threat of the nationalist population.

Between them, the Special Powers Act and the B Specials provided the state with draconian powers and a force prepared to make use of them when the government deemed it necessary. Political violence was widely seen on the Unionist side as the product of Irish republican nationalism determined to overthrow the new state. Between July 1920 and July 1922, there were 557 political deaths in Northern Ireland.[34] The Catholicism of the minority in Northern Ireland was considered to be associated wholeheartedly with such an aim, and in those circumstances many Unionists saw the minority as irreconcilably disloyal. The leaders of Unionism were frequently prepared to voice such opinions, as when Craig stressed that he believed that Northern Ireland was a Protestant state for a Protestant people. It has been pointed out that the speech was made in response to the declaration in the constitution of Éire in 1937 that gave a 'special position' to the Catholic Church within the state.[35] However, government ministers were prepared to initiate episodes in which the loyalty of Catholics was questioned. In 1932, Sir Basil Brooke, a Parliamentary Secretary at the time and later Prime Minister, told an Orange meeting that 'There was a great number of Protestants and Orangemen who employed Roman Catholics. He felt he could speak freely on this subject because he had not a Roman Catholic about his own place.'[36] In the controversy that followed, Brooke argued that he discriminated not on religious but on political grounds. He refused to employ Catholics not because they were Catholic but because he considered them to be disloyal. This was a common stance among Unionists and it discouraged attempts to reconcile Catholics to the state.

The greatest division within Unionism was that arising from perceptions of the politics of social class. Bew, Gibbon and Patterson have seen the Unionist leadership's discussion about strategies for reconciling the interests of the Protestant working class as forming the central political debate of the Northern Ireland state.[37] They feared that their coalition was fundamentally unstable because the working class might form a class consciousness incompatible with Unionism.[38] Two camps emerged. The 'populists', Sir James Craig, John Andrews and R. Dawson Bates, utilized a strategy entailing sectarianism and the extensive use of public funds to retain working class support for the Unionist Party during the long periods when there was no realistic republican threat to the state that could be mobilized to maintain the loyalty of the Protestant working class to the Unionist Party. On the other side were the 'anti-populists', represented by Sir Wilfred Spender, the head of the Northern Ireland civil service, and two finance ministers, Hugh Pollock and John Milne Barbour.[39] This group sought to retain the stability of the state by strict financial parsimony and some level of integration of the Catholic community.

The debate reflected the perceptions about which section of the working class constituted the greatest threat to the stability of the state. While the anti-populists considered that the Irish nationalist orientation of the Catholics could be lessened by the application of 'British' standards to housing and employment, the populists pandered to the view of the Protestant fundamentalists that the Catholics were irreconcilable. The populists, therefore, saw the major role of the state to construct a platform around which the Protestant working class could be gathered in support of the Unionist Party, which alone could be trusted to avert crisis. The populists saw their major rivals as independent and especially labour unionists who might divide the Protestant working class. The Unionist leaders saw every election between the 1920s and the 1960s as contests between the Unionist Party and labour.

The Government of Ireland Act came into effect on 1 May 1921 and elections were called for 24 May, Empire Day. Craig's major concern was that in the wake of the working class militancy following the First World War, the labour candidates would draw support away from the Unionists. In Belfast, three labour candidates, James Baird, John Hanna and Harry Midgley, booked Ulster Hall for a meeting only to find it invaded by loyalist shipyard workers, who subsequently sent a telegram to Craig asking him for support.[40] His reply validated their actions. 'I am with them in spirit,' he wrote from London. 'Know they will do their part. I will do mine. Well done big and wee yards.'[41] While Labour performed poorly in the election Craig's concerns were not lessened.

The 1920 Act had legislated for proportional representation in local and parliamentary elections in Northern Ireland, as a safeguard for the Catholic minority. The effect can be seen in the elections to Belfast City Council in 1920. Before proportional representation, the Unionists had won 52 wards to the nationalists 8, but under PR official Unionist representation fell to 35, with 2 independent Unionists, 13 Labour and 10 nationalists elected. The 1925 Northern Ireland general election confirmed the beneficial effects of PR for labour, when Belfast saw official Unionist representation fall from 15 to 8, with 4 seats going to independent Unionists and 3 going to labour.[42] Craig's concern was that, while Protestant working class voters would never vote nationalist, they could be won over to other variants of unionism that might form some sort of arrangement with nationalists, weakening the control of his party at Stormont and within the United Kingdom. In such circumstances he wished each election to be fought on the dichotomous question of 'Who is for Empire and who is for a Republic?'[43]

Proportional representation obscured the dichotomy. To the west of the River Bann where Protestants were in a less secure majority or indeed, as in Fermanagh, Tyrone and Londonderry City, formed a minority, there was strong grassroots pressure to abolish PR. Craig's decision to do so therefore served two useful purposes. It drove politics back to the issue of the Union at the same time as demonstrating his responsiveness to the wishes of his supporters. PR was abolished in local elections in 1922 and in parliamentary elections in 1929. The effect on local councils was dramatic. Under PR, nationalists and labour had controlled 32 per cent of councils, without PR they controlled only 16 per cent.[44]

The other side of the populists' strategy was more positive. The Unionist Party needed to appear as a party alert to the material needs of the Protestant working class. Craig promised to follow British social policy 'step-by-step'. Again, the advantages were two-fold. There was the direct material appeal to working class voters in living in some of the United Kingdom's poorest conditions, but in addition contrasts with the Irish Free State could be drawn. Britishness meant progress, while Irishness was associated with neglect of social policy and with the interference of the Catholic hierarchy in the affairs of state.

The major advance in British social policy during the Second World War emphasized the political imperatives associated with the populist strategy. The Westminster government began to move far ahead of what the anti-populists considered possible in Northern Ireland, yet the Ulster electorate was radicalized by war. This did not lessen the unionism of the Protestant working class but there was a substantial shift to the left in politics. The Prime Minister Sir Basil Brooke called an election immediately after VE Day, attempting like Churchill to bask in the glory of victory. Where Churchill failed, Brooke succeeded, though with substantially reduced support. In 1938, labour candidates had secured only 7.4 per cent of the vote, with nationalists and republicans taking 4.9 per cent. The official Unionists had won 56.5 per cent of the vote. In June 1945, labour candidates won 32.9 per cent of the vote, with nationalists and republicans gaining 9.2 per cent. The official Unionist vote was a bare majority at 50.4 per cent.[45] The first-past-the-post electoral system saved the Unionist Party but it was clear that the dichotomy had to be re-established.

Brooke was convinced that his government had to follow the path taken by the British Labour government. Others within his cabinet believed that Labour's socialism was contrary to Northern Ireland's Conservative Unionism. Brian Maginness and Sir Reginald Nugent considered the solution to be dominion status, which would give them constitutional parity with Australia, New Zealand, Canada and South Africa. They could remain culturally British while becoming legally separate from the United Kingdom. Brooke, however, warned against separating Northern Ireland from the United Kingdom because it could fracture the Unionist alliance with the Protestant working class. In a speech in Larne he counselled against dominion status:

> To attempt a fundamental change in our constitutional status is to reopen the whole Irish question. The government is strongly supported by the votes of the working-class who cherish their heritage in the Union and to whom any tendency towards separation from Britain is anathema ... The backbone of Unionism is the Unionist Labour party. Are those men going to be satisfied if we reject the social services and other benefits we have had by going step by step with Britain?[46]

Brooke was aided in his scheme to maintain the polarization of Northern Irish politics around the question of the Union, to the detriment of labour, by the governments of the south. In September 1948, John Costello, the Irish Taoiseach, withdrew Ireland from the Commonwealth. Brooke handled the situation skilfully. He visited the British Prime Minister Clement Attlee at Chequers and persuaded him to make a declaration on Northern Ireland's constitutional position, which Attlee did in two speeches affirming that the will of the people of Ulster expressed through the Stormont parliament would be the deciding factor in the constitutional destiny of the province.

Bolstered by Attlee's assurances, Brooke called a general election with a manifesto that declared:

> Our country is in danger ... Today we fight to defend our very existence and the heritage of our Ulster children. The British government have agreed to abide by the decision of the Ulster people. It is therefore imperative that our determination to remain under the Union Jack should be immediately and overwhelmingly re-affirmed ... No Surrender, We are King's Men.[47]

In the late 1940s the Anti-Partition League had been active and had encouraged some British Labour MPs to voice criticisms of the

Northern Irish state. Costello's announcement stifled their calls for reform. Instead, in what might be considered the high point of the Union, the Labour government passed the Ireland Act, which gave statutory force to Attlee's declarations about the position of Northern Ireland. Winston Churchill had seen Ulster's war record as entitling it to firm support. The neutrality of Ireland in the war, however benevolent, had emphasized that 'by the grace of God Ulster stood a faithful sentinel'.[48] Now Labour, traditionally sympathetic to Irish nationalism, established itself as consciously unionist. The Act secured the Unionist state's constitutional position for the next quarter century.[49] The King's men election routed labour, rallying Protestants back to electoral support for the Unionist Party.

Developments of the late 1940s brought Northern Ireland into the welfare state and this continued the process of the province's 'de-insularisation' from Britain.[50] The decision to follow Labour's welfare policies step-by-step was not taken easily. It seemed that Ulster's independent position would be threatened, but the Unionist government reached financial agreement with the British Treasury to fund the welfare state in Northern Ireland at the same time as the Ireland Act confirmed the sovereignty of Stormont over the constitutional position. Integration of social policy had proved entirely compatible with the devolution of constitutional policy. The Union was operating to accommodate the diversity of Ulster within the United Kingdom.

It was the problem of the nationalist minority that encouraged most British politicians to consider that devolution was a necessary device for avoiding difficult issues in Northern Ireland. Faced with militant Irish nationalism, the British had sought a disengagement from Ireland. The strategy of Gladstone and Asquith had been to maintain Ireland within the United Kingdom but with sufficient devolution of powers to an Irish parliament so as to marginalize the Irish within British politics. This was a policy of pluralism combined with self interest. Ulster Unionism stood in the way of disengaging from Ireland but Lloyd George's settlement in 1921 provided a way out, in which devolution to a region (not a nation) within the United Kingdom enabled Northern Irish politics to be retained within the United Kingdom but outside of British politics. In consideration of Northern Irish politics perspective is everything. From the perspective of nationalists, Catholics and some socialists, the Northern Irish state seemed like a carnival of Protestant reaction. From the perspective of many British politicians and for most Ulster Unionists, the state was a success. As Bardon has argued, 'For just over fifty years Northern Ireland had been a self-governing part of the United Kingdom. Except for a violent beginning, nearly all of those years until 1969 had been so peaceful that Westminster felt able to leave the devolved administration largely to its own devices.'[51]

The following two chapters examine the way in which unionism in Ulster mobilized support from a variety of sources. Ulster unionism was a cross-class and cross-gender coalition. Over three decades, from the 1920s to the 1950s, Harry Midgley constructed a political programme from a combination of Belfast socialism, imperialism and, ultimately, Protestant Unionism. Dehra Parker came from a rural and landed family and against the advice of the Ulster Women's Unionist Council stood as a candidate for the Northern Ireland parliament. She was elected as a Unionist. Like Midgley, she remained in politics for three decades. She was instinctively a Unionist. Her gender did not serve as a source of tension in the highly masculine world of Unionism, though it did limit her career. Both Midgley and Parker, through the assertion of their ideas, helped to maintain the Union while also proclaiming Ulster's distinctiveness.

9
Ulster's Ramsay MacDonald? Harry Midgley (1892–1957)

The Unionist Party believed that its coalition of support could be fractured if working-class identity provided a focus of loyalty that was irreconcilable with the Union. Elsewhere in the United Kingdom, Northern Ireland was seen as 'a place apart' because it was divided by the fundamental political dispute between Irish nationalism and Unionism. The conceptualization of class as the primary identity of individuals in modern society meant that the existence of labour parties was seen as natural and inevitable. The Unionist Party sought to obstruct the 'forward march of labour' in Northern Ireland and their success suggested to the British Labour movement that the (Northern) Irish were deviating from the normative politics of the rest of the United Kingdom. Given their debt to late nineteenth-century Liberalism, which under Gladstone and Asquith was being forced to confront the pluralist nature of the British Isles, many early labour activists had an intense sympathy for Irish nationalism.[1] The presumption was that Unionist-labour in the north of Ireland was a departure from the true interests of the working class.[2] These presumptions have followed through into the historiography of the labour movement in Northern Ireland. As Henry Patterson has remarked, 'The problem with such histories is their tendency to treat the main ideological currents among Protestant workers simply as obstacles to be overcome. From the outset they are defined as "problems."'[3]

Henry Cassidy (Harry) Midgley, born on 8 September 1892 into a Protestant working class family in North Belfast, is particularly poorly served within such tendencies. Midgley was a pioneer of labour politics in Belfast but ended his political career as Unionist Minister of Education in the 1950s. This has led to accusations that Midgley was 'Ulster's own Ramsay MacDonald', betraying labour for the sake of his career.[4] The final controversy of his controversial political life showed the distance he had travelled from politics based on identities of class to those based on religion. He made a speech in 1957 in which he was alleged to have said that 'all the [Catholic] minority are traitors and have consistently been traitors to the Government of Northern Ireland'.[5] Graham Walker's biography of Midgley is rigorously researched and coherently argued, yet its title, *The Politics of Frustration: Harry Midgley and the Failure of Labour in Northern Ireland*, summarizes the sense that Midgley's actions were essentially negative reactions to the sectarianism that 'distorted' the natural growth of labour in the Ireland before and after partition.[6] Walker sees Midgley as unable to overcome sectarian divisions, so surrendering to them. This obstructs full consideration of Midgley's agency to formulate and develop what might be called a 'social Unionism' that eventually found him a home within the Unionist Party because of that party's acceptance of the step-by-step policy in relation to British Labour government's welfare state of the late 1940s.

Midgley is seen as even more problematic because he appears as a serial turncoat. He left the Northern Ireland Labour Party (NILP) in 1942 to form his own Commonwealth Labour Party, which he abandoned in 1947 to join the Unionist Party. In British politics, where the party system was fairly securely fixed between the Conservative, Liberal and Labour parties between 1900 and the 1970s, those who have defected from parties have been seen renegades, such as Oswald Mosley and James Ramsay MacDonald.[7] The longevity of the Unionist Party in Northern Ireland suggested that a similar condition of party stability was in place. Therefore, Midgley's abandonment of two parties seemed to be both unprincipled and a matter of expediency.[8]

However, the permanent electoral majority enjoyed by the Unionist Party encouraged the fluidity of oppositional party politics. Here was the politics of frustration as Catholic, nationalist, republican and labour groups and individuals faced the reality of the unresponsiveness of the Unionist government to their separate and diverse demands. New organizations emerged to attempt to galvanize nationalist, republican and labour politics, only to disintegrate in disappointment and disillusion. Nationalist politics moved through a variety of organizational forms, from the United Irish League to the National League of the North to the Anti-Partition League. Harry Diamond, for example, moved from the Nationalist party to form his own Socialist Republican Party in 1945, which became the northern section of the Irish Labour Party in 1949, from which he was expelled in 1951. Diamond formed the Republican Labour Party in 1965, with Gerry Fitt, who in turn founded the Social Democratic and Labour Party in 1970.[9] In this context, Midgley's party fluidity can be seen as in the mainstream of oppositional politics in Northern Ireland, and should leave us free to consider his political ideas rather than his political manoeuvring.

Midgley's passage to Unionism entailed the formulation of positive ideas and policies. These were constructed in the context of the centrality of the Union in Northern Irish politics. Midgley did not unthinkingly support the Union but arrived at a position in which he came to believe that the Union provided a beneficial political and social state of affairs for the Protestant working class in Northern Ireland. This suggests a certain parochialism, and it is indeed the case that the existence of the Stormont parliament did encourage an insular and inward-looking politics among most political forces within the province. Again, rather than seeing this as signifying Northern Ireland as a place apart a more appropriate conceptualization might be to see such localism as operating within Midgley's wider concerns with British standards of citizenship. When he left the NILP it was to form the Commonwealth Labour Party, which had a wider perspective on the place of Ulster in world politics.

This chapter examines Midgley's political life in relation to his attitude towards the politics of nation, where he was located between Britain and Ireland. He did not abandon national political identity but this should not be seen as a deviation from class politics but as the integration of his class and national identities. The British Labour Party, content with its own position within the consensual British nation, abstained from Northern Irish politics, leaving the NILP alone to cope with the complexities of identity politics in Ulster. Midgley sought to resolve the tensions of class and nation in Northern Ireland through his imperial turn, when he came to see the Commonwealth as providing a political space to emphasize Ulster's distinctive Britishness without abandoning the politics of class.

Labour and the Irish nation before partition

Midgley's political ideas were developed in the ferment of Edwardian labour politics. Attitudes towards the Union were central because the emergence of labour politics coincided with the development of Ulster Unionism as a cross-class movement. Midgley's entry into politics came early in his life. He became an apprentice joiner aged fourteen and soon began speaking at meetings of the Independent Labour

Party.[10] Parts of the labour movement in Belfast considered the ILP, as a British party, to be inappropriately organizing in Ireland. The Edwardian period saw debates between nationalist and unionist labour activists about the direction that they should take towards socialist and labour advance.

Developments in British politics brought this debate to the forefront of Irish labour's attention. The Liberal government elected in 1906 had attempted to close its eyes and ears to the demands of the eighty-strong Irish party in the House of Commons, bolstered by its over-whelming parliamentary majority. The constitutional conflict over Lloyd George's 'People's Budget' in 1909 and reform of the powers of the House of Lords in 1910 resulted in two general elections which left the Liberals without an overall majority and reliant on the support of the Irish and Labour parties to govern. Under these conditions, the Liberal Party's pluralist outlook on United Kingdom politics re-emerged and Asquith introduced the third Irish Home Bill to the House of Commons in 1912.

Opposition to Home Rule had been invigorated in 1905 by the formation of the Ulster Unionist Council when faced with the mildly devolutionist plans of the Conservative Irish Secretary George Wyndham. The debates over the strategy that labour in Ireland ought to adopt therefore took place against the background of a contest over attitudes towards British and Irish national identity, in which the majority of the Protestant working class were opposed to repeal or reform of the Union. In Belfast, the best-known Protestant labour leader was William Walker, a joiner at the Harland and Wolff shipyard, itself a bastion of skilled Protestant workmen.[11] Walker sought to build working class unity between the skilled and unskilled workers but remained convinced that the Irish people were better served within the Union than without. He wanted to integrate Irish labour into the British Labour Party, which had succeeded in electing thirty MPs in the general election of 1906. He declared that he was 'determined that the Union shall be beneficial to Ireland, that every advantage which can be obtained through the Union shall be conferred upon the Irish people'.[12] On the nationalist side, James Connolly argued that socialist politics in Ireland should be republican to establish without doubt their anti-imperialist nature and that labour should be organized on an Irish basis in order to be able to operate within Ireland that seemed likely to achieve Home Rule within the next few years. Walker's strategy entailed a strong labour party at Westminster. While Walker was more in tune with the outlook of the Belfast Protestant working class, the British Labour Party supported Irish Home Rule. In 1912, with the backing of the Irish Trade Union Congress the Independent Labour Party (Ireland) was formed. Defeated, Walker retired from politics.

Midgley's position in regard to the debate over the way labour should face in Ireland is obscure. He supported Walker in the Belfast North by-election of 1907 but subsequently broke with him. Graham Walker has suggested that this entailed support for the Connollyite Irish position, but John Gray has argued that the evidence for such support is tenuous.[13] In 1912 Midgley left Ireland for the United States. This does seem to imply that he was dissatisfied with the disputes within labour politics, and it also means that he was absent from Belfast during the period of the greatest anti-Home Rule militancy supported by the bulk of Protestant workers. Nonetheless, when Midgley returned to Belfast for a holiday and European war broke out, he joined the Royal Inniskilling Fusiliers with his brothers, Alex and Eddie. While there were many possible reasons for enlisting, Midgley was clearly distancing himself from the republican socialism of Connolly, which saw the war as an imperialist struggle and nationalist Ireland's opportunity to achieve independence.

There were some parallels between the experiences of Midgley and Huw T. Edwards. Both had been active in socialist and trade unionist politics before the war but both joined the British Army in 1914. In each case the experience of war seemed to confirm their socialist politics, which did not entail a fundamental break with a sense of loyalty to the United Kingdom. This reflected the general impact upon British Labour. Ramsay MacDonald resigned as chairman of the Parliamentary Labour Party because the majority of the party decided to support the war. The ILP opposed the war but through the argument of respect for the individual's conscience it made no pronouncement on enlistment. It is also sometimes presumed that as the war continued there was a growing sense of war weariness that contributed to the significant growth of anti-war feeling. Undoubtedly, the British population was subject to great emotional strain as the casualty lists lengthened. The Russian Revolution and the Bolshevik withdrawal from the war provided some sense of an alternative to the war. However, British Labour continued to support the war effort right through until the Armistice on 11 November 1918. The party did formulate war aims that included making the world safe for democracy, an end to secret diplomacy, and international arbitration to prevent future wars, but their achievement rested upon determination to see Germany defeated.[14] As British Labour reorganized its structures in preparation for the coming political battles, it also reaffirmed its commitment to the nation through its desire to establish a 'National Memorial of Peace and Freedom,' a war memorial 'to commemorate the heroic deeds and unselfish devotion of those members of the British trades unions and other Labour organisations who fell in action … in the great struggle for freedom and peace'.[15] There was a suggestion that the subscriptions raised could be used to build a new headquarters for the party that would act to permanently remind the nation of the party's patriotic credentials.[16] Midgley and Edwards therefore shared the combination of war service and labour politics with the mainstream of British Labour.

The position in Ireland, however, diverged from that in Britain. Irish nationalism was divided by the war.[17] The constitutional nationalists, led by John Redmond, who had the overwhelming support of Catholic Ireland in 1914, supported the war. Physical force nationalists, however, staged a rebellion in April 1916. The suppression of the Rising, the execution of its leaders, war weariness and the decision to implement conscription in Ireland in April 1918 destroyed Redmondite constitutional nationalism. In Protestant Ulster, such events acted to confirm the sense that Catholic Ireland was fundamentally disloyal. In July 1916, three months after the blood sacrifice for the Irish Republic, loyal Ulster gave the blood of its sons to the British nation and the Protestant religion in the Battle of the Somme. Midgley's war service strengthened his labour politics at the same time as reinforcing his commitment to the Protestant working class. In 1924 he published a volume of war poems called *Thoughts from Flanders*. The message of the verses was of remembrance. In some he hoped that armistice would 'bury all divisions in remembrance of this day',[18] but the politics of the war meant that the act of publication placed him within the loyalist camp. He memorialized the Ulster-British war dead, not the martyrs of Easter Week. *Thoughts from Flanders* celebrated 'our mighty dead' collectively and individually and the causes for which they had fought:

> Lest we forget, I call once more to mind
> His smiling face, his manner strong and mild,
> His actions ever faithful, true, and kind,
> Strong as a man and faithful as a child,
> Dauntless his courage, his confidence serene,
> Quick to resist a wrong, earnest for right;
> Forward he walked through life with sense ever keen,
> Working for justice and freedom's golden light.[19]

In the years immediately following the First World War, the contest over national identity in Ireland became a war. While some labour activists in southern Ireland subordinated themselves to nationalism,[20] other activists, including Midgley sought to abstain in the debates about partition. The immediate post-war years saw massive industrial unrest in British cities, and Belfast workers showed common experience with Britain by similarly engaging in strike action, whereas southern Irish town and cities were engaged in the nationalist struggle. There was a four-week engineering strike in Belfast in early 1919, and in this situation, labour was able to make some headway in Belfast's municipal politics. Twelve labour councillors were elected to Belfast Corporation in January 1920.[21] As Walker comments, 'Most of the seats were won in Protestant areas with the Labour Party ... careful to avoid the national question and to concentrate on economic issues.'[22]

Unionist Party leaders were certainly worried that the politics of class might act to weaken the politics of nation in such a crucial period. Loyalist workers in the shipyards and engineering, if not encouraged were certainly condoned in their expulsion of Protestant labour activists when Catholic workers were driven out. In these circumstances, Midgley stood as an independent labour candidate in the elections to the new Northern Ireland parliament in May 1921.

This election is seen as the measure against which Midgley's subsequent desertion from non-sectarian politics is judged. With John Hanna and James Baird, Midgley released a joint statement declaring that 'We are completely against partition. It is an unworkable stupidity ... the interests of the workers of Ireland are politically and economically one.'[23] The labour candidates ran an advertisement in the *Irish News* saying that 'We stand for an unpartitioned Ireland based on the goodwill of all who love their native land – north to south and east to west.' Walker argues that 'Midgley, therefore, had come out explicitly against partition.'[24]

This was not the same as declaring support for nationalism. The labour candidates equivocated by delivering a less stark message to the Unionist press, calling only for 'Civil and religious liberty!'[25] In addition, the labour candidates stance supported the unity of the island of Ireland but did not endorse the establishment of the Dáil Éireann in Dublin. Too much can be made of Midgley's anti-partition declaration in 1921. The threat from Ulster Unionists had always been seen as a device to prevent Home Rule for all Ireland. In the early 1920s, partition was opposed by some as a betrayal of those Unionists who were to fall under the sway of the Dublin parliament. Midgley certainly was not among those complaining of betrayal but the labour candidates' declaration against partition should not be seen as positive support for establishment of the Home Rule parliament in Dublin. Rather, it can be read equally as a statement of support for the *status quo ante*, keeping Ireland united for the benefit of the working class in the north and south. With expulsions from the shipyards of Catholic and 'rotten Prod' workers and with sectarian violence an everyday occurrence, the subtlety of the labour position was missed. The labour candidates lost their deposits as voters rallied either to Unionism or nationalism.

Midgley did not make another statement in opposition to partition or in support of the unity of the northern counties with the Irish Free State. Sometimes he argued that the border was an irrelevance for labour, as in October 1923 when he told a meeting at the Ulster Hall that

> I notice the orthodox politicians in Northern Ireland are at present preparing their new bogey for the next election – that is the Border Question … I tell you, both from an international point of view, and also from the point of view of the love that ought to dwell in our hearts, there is no border on God's earth worth losing one's life over.[26]

There was an implication here that nationalists, who believed the border was worth dying for, were the targets of Midgley's criticism. This point is further emphasized because Midgley made his point at a meeting addressed by Josiah Wedgwood, a British Labour MP. In the same year, Midgley told an audience on the protestant Shankill Road that he was as loyal as Craig on the boundary issue, and when asked 'Where's your [union] flag?' he responded 'Flying over the grave of my brother on the Western Front.'[27]

Midgley's position, therefore, wavered between avoidance of the partition question and asserting its insignificance for labour in Northern Ireland. However, he always fell on the side of support for the newly negotiated Union, with Northern Ireland within the United Kingdom. In 1928, while he called for a third tradition between Walker's labour Unionism and Connolly's socialist nationalism,[28] he continued to see the politics of Northern Irish labour falling within the realms of British Labour.

Midgley and British Labour

In the 1923 Westminster general election, Midgley stood on a programme that was virtually identical to that of the British Labour Party.

He supported the capital levy and the minimum wage, and like many British Labour candidates, he emphasized his war service.[29] In the debate within the NILP as to whether the party should face towards Irish or British Labour, Midgley now consistently favoured the British aspect. The NILP's position of neutrality on the border question meant that it accepted operation within the Northern Irish state, which made Midgley's stance logical and largely unassailable.

The NILP wanted recognition from the British Labour Party but was treated as if it was the illegitimate outcome of a regretted sexual liaison. While not devoting much attention to the issue, British Labour had supported the demand for Home Rule in Ireland before the First World War. This did not mean that the party supported the separation of Ireland from the United Kingdom. The party's position was one of pluralism within the United Kingdom, not of Irish nationalism. The June 1918 party conference passed a resolution that expressed such a view, declaring 'that the conference unhesitatingly recognises the claim of the people of Ireland to Home Rule and to self-determination in all exclusively Irish affairs'.[30] Even when the 1920 conference removed the limiting final clause, party leaders told the House of Commons that Labour supported only dominion status for Ireland, with William Adamson saying that 'I do not believe in their heart of hearts [that the Irish people] really want a republic; they are simply putting forward, in my opinion, their maximum demand'.[31] Labour's position on Ireland reflected its belief in the 'imperial standard' – that British standards were the most advanced in the world and that all nations benefited from being judged against their measure. In the case of the white dominions, Labour believed that the imperial standard was fully compatible with legislative devolution. In the Irish case, as Terry Cradden has explained, while 'Labour was ... opposed to Ireland leaving, or being removed from the United Kingdom; it was, at the same time, ideologically committed to as much legislative independence under Home Rule as the Irish themselves demanded; and it was also against partition.'[32]

After the passage of the Government of Ireland Act, British Labour wanted to abdicate responsibility for Northern Ireland. Parts of the party sympathized with the position of the northern Catholics; few understood the position of the Unionist working class. In the 1920s, British Labour breathed a 'sigh of deliverance' from the complications of Ireland.[33] The existence of the NILP was, therefore, something of an embarrassment to British Labour. The NILP, and especially Midgley, attempted to build links with British Labour, believing that

Westminster Labour governments would provide improved standards of living and political conditions for the working class in Northern Ireland. Labour's śuccess in Britain, they hoped, might be emulated within Northern Ireland to establish the NILP as the chief opposition to the Unionist Party, which they always branded as Tory. Midgley and the NILP therefore sought the normalization of Ulster politics within the British model. Given the determination of the Unionist Party to maintain politics in frames of attitudes towards the Union, the NILP needed all the help it could get to turn the issue back to interests based upon class.

The events of the 1930s seemed to offer some promise to labour politics, but Northern Ireland's economic and ethnic conditions pushed Midgley further towards support for the Union and British Labour. Reliant on exports, Northern Irish workers were laid off in large numbers during the world depression of the early 1930s. Between 1931 and 1939 more than a quarter of the insured workforce were out of work. In 1932 unemployed workers ignored their religious divisions in protests against the harsh conditions and low allowances imposed on outdoor relief workers by the Poor Law in a period of mass unemployment.[34] Influenced by Communists in the Revolutionary Workers' Group (RWG), the unemployed staged a series of strikes and demonstrations in September and October, which turned into battles with the Royal Ulster Constabulary. This has seemed to some left historians to suggest the possibilities for labour uniting across the sectarian divide,[35] though Tom Hennessey suggests that 'Non-sectarian class unity was short-lived ... [the 1932 riots] might ... be interpreted as an aberration in a highly sectarian society.'[36]

Midgley did not respond to the riots with a heightened sense of the possibilities for labour unity. As a constitutionalist, he was hostile to street politics, particularly because in Northern Ireland they were usually associated with sectarianism. Instead, he condemned the workers who had fallen under the influence of the Communists. Midgley described how the rioters 'in their hour of need, brought about by their own political stupidity ... turn to counsels of despair' of the 'political knaves and adventurers' in the RWG.[37] Midgley came from a tradition of self-improvement, associated with his position within the skilled working class. He enjoyed classical music and opera, and lived a happy domestic life with his wife Eleanor and his children. His was a political vision of order, education and reason, which he believed could only be accommodated within constitutional procedures, associated with British Labour and the Union. He associated sectarian politics with a lack of education on the part of the working class. '[H]erded together', he said, 'their mentality is not so keen' and so they danced to the 'sectarian tune'.[38]

Nationalism and Catholicism seemed to Midgley to provide continuing obstacles to the political success of labour, which he believed could contribute so much to stability and social progress within Northern Ireland. Between 1932 and 1942 he was leader of the NILP and he consistently argued his case within the party. His platform was based on the Protestant working class, but he frequently also needed the votes of Catholics to secure his election. The attitude of the nationalists towards Midgley was therefore crucial. His attitude to them was hostile. The other NILP leaders, Jack Beattie, Sam Kyle and William McMullen were all Protestants like Midgley but forged much easier relationships with northern Catholic nationalism. Their links were with Irish rather than British trade unions. Beattie was expelled from the NILP in 1934 for becoming Northern organizer of the Irish National Teachers' Organization and refusing to move the writ for a by-election in Belfast Central after the death of veteran nationalist Joe Devlin, and he retained his Stormont seat by virtue of solid Catholic votes in Pottinger. In 1932 Sam Kyle moved to Dublin to lead the Irish Amalgamated Transport and General Workers, becoming chairman of the Irish TUC in 1940. McMullen had been President of the Irish TUC in 1928–29 and moved to Dublin in the 1930s becoming President of the Irish TGWU. Both Kyle and McMullen became members of the Southern Senate. Midgley never enjoyed the same relationship with the south. His life, political and personal, was embedded entirely within Ulster.

His lack of sympathy for the Catholic population became increasingly evident. This was not yet direct hostility to Catholics, but rather disdain for Catholic nationalism. In the summer of 1935, the silver jubilee of George V provided the opportunity for extended sectarian rioting in which Catholics were the victims of intense loyalist violence. There were thirteen deaths, eight Protestants and five Catholics, but the direction of violence is better represented in the driving of 2000 Catholics but only a handful of Protestants from their homes.[39]

Historians of various political complexions recognize the role of Unionist leaders in exacerbating tensions in the mid-1930s.[40] Midgley had been elected to Stormont in 1933 for the Belfast seat of Dock. In 1935 he was criticized within nationalist and Catholic circles for his 'silence' on the riots, though he was re-elected unopposed as alderman for the Dock ward in 1936.[41] Midgley condemned all sides in the riots, but given that they were chiefly loyalist attacks on Catholics and that in some respects they had been encouraged by Unionist leaders, they signified his increasing distance from his Catholic constituents.[42]

War and Commonwealth

Midgley's concerns were not entirely with the domestic situation in Northern Ireland. In 1934 his chairman's address warned the NILP conference of the dangers of the fascist threat in Europe. Midgley began to consider the global aspect of Northern Ireland's British connection. At the 1936 NILP conference he called for close cooperation with labour movements 'throughout the British Commonwealth of Nations'.[43] This was a theme to which he would increasingly return over the next decade. In the late 1930s, however, he was diverted, not entirely against his will, into seeing the threat of fascism in a religious context.

The occasion was the Catholic nationalist rising against the republican government in Spain. Successful republican resistance turned the attempted coup into civil war. The reaction of some Catholics in Northern Ireland was hysterical. While the Catholic *Irish News* condemned the 'Godless reds'. Midgley fully supported the republican government. He was honorary secretary of the NILP's Ulster Medical Aid for Spain Committee. He accommodated in his own house the crew of a republican ship impounded in Belfast as a result of the non-intervention agreement among European powers.

Midgley, however, felt the need to take on Northern Irish Catholicism as well as Spanish fascism. He responded to the *Irish News'* campaign with a series of letters that denounced the desire of Catholicism to prevent individual faith. Midgley was not defending Protestantism but his tone certainly coincided with that of evangelical anti-Catholicism. As John Gray has suggested, Midgley's position was not anticlericalism, but was 'rather one in the Walkerite tradition of equating socialism and Protestantism'.[44]

In case any of his Catholic constituents missed his letters to the press, he republished them in a pamphlet called *Spain: The Press, the Pulpit and the Truth.*[45] In 1935 Midgley had declared a plague on both Catholic and Protestant sectarianism. In 1936 he linked Irish nationalism and Catholicism to fascism. The plague was now confined to one house.

The question of the Union was restored to its primacy in Ulster politics by Éamon de Valera's decision as Irish Taoiseach to frame a new constitution for the Irish Free State. Always keen to bolster the position of the Unionist Party, Craig called a general election to assert Northern Ireland's separation from Éire, as de Valera renamed the Free State. In the election, Midgley was faced by both Unionist and Nationalist candidates. He was subject to the full ferocity of Catholic sectarianism, with his meetings disrupted by cries of 'Up Franco!' and the singing of the Irish national anthem.[46] Midgley was defeated, coming third in the seat he had won by a large majority in 1933.[47]

Undoubtedly, this had a major impact on Midgley's attitude towards Catholics. He condemned 'the peculiar whims and fluctuations of people swayed only by sectarian impulses and who are likely to be carried away by such emotions at each succeeding election'. Midgley's disillusionment with the rationality of the electorate was not wholly unsurprising. He had been on the receiving end of crowd hostility in nearly every election he had contested. He was frequently open to the accusation of being a 'rotten Prod' because of his association with anti-partitionists in the NILP. His response had been to attempt to place politics on class lines through concentrating on labour issues and in the 1930s through his concern for international relations. However, his anti-fascism had brought conflict with the Catholic Church. Increasingly, Midgley associated Catholicism with Irishness, while his attention was falling more and more on the progressive possibilities of the British Commonwealth.

Labour movements within the British Commonwealth had cross-fertilized ideas and policies since the late nineteenth century. The labour movement in the United Kingdom might not have fully and unconditionally endorsed imperialism but it operated within an imperial context. British trade unions had branches in the white dominions and many British socialists had made visits of different lengths to different parts of the Empire. With successful labour parties in Australia and New Zealand, the white dominions were seen as models to be followed by labour activists in the motherland. With the threat of expansionist fascism in Europe, Midgley increasingly pinned his hopes on the Commonwealth as defender of democracy and vehicle for the advancement of the social condition of the working class.

Alvin Jackson has argued that a local perspective always framed popular imperialism in Ulster, and that frequently it took personal experiences to initiate enthusiasm for Empire.[48] Midgley certainly took a local perspective on the Commonwealth. He always held Northern Ireland at the core of his concerns. The Commonwealth was the vehicle through which Northern Irish distinctiveness could be expressed on the world stage. The outbreak of the Second World War provided Midgley with his opportunity to develop and refine his ideas about Ulster's role in the Commonwealth. The war was the watershed in Midgley's political career. It led him towards the assertion of the primacy of Unionism.

The imperial aspect of the Second World War has certainly been underplayed in British historiography and popular memory because it seems to jar with the notion of a war for freedom against Nazi imperialism. Recently, however, some historians have argued that the Second World War saw the construction of the notion of a 'people's empire' to complement the domestic idea of the 'people's war'.[49] The development of Midgley's ideas certainly accords with this interpretation. In the early 1940s imperialism could still be framed as a positive and democratic force because the Commonwealth could be represented as a partnership. In 1914 George V had declared war on behalf of the Empire including the dominion nations. In 1939, however, the dominion governments themselves decided the issue. All, except Éire, made the decision to fight alongside the United Kingdom. In this context, using the contrast of Irish neutrality, loyal Northern Ireland stressed its distinctive role in the war effort, and Midgley was at the forefront in doing so. As a representative of labour, Midgley was invited to broadcast on the BBC. He told listeners that 'Here in Northern Ireland we regard ourselves as being in the front line of defence and attack with Great Britain.' He went further and explained the constitutional situation: 'Though we are not a self governing dominion in the complete sense of the term, we have our own Government with complete autonomy in all domestic matters and an associated arrangement with the Imperial Government whereby our great Social Services are identical in every respect and reciprocal with those of England, Scotland and Wales.'[50] Midgley was establishing a sense of ownership over the (Unionist) government and stressing the social benefits of the Union and Commonwealth. He emphasized that 'Northern Ireland linen, engineering and shipbuilding ... along with our newer but equally important great Aircraft industry, shall once again play an important part in smashing tyranny and liberating the peoples of the earth.'[51] Midgley hinted at divisions within Northern Ireland but suggested that they had been overcome, saying that 'practically all sections of our community are agreed that Nazism must be destroyed'.[52]

Midgley was criticized within the NILP for his willingness to appear on recruiting platforms with Unionist government ministers. He had also moved closer still to British patriotism associated with social reform. For British Labour such a stance was uncomplicated after their entry into Churchill's coalition government in May 1940. In the NILP, Midgley's position was more difficult to sustain, especially since the anti-partitionist tendency in the party was strengthened when two Belfast Nationalist councillors joined the party and Jack Beattie was re-admitted.[53]

Northern Ireland was not fully integrated into the war effort because conscription was not extended to the province, despite Unionist demands. The imperial government was unwilling to conscript Catholics.[54] In addition, as James Loughlin has explained, 'there was a persistent concern at Westminster throughout the war about the North's inadequate output, its poor record of contract completion in war industries, poor workmanship, resistance to the "dilution" of restrictive practices in industry, high absenteeism among workers, strikes and strained labour relations'.[55] Craig's government seemed complacent in its attitude to the war. The position was little improved when John Andrews succeeded to the premiership after Craig's death in November 1940. Within the Unionist government there was a campaign to replace Andrews. Outside the government, Midgley provided a conduit for discontent.

There were severe air raids on Belfast in April and May 1941, which left 1,100 people dead and 56,000 houses damaged. The raids revealed the extent of the government's inactivity and raised levels of popular disenchantment.[56] The fundamental issue was how the Protestant working class would react. They could not support the Catholic parties, which tended to support the neutrality of the Éire. They needed an acceptable method of voicing political opposition to the government's handling of the war effort without abandoning allegiance to the Union.

In these circumstances, the Willowfield by-election in December 1941 was an important test for the government. The seat was mainly Protestant and working class and had always elected a Unionist. The NILP decided to contest the seat, with Midgley as its candidate. He campaigned as a labour patriot. He emphasized social policy but constantly stressed his patriotism, which entailed loyalty to the British connection. Midgley wore his First World War medals during the campaign and the national anthem was played at the end of one of his meetings. The chairman, Bob Thompson, told the meeting that 'There were no stronger upholders of the constitution than the Labour Party.'[57] Midgley defeated his Unionist opponent by 7209 to 2,435 votes in what Graham Walker has described as the biggest electoral upset since the formation of the state.[58] There were limits to the impact. The loss was a blow to the Unionist Party, but emphasized the strength of the Union and commitment to the war effort. Midgley won the seat with a variant of unionism, which he sought to develop over subsequent months.

This development led to his removal from the leadership of the NILP and the formation of his new party, the Commonwealth Labour Party. Midgley first tried to convert the NILP to his programme. In November 1942 he issued his 'Declaration of Policy', which asserted its claim to unionism: 'We accept the present political position in Northern Ireland and are prepared to work for a government ... which will co-operate with Great Britain and the British Commonwealth of Nations. This means that we reject the claims of those who stand for separation from Great Britain and the Commonwealth.'[59] This was a direct challenge to the anti-partitionists. At a meeting held in Midgley's absence, Beattie was elected to the leadership of the three-member parliamentary party. The position of chief whip went to the other MP, Patrick Agnew, a labour nationalist, with Midgley as deputy leader. Midgley was only informed nine days later. Because of his objections a further meeting was held. As well as arguing that he had been recognized as the virtual leader of labour for twenty years and that Beattie had only recently returned to the party after eight years' expulsion, Midgley again stressed that the matters involved were his 'association with the British Commonwealth at a time when Mr Beattie did not associate himself with such issues' and that 'Mr Beattie had repeatedly made speeches in the northern Parliament which indicated, beyond all doubt, that he did not believe in the present political status of Northern Ireland.'[60] Before the executive made a decision, Midgley declared that he would not accept the deputy leadership. He told the press that he had resigned from the party and the party executive expelled him. On 19 December 1942, he formed the Commonwealth Labour Party.[61]

Midgley had seen the British Commonwealth as a progressive force for internationalism and social improvement for a long time. He considered that the war strengthened his position, telling the 1942 NILP conference that the party 'is proud to associate itself with the labour movements of the British Commonwealth and, indeed, the United Nations, in their resolve to free the world from the barbarities, fears, bestialities, and injustices of Nazi-Fascist totalitarianism'.[62] The position adopted by Midgley and the CLP, which probably had 800–1,000 members, was that Northern Ireland could flourish through its connection to Britain, British Labour and the Commonwealth. The party stood for an equality of social services with the rest of the United Kingdom. Where it differed from the Unionist Party was that it argued for a universal social security system, whereas the step-by-step policy of the Unionists followed British moves. 'It is very cowardly,' Midgley said, 'all the time to shelter behind the British government.'[63] The CLP emphasized the shared Britishness of Labour in the UK. Hennessey has argued that 'Ultimately, the Second World War reinforced the psychological gap between Ulster unionism and Irish nationalism.'[64] This was certainly the case for Midgley and the CLP. Their commitment to the war effort around an ideological axis of anti-fascism, progressive imperialism and social reform divorced them from the anti-partitionist tendencies within the NILP.

From unionist to Unionist Party

In April 1943, after months of internal cabinet and party discord, Andrews resigned as Prime Minister and was replaced by Sir Basil Brooke. Responding to pressure from London, Brooke sought to give the impression that his was a more inclusive government than those of his predecessors. Most of the Unionist old guard was removed from the cabinet and William Grant, a veteran labour Unionist was appointed as Minister of Labour. Midgley was appointed as Minister of Public Security. He was the first non-Unionist to serve in the Northern Ireland government, but as Bardon has commented, 'this was no all-party government: no Nationalist or Catholic was invited to join'.[65] There was some hostility to Midgley from within the Unionist Party but his frequent assertions of loyalty to the Union and Commonwealth served to reassure Brooke. According to Walker, Midgley believed his appointment offered great opportunities: to advance the cause of the CLP and to enable him to promote socially progressive legislation.[66] In 1944 he hoped that he would be appointed as Minister of Health, a position that would have seen him presiding over social policy, but his appointment was blocked from within the Unionist Party and he took the Ministry of Labour instead. Midgley was soon diverted from social reform to sectarianism. He and other labour MPs had frequently raised the question of persistent unemployment during the war. The demands for labour had resulted in an influx of skilled workers from the south. Midgley was concerned that after the war the Protestant working class would be as disaffected as after the first war. He joined the issues of the anxieties over post-war unemployment with the fear of a 'deluge' of southerners, who would heighten unemployment, place a burden on the Beveridge welfare measures and 'would gravitate to the disloyal element of our population and increase our political difficulties'.[67]

Midgley's increasingly public hostility to Éire and Catholicism coincided with the strengthening of labour politics in Northern Ireland. The Unionist Party fought the 1945 Stormont election as a referendum on the autonomy of Northern Ireland from the British Labour government.[68] They argued that socialism would mean centralization and the lessening of Ulster's independence. The results of the election, however, suggested strongly that substantial parts of the Protestant working class saw nothing incompatible between their unionism and their desire for British Labour's welfare state. Midgley resigned from the government to fight the election and the CLP campaigned on a programme that committed the party to 'The maintenance of Ulster's position as an integral part of the United Kingdom and the British Commonwealth,' and incorporating 'a Commonwealth Parliament ... and the raising of our Social Services to the highest Commonwealth level, namely that of New Zealand which has the highest standards in the world'.[69] The combined labour parties won a third of the vote with the Unionist Party achieving only just over half. The CLP faired well in terms of votes, but divisions among the labour parties meant that Midgley was the only successful CLP candidate.

Midgley had hoped that a socially progressive but clearly unionist, indeed imperialist, party would be able to break the dominance of the official Unionists over the Protestant working class, particularly in Belfast. The outcome of the 1945 election, while promising, suggested that the task was extremely difficult. If the special circumstances of the war, when trade unionism and class consciousness were strong, could not shift the Unionist Party from power then few circumstances could be foreseen that would do so. At the same time labour's strong performance in the election had meant that the debate within the Unionist government about attitudes to the British Labour government's welfare reforms had been resolved in favour of those who wanted to continue the step-by-step policy of keeping up with British social policy, a resolution made easier by the British Labour government's agreement to underwrite the costs of the welfare state in Northern Ireland.[70]

Midgley saw British Labour as the model for his own politics. The acceptance of its programme by the Unionist Party went a long way towards convincing him that the party's Toryism was no longer an obstacle to the development of a socially progressive Northern Ireland within the Commonwealth.[71] In September 1947 he resigned from the CLP and joined the Unionist Party. He told Brooke that 'there is no room for division among those ... who are anxious to preserve the constitutional life and spiritual heritage of our people'.[72]

The NILP was also clarifying its unionism in the late 1940s. There had been a backlash against anti-partitionists within the party, driven by Protestants who were members of British trade unions. Indeed, there had been requests for a meeting with the British Labour Party to ask for affiliation as a local section of the party. Michael Farrell has argued that this was an attempt to respond to Éire's pronouncement as a republic outside the Commonwealth and to 'claim Attlee's declaration on the constitution as their own and point to their links with London as proof that their loyalty lay with Britain and not with the South.'[73] Leading anti-partitionists, such as Bob Getgood MP, resigned from the NILP and formed a northern section of the Irish Labour Party. This opened the way for the NILP to declare, in time for the general election of 1949, that 'The Northern Ireland Labour Party, being a democratic party, accepts the constitutional position of Northern Ireland and the close association with Britain and the Commonwealth.'[74] The nature of the election confirmed Midgley's view that there was little political space for division among Unionists in Northern Ireland. The NILP vote fell from 66,053 in 1945 to 26,831 in 1949.

Midgley was not, therefore, an isolated individual moving in the opposite direction to labour in Northern Ireland, nor was he was the only labour figure to join the Unionist Party. In 1953 Harry Holmes, former NILP chairman, was elected Unionist MP for Shankill. Now in the Unionist Party, Midgley set out to explain the politics of his social Unionism.

Ulster's British heritage

Just before joining the Unionists Midgley argued that the 'conservatives of today often sponsor legislation that would have been considered revolutionary a few years ago. That is essentially true of legislation in Ulster'.[75] His support for the welfare state underlay his Unionism. He explained in 1953 that the benefits of the connection between social welfare and the Union: 'All the fine Conditions and Standards we enjoy today, combined with our splendid achievements in Education, Health Services, Social Justice and Social Security, have been made possible by the preservation of our Ulster-British citizenship and Way of Life.'[76]

The main theme of Midgley's speeches and writings from the late 1940s to his death in April 1957 was his assertion of Ulster's British heritage. Midgley declared that he joined the Unionist Party because 'it is imperative that all those who cherish Ulster's heritage and birthright should present a united front to those who are striving to force Ulster into a political State based upon principles which are alien to Ulster's ideals and spiritual convictions and which aims at destroying our British unity and citizenship.'[77] Midgley frequently emphasized cultural differences between the twenty-six counties and Northern Ireland. As a consequence, he stressed the Protestantism of the north and the Catholicism of the south. The Unionists had seized on the 1936 declaration of the Irish Free State as Éire because it emphasized the Gaelic nature of nationalism. Midgley took up this use of terminology to emphasize that Éire and Northern Ireland were the products of deep underlying differences. In November 1947 he told a Unionist audience that the Éire-British difference was one of incontrovertible fact: 'It followed ... as the night the day, that the vast majority of the people of this area differed in faith, tradition, culture, organization and politics, from the people of Eire.'[78] He pointed to cultural differences in language and material differences such as the Northern membership of British trade unions and the lower level of state provision for the population in the south.

Midgley became increasingly hostile to the Catholic Church and its influence on the Republic of Ireland state.[79] This gave him an influential voice among the most sectarian elements of Unionism. Institutionally, Midgley asserted his Unionism through joining the Orange Order and its senior lodges, the Royal Black Preceptory and the Apprentice Boys. This established the Protestant nature of his Unionism. He had never discarded his religion. In 1934 he had told Stormont that 'I am fundamentally the same Protestant now as I was when I received my first religious instruction from my father in my own home. I have never deviated from the faith of my father and mother.'[80] He claimed a belief in religious liberty and the equality of treatment of all of Northern Ireland's citizens. His appointment as the Minister of Education in 1950 put such claims to the test.

This was very much a shock appointment. Midgley had returned to the cabinet as Minister of Labour and National Insurance in 1949. He immediately became an opponent of the relatively liberal Minister of Education, Colonel Hall-Thompson, who wanted to provide additional support to the mainly Catholic voluntary schools. The state already paid the salaries of teachers in these schools and Hall-Thompson sug-

gested that the state should also pay their national insurance contributions.[81] Midgley had always seen Catholic control of Catholic
education as reactionary and an obstacle to the unity of labour. His
opposition to the plans for education provided an opportunity to gain
prominence in the Unionist Party, since the Orange Order was leading
a campaign against Hall-Thompson. Abandoned by the Prime Minister,
Hall-Thompson resigned. Civil servants at the Ministry of Education
greeted rumours of Midgley's appointment 'at first with derision, then
... with annoyance ... the announcement ... brought dismay and
shocked surprise'.[82]

Michael McGrath has argued that in a number of areas, Midgley's
actions as Minister, 'limited the educational opportunities available to
thousands of Catholic children'.[83] He argues that Midgley treated
Catholic voluntary schools unfairly, limited the state's contribution to
a Catholic teacher training college and refused to recognize teacher-
training qualifications from the Irish Republic. In 1956 Midgley
requested Protestant landowners not to sell land for building Catholic
schools.[84] Midgley decided that the Catholic Church was a regressive
and reactionary force which was damaging children's education.
Influenced by the writings of the Protestant theologian Paul Blanshard,
Midgley adopted a totalizing view of Catholicism seeing it as a tyranni-
cal power that sought complete control over conscience.

Midgley reasserted his Protestantism in the 1950s. As Walker argues,
'Midgley ... had come to view the British way of life, the substance
of which he derived from the principles of individual liberty won by
the reformation and consummated in the British constitution after the
"glorious revolution" of 1688–9.'[85] His perspective on the contrast
between Ireland and Northern Ireland were shaped by this perception.
He argued that 'there is simply no doubt about it that Northern Ireland
is a much freer and more tolerant community than Eire; for it is an historical fact that the Constitutions of Protestant countries are always
more liberal and contain fewer inhibitions and prohibitions than those
of Catholic countries.'[86]

It was these absolutes that led towards Midgley's speech in February
1957 in which he declared that 'all the minority are traitors'. While the
Northern Irish government and the Protestant people reasserted their
Britishness through the Festival of Britain and the coronation such
stark assertions of loyalty raised opposition from the nationalist minority.[87] The early 1950s saw the emergence of Saor-Ulaidh (Free Ulster), a
breakaway from the IRA, and the election of its military commander,
Liam Kelly, for the Stormont seat of Mid-Tyrone. In 1953 a number of

nationalist MPs and senators repudiated 'all claims now made ... on behalf of the British Crown and Government over any portion of the land of Ireland'.[88] In 1955 republicans secured their highest vote in a general election since partition, and in the same year the IRA launched an armed campaign that was to last six years.[89] As well as using the Special Powers Act, the government passed the Flags and Emblems Act in 1954, which gave special protection to the Union Jack and allowed the RUC to remove any other emblem whose display might cause a breach of the peace.[90]

There were divisions within the Unionist Party about attitudes towards the Catholic minority and their treatment by the state. Some hoped that the welfare state and rising standards of living might reconcile Catholics to the state, and Brooke suggested in 1951 that 'even in Nationalist areas electors are beginning to realise that life in British Ulster is to be preferred to existence in a Gaelic republic'.[91] Walker has suggested that Midgley tried to put himself at the head of the hardliners in order to challenge for the leadership of the Unionist Party.[92] Midgley's development of ideological underpinnings to his anti-Catholicism suggests more than expediency alone but he certainly knew how to play to sectarianism. In February 1957 he was challenged in the House of Commons over the allegation that he had said that 'all the minority are traitors'. Brooke defended Midgley arguing that he had been quoting from Blanshard's *The Irish and Catholic Power*. While Midgley agreed that this was the case, he concluded that 'it was true that the vast majority of the minority in Northern Ireland were disloyal to the Government here. There was no doubt about that.'[93]

This was Midgley's testament. He died in April 1957. The *Belfast Telegraph* declared his life and career 'one of the romances of Ulster political life'.[94] Midgley had, it seemed, travelled a long way. He began his political life as a socialist in the ILP, which supported Home Rule for all Ireland. Midgley considered that Home Rule was likely and had, therefore, differed from William Walker, who was unequivocally unionist in outlook. Yet Midgley was a unionist for most of his political life. The ILP was a British party, supporting Home Rule only within the United Kingdom. The furthest British Labour was prepared to go in its support for Irish nationalism was to dominion status – for Ireland within the Empire. Midgley fought the 1921 election alongside anti-partitionist labour candidates, but there is little evidence that he held to such a view himself after the formation of the Northern Irish state. He was a Protestant, retaining attachment to his religion throughout his political life, and also to the cultural expressions of Protestantism in popular culture. He was, for example, a life-long supporter and later club chairman of the Protestant and loyalist Linfield Football Club.

Midgley was less uncomfortable with Protestant displays of violence than with those of Catholics with whom he had little sympathy other than as people who shared a class position within society with him. As long as working-class Catholics asserted their class identity above their religious identity, he was content to represent them politically. When Catholic identities were displayed he found himself antagonistic. Over time, this advanced to become all-out enmity against the Roman Catholic Church. The Union took on greater importance for him, for it provided the bridge to the British Commonwealth, which he saw as an internationalizing and socially progressive group of nations with a powerful role for labour parties. Midgley did not give up his labour identity. He frequently referred to his class origins in the shipyards. He forged a conglomerate identity for himself, at once Protestant, Unionist and working class. In Ulster, and in Belfast in particular, such an identity was far from unusual.

For this reason, Harry Midgley was not Ulster's Ramsay MacDonald. MacDonald had abandoned the Labour Party. In Northern Ireland, the British Labour Party abandoned the working class. This made the possibilities of building a successful party based on working-class identity virtually impossible. The Unionist Party exploited labour's weakness to maintain politics along the lines of the ethnic-sectarian divide rather than allowing politics to be fought on social and economic issues. Midgley believed that the social condition of the Ulster working class was better in the Union. When the Unionist Party accepted British Labour's welfare state, Midgley accepted the Unionist Party.

10
Fur-Coat Unionism: Dame Dehra Parker (1882–1963)

Ronald MacNeill, in what amounts to the official history of Ulster Unionism before partition, paid tribute to 'The women of Ulster [who] were scarcely less active than the men in the matter of organization. Although, of course, as yet unenfranchised, they took as a rule a keener interest in political matters – meaning thereby the absorbing question of the Union – than their sex in other parts of the United Kingdom.'[1] Yet MacNeill devoted only one and half pages to women's Unionism. Mainly because women were kept in subordinate and auxiliary positions within the movement, the sources for examination of the day-to-day politics of women's unionism are sparse and women have been largely absent from the historiography of Ulster Unionism.[2] Women in the north of Ireland were, however, a significant force in the spread of unionist ideas outside the normal channels of masculine politics. They strengthened unionist ideas within the home and in voluntary organizations.[3] After 1910, with the Irish MPs holding the balance of power in the House of Commons, the urgency of the threat of Home Rule did afford women a greater role in Unionism. Dehra Parker was one such woman. After the accomplishment of the exclusion of the six counties from Home Rule and the formation of Northern Ireland women's role in politics was restricted, as the running of the state fell overwhelmingly into the hands of men. Irish politics, both Unionist and nationalist, had privileged masculinity since the Act of Union. Nationalist men were called on to restore honour to Ireland as a feminine nation and northern Unionists celebrated the notion of staunch and independent Ulstermen ready to defend the Union.[4] Despite this, Parker remained prominent in Unionist politics for the next three decades.

Dehra Parker was truly exceptional. She was the only woman to serve in Northern Irish government between 1921 and 1972 when Stormont was prorogued by the United Kingdom government. She was born in Dehra Dun, northern India, in 1882 and married Colonel Robert P.D. Spencer Chichester in 1901. He had extensive imperial service in Africa and died in 1921.[5] She was married again in 1928 to Admiral H.W. Parker. He commanded HMS Benbow at the Battle of Jutland 1916 and commanded a cruiser squadron in the Mediterranean in the late 1920s. He retired in 1934 and died in 1940. Dehra Parker was, therefore, connected by marriage into service to the Empire. She represented Londonderry County and City as a Northern Ireland House of Commons MP between 1921 and 1929, returning to the House to represent South Londonderry between 1933 and 1960. She served as Parliamentary Secretary to the Ministry of Education between 1937 and 1944 and entered the cabinet as Minister of Health and Local Government in 1949, resigning in 1957.

This was a long and important career. The absence of any collection of personal and political papers has contributed to the neglect of Parker as a political figure.[6] Accounts, including this one, are forced to rely on public utterances and the limited number of other people's memoirs that refer to her career. This chapter considers the relationships between Parker's gender and Unionism through an examination of the role of women in the organizations involved in defending the Union before and after partition. It discusses Parker's political ideas in the 1920s and 1930s as a woman MP and some aspects of her ministerial career. Parker was also interested in the politics and administration of culture and this interest is discussed in so far as it relates to her thinking on Unionism.

Women and Unionism before partition

Women have certainly played a substantial and significant role in the construction of national identities, even when the relationship between them and the nation was often considered as ambiguous and entailed subordination.[7] Irish Unionism was generally under the leadership of men who held to conservative political and social philosophies. This did not preclude the effective organization of women, but since only men had the parliamentary vote until 1918 the organization of women was to secure the more efficient mobilization of male voters. In Britain, Conservatism sought to mobilize the electorate on issues of manliness, such as the defence of popular culture and manly independence, and the obverse of this platform was the defence of feminine domesticity.[8] In Northern Ireland, a robust Unionism confirmed the active nature of men and the passive nature of women. These were extremely popular ideas across the United Kingdom. The largest women's organization in Britain in the late nineteenth and early twentieth century was the Mothers' Union, attached to the Church of England and encouraging 'traditional' notions of motherliness and domestic order.[9]

Ulster Unionists overwhelmingly shared these ideas of separate, intertwined and complementary spheres for men and women. In 1911 the Parliament Act that removed the power of veto from the House of Lords served to make Irish Home Rule inevitable. The 1910 elections had given the Irish parliamentary party the leverage to ensure that if the Liberal government did not deliver on their pluralist policy it could be turned out. With about 40 Labour MPs supporting Home Rule, the parliamentary majority for reform of the government of Ireland was secure. Asquith's Home Rule Bill, introduced first in 1912, had only to pass through the House of Commons three times to become law.

The ultimate act of the male citizen was to take up arms in defence of his nation. In 1913 Irish politics was militarized when the Ulster Volunteer Force was formed to resist Irish Home Rule by force of arms. This built on an idea of the "Ulster' character as 'dour but hospitable, shrewd, self-reliant, steadfast and industrious, blunt of speech, and gifted with the capacity to govern less fortunate peoples.'[10] These were masculine virtues and the drilling and arming of Ulstermen relegated women to increasingly subordinate roles within Unionism.

Women in the 1880s and 1890s had played an ancillary role in opposition to the first two Home Rule Bills. As Diane Urquhart observes, 'Women seemed content to accept this essentially conservative, but nonetheless important role: petitioning, fund-raising, canvassing and organizing demonstrations of their own sex. Thus, by the early twentieth century a clearly defined role for women within Ulster unionism had emerged.'[11] Many of the leaders of female Unionism were the wives of the aristocratic leaders of male Unionism, for example from the Abercorn, Dufferin and Londonderry families.[12] While they were able to apply some personal and political influence, their husbands and other men formed the policies and strategies of Unionism. This mattered little, since female Unionists shared most of the assumptions of Protestant Ulstermen. When Sir Edward Carson presented his English wife, Ruby, to a unionist meeting in Belfast he said that she was 'as good Ulsterman and as good Unionist and as good Protestant as I am'.[13] Unionists celebrated unity of the Protestant people, and women were expected and content to be united with their men.

The Ulster Women's Unionist Council was formed in January 1911 and saw itself in this light. It represented women's sexual difference from and political unity with men. In January 1912 it declared that 'We, the members of the Ulster Women's Unionist Council, assembled at our Annual Meeting, hereby affirm unswerving loyalty to the Person and Throne of our gracious sovereign King George V, and unalterable attachment to the Constitution of the United Kingdom, the unbroken centre of our world-wide Empire.'[14] The UWUC quickly gathered a mass membership. Within a year it claimed between 40,000 and 50,000 members and by 1913 more than 115,000.[15] MacNeill claimed that of the 4,000 West Belfast members who joined in the first month four-fifths were mill-workers and shop-girls, but the leadership remained firmly in the hands of landed Ulster, with more than one-third of the first executive committee being titled.[16]

The UWUC emphasized defence of domesticity in its reasons for defending the Union. As Urquhart has argued, 'the home, the traditional sphere where a woman's influence was socially acceptable, featured prominently in the iconography of women's unionism'.[17] UWUC meetings frequently began with the hymn 'Our God, our help in ages past/ Our hope for years to come, / Our shelter from the stormy blast, / And our eternal home,' sanctifying the unionist home.[18] In June 1911 the UWUC unanimously passed a resolution declaring that 'the civil and religious liberty of the women of Ulster and the security of their homes can only be guaranteed under the Legislative Union of Great Britain and Ireland'.[19] On 28 September 1912, named as 'Ulster Day' when the Solemn League and Covenant was signed by 218,206 men, an alternative declaration was signed by 234,046 women. The men's covenant pledged 'men of Ulster ... to stand by one another in defending for ourselves and our children our cherished position of equal citizenship in the United Kingdom and in using all means which may be found necessary to defeat the present conspiracy to set up a Home Rule Parliament in Ireland'. The 'Women's Declaration of the Covenant' was more limited. They signed to 'associate ourselves with the men of Ulster in their uncompromising opposition to the Home Rule Bill now before Parliament'.[20]

Parker's entry into Unionist politics occurred during the third Home Rule crisis. In 1927 she recounted some of her early life to the Northern Ireland House of Commons. She suggested that the age of voting should be set at 25 years, for she argued, few young people were interested in politics, and they were 'not perhaps so stable in their political views'. To illustrate her argument, she told the House that as a girl she had been 'very ardently interested in Irish politics, in Irish poetry, in Irish literature and Irish history'.[21] After her marriage at 21, she 'was far too interested in my home and two children to pay any attention to political matters of any kind'. She had married a Unionist military officer and local JP and this led her into the social circles of Unionism. As she told the Commons, 'I was 27 years before I opened my first Orange Hall (Hon. Members: Hear, hear.) Personally, I call that the dawn of commonsense.'[22] Parker's early life, therefore, followed the traditional path of the daughter and wife of the Irish gentry. Her engagement with politics emerged at least in part from being the wife of a Unionist. Opening Orange halls was the fabric of the social politics of the wives of the Unionist elite. The third Home Rule crisis, however, allowed a more independent role for many upper and middle class women, including Parker. She became active within the UWUC, establishing herself on a number of its sub-committees and participating in its strategy discussions.[23]

The outbreak of war in Europe in August 1914 diverted the attention of the Unionist movement to wider issues of patriotism. Women's activism in the Unionist movement in Ireland (and in patriotic leagues in the rest of the United Kingdom) prepared them for patriotic efforts in the Great War. Much of the organization was readily transferable to the needs of supporting the men of the Ulster Volunteer Force, many of whom joined the British army to form the 36th (Ulster) Division. Before the war, Unionist women had established ambulance and other medical services in preparation for the armed resistance that might prove necessary against Home Rule. During the war the UWUC established the Ulster Women's Gift Fund to collect and send comforts to Ulster's Protestant soldiers. By the end of the war it had collected £119,481. The UWUC also funded the Ulster Volunteer Hospital in France and established the Ulster Sphagnum Moss Association.[24]

Parker continued to play a prominent role in the activities of the UWUC. On the executive committee in February 1916, she proposed a resolution responding to a call to women by the Lord Mayor of Belfast's to rally to greater efforts. The resolution, which was passed unanimously, indicated the manner in which women Unionists saw their role and the place of Ulster in an imperial context. She proposed 'That this meeting ... desires to assure the Lord Mayor of Belfast that the members of the Council ... have since the outbreak of War done everything in their power to aid the Empire in the great struggle in which it is engaged and have in particular done their utmost to secure recruits for the Ulster Division and the Imperial Forces generally.'[25] As with other women's organizations, the UWUC listed its war activities with great attention to detail to ensure that the efforts of its members were recognized.[26] The patriotism of thousands of women was validated by the award of honours, and Parker was granted an OBE for her work under the auspices of the Soldiers' and Sailors' Family Association.[27] The war served to encourage domesticity linking it more closely to the idea of the nation. Parker's patriotic role had been domestic and encouraged her belief in the Union as essential to the safety of 'British' homes.

One outcome of the war had, therefore, been the reinforcement of women's domestic role. As Nicoletta Gullace has argued, the war saw citizenship redefined, as it became associated with service to the nation rather than the male body.[28] The war service of many women, like Parker's, had been within the home or in support of the familial relationships of servicemen. The granting of the parliamentary vote to women over the age of 30 might be seen in this light, both as recognition of women's public patriotism and of the continuing expectation of their domesticity. That younger women were excluded from the vote suggests that the essentially domestic role of older women was privileged over the military service and industrial work of younger women.

In Parliament in the 1920s

The UWUC wanted to ensure that as many Unionist women as possible were registered to vote.[29] In the years immediately following the war, they did not seek to use their votes as women but as Unionists. In 1921 the UWUC argued that the 'time was not yet ripe' for women candidates because 'the essential thing in the first Parliament was to preserve the safety of the Unionist cause'. For this work, they agreed, 'perhaps women had not the necessary experience, and except in the case of outstanding qualifications, men candidates were preferable'.[30]

Parker was elected a vice-chairman of the UWUC in 1918. In February 1919 she was appointed to a sub-committee to consider the organization's future policy. She was in favour of a resolute programme of Unionist propaganda, particularly in America against Sinn Fein. She also offered to interview Sir James Craig and Captain Charles Craig in London to gauge their opinion of a possible UWUC campaign in England.[31] There are, however, no records as to her attitudes towards the representation of women in the new Northern Ireland parliament. Nonetheless, she was elected as MP for the five-member constituency of Londonderry County and City in the first elections to the Northern Ireland parliament in May 1921. Julia McMordie was also elected as a Unionist for South Londonderry. It might be speculated that the proportional representation system, which Parker opposed, acted as a pre-requisite for the selection of female candidates at all. With multi-member constituencies, Parker and McMordie could not be seen as preventing the election of Unionist men, but instead could be seen as a way of mobilizing the female vote.

The UWUC continued to see its role as limited by the sex of its members. It championed patriotism though consumerism, encouraging its members to buy Empire goods, with an imperial cake competition held in 1927.[32] In some ways, Parker followed this gendered path in the 1920s. She concerned herself with women's political issues such as the Illegitimate Children Act and argued that women were suited best to the domestic concerns of local government, but as McNamara and Mooney bluntly state, she did not 'contribute to any feminist agenda in the house'.[33] She warned against putting 'sex before party principles'.[34] Above all, from her entry into parliament in 1921 to her retirement in 1960, Parker saw herself as a Unionist. When she claimed to speak for women, it was for Unionist women. In 1924 she was selected to move the address following the King's speech in the Northern Ireland House of Commons. She made it clear that she considered this an honour because she represented women within the Empire. She also emphasized the honour it bestowed on her constituency, linking localism and imperialism:

> I fully realize that it is not a personal honour, but that it is, first of all a compliment to the city and county of which I am one of the representatives, and also that it is a tribute – if I may take it as such – to the sex to which I belong. (Hon. Members: Hear, hear.) I believe I am correct in saying that I am the first woman, at any rate in the British Empire, who has had this privilege – (Hon. Members: Hear, hear.) – and, also coming nearer home, as a recognition, perhaps, of the work which has been accomplished by the women of Northern Ireland. (Hon. Members: Hear, hear.)[35]

Parker therefore expressed a range of identities, local, national and imperial, embedded within each other and combined with her gender identity. Gender and place were not opposed but were complementary. She saw herself as a Northern Irish Unionist woman.

West of the Bann

This was made clear in Parker's contributions to debates over constitutional legislation relating to voting and in her general attitude towards politics. Across her political career, Parker represented constituencies in the west of Northern Ireland, where Protestants were in the minority. In these circumstances there was sometimes a tension between Unionists in Belfast and the Protestant heartlands of counties Antrim and Down and those living to the west of the River Bann in Fermanagh, Tyrone and Derry.[36] The formation of Northern Ireland from six counties had been designed to ensure a safe Protestant majority. The counties of Monaghan, Cavan and Donegal, within the historic province of Ulster and with substantial Protestant minorities, had been jettisoned. Living with a Catholic majority in a loyal and Protestant state encouraged the sense of siege felt by Protestants to the west of the Bann, and Parker used the Northern Ireland House of Commons to represent these anxieties.

The Government of Ireland Act of 1920 had implemented proportional representation voting system for councils and parliament in Northern Ireland, in an attempt to ensure the political representation of minorities. In the Catholic majority areas, the effect was to ensure that the nationalists controlled the councils. Parker acted as the parliamentary voice of rank and file demand from within the Unionist Party for the abolition of proportional representation at local level.[37] In 1689 Londonderry had been besieged for 105 days by the Catholic James II. The privation of the Protestant population, its resistance and ultimate relief was part of the foundation myth of the Ulster unionism. Parker's parliamentary contributions to debates on proportional representation employed the tone and rhetoric of such Protestant martyrdom.

Where nationalist councils and local government boards had refused to co-operate with the new state, claiming allegiance instead to the Irish Free State, they were dissolved and commissioners took over their administration. Parker had been a member of one such board. She warned the Commons of the impact of Catholic rule on the 'Loyalist minority'. She argued that the Catholic religion, because of its commitment to higher powers, made for disloyalty to the Northern Ireland state. In addition, she claimed that the nationalist and Catholic councils and boards had discriminated against Protestants to the point of persecution.

[L]et us not forget the insults which we had to endure in the past [she urged], and the tyranny with which they ground the minority under their heel. May I remind hon. Members that I come from an area where ... 247 labourers' cottages were built, and of those only 47 were given to Unionists ... We have had to sit there and listen to our King being insulted, to our Government being derided ... I remember a scene in which one of the [Catholic] majority said that rather than recognise the Northern Government the hillsides would be running red with blood.[38]

Proportional representation was abolished and ward boundaries were redrawn to make Catholic majority areas safe for Protestantism. 'Gerrymandering' ensured, for example, that Londonderry with its Catholic majority of around 60 per cent of voters elected a council that was 60 per cent Unionist. Before the redrawing of boundaries, Parker's own council of Magherafelt had a nationalist majority of 17 to 11 but after 1924 the Unionists secured a majority of 18 to 11.[39]

Parker's contributions to the debate gave her a reputation for sturdy and vigorous Unionism. She attempted to develop this in a populist direction, to enhance her position within the Unionist Party. She staged a robust defence of the Unionist government and of the Prime Minister at every possible opportunity.[40] In December 1927, when the nationalists moved a vote of censure against the government, Parker described the Ulster character as meaning that 'the people of Ulster perhaps like to criticize. The people of Ulster might like to grumble'. However, it became clear that this was a character exclusively held by the Protestant people, for 'the people of Ulster are even watching the Government to see they do not play in any way, if that were conceivable, into the hands of those people represented by the hon. Members opposite'. 'The people,' she declared are the watchdogs of Ulster.'[41]

Parker's background and upbringing, indeed her personality, made her an unlikely champion of the people. In a general critique of the class nature of the Unionist government in February 1944, the NILP MP Jack Beattie condemned the 'county family ... and old school tie' character of Sir Basil Brooke's government and included Parker within his criticism.[42] She was seen as part of 'fur-coat Unionism', removed from the material interests and specific spiritual needs of urban, working-class Protestantism.[43] She aroused much hostility, and not just from the nationalist and labour opposition. Thomas Henderson, an independent working-class unionist was a long-term and bitter adversary in the Commons. In response to Beattie's attack, Henderson added one of his own by saying that Beattie 'had made a mistake when he mixed the hon. Lady up with one of the old county families ... she is no more a member of an old county family than I am'.[44]

Some of this hostility was undoubtedly based on her sex, and her Conservative politics also distanced her from working-class Unionism. She considered that 'over-legislation was as bad, if not worse, than no legislation at all', and that the rates and taxes of her rural constituents should not be increased for the benefit of the towns.[45] This put her firmly in the camp of the anti-populists within the party. Some of the antagonism towards her was also in reaction to her style of parliamentary performance. She was aggressive in her attitude towards the opposition and dismissive of their claims of discrimination against Catholics. During the censure debate in 1927, she referred to the opposition MPs as 'the jazz band opposite' with 'the Hibernian drum beating as usual ... the Socialist drum ... [and] other somewhat ill-assorted instruments which find their place in the orchestra opposite'. She condemned the 'consistent inconsistency' of the nationalist opposition for their criticism of the government but abstention from the parliament.[46]

Her response to accusations of Catholic disadvantage within Northern Ireland was to brand them as manufactured or to point to discrimination against Protestants in the Free State and under nationalist controlled councils. Alleging that Tyrone County Council had not appointed any Protestants to office between 1920 and 1924, she asked 'Which party is the bigoted one?' Accusations of discrimination against Catholics were 'false and inaccurate statements', she said, and she sought to show how 'all these stories are manufactured'.[47]

Denials of the subordinate position of Catholics in Northern Ireland had implications for Parker's attitude towards Catholics. She always claimed to represent all her constituents, whether they had voted for her or not and whether they were Catholic or Protestant.[48] But she could use such an argument to oppose measures that would have benefited the Catholic population and which may in some small measure have contributed to their reconciliation to the state. In 1947 she opposed the restoration of proportional representation because, she said, it created constituencies that were too large to enable the effective representation of all the people within them.[49] Parker argued, as did many other Unionists, that she did not resent Catholics but their religion which she believed bred disloyalty. She told MPs that Catholics'

particular faith is identified with a particular form of politics, and that particular form of politics is identified with what we call disloyalty. And what is disloyalty? Disloyalty to the Union for which we stand. They wish to divide us. They wish to take away our liberties. They admit it. They wish to take from us everything which to-day we hold and are determined to hold, and we have to use every means in our power to see that they do not get an opportunity to take it away. It is for this reason that we unite in order to keep out those who are disloyal.[50]

For Parker, the Union was the crux of her politics and Catholicism was innately disloyal, which in turn encouraged a continuing siege mentality and defence of the Union through the exclusion of Catholics from power.[51] One of her civil servants at the Ministry of Health and Local Government in the 1950s described her ministerial position on discrimination against Catholics:

> She could grasp every bit as well as we officials could and perhaps a lot better, the arguments in favour of changes in electoral affairs or in housing allocations or (more aptly) in the relationship between the two; but she could grasp even more clearly the political case for leaving such sensitive matters as they were. She would not be moved; and that was her right.[52]

Parker's attitude to the nationalist opposition, to claims of discrimination and to the question of Catholic loyalty were nothing unusual in the Unionist Party. Indeed, Parker was exceptional in that she was a woman active at a prominent level of politics, but her Unionism was representative.

Education and war: 'A Woman is the Best Man for the Job'[53]

Parker re-married in 1928 and gave up her South Londonderry parliamentary seat in the 1929 election to her son-in-law, James Chichester-Clark. She returned to parliament at a by-election when he died in 1933, unopposed, as she was to be in all the subsequent general elections except 1949.[54] She resumed her loyalty to the Union and the government and was rewarded by appointment as Parliamentary Secretary to the Ministry of Education in late 1937. This might be seen as having been a suitable ministry for a woman, but given that Parker was the only woman to serve in Northern Ireland governments between 1921 and 1972 it would be more apt to see her appointment as exceptional rather than representative of the idea of women having appropriate roles within government.

Parker had already shown an interest in education having served on the Lynn committee on educational services, which reported in 1923. On that occasion, she had issued a minority report, with William Miller, opposing the recommendation of the committee that the state should support the teaching the Gaelic above fourth standard. They had pronounced that they 'most strongly object to the minds of our children being burdened with such useless work; and we have still stronger objection to the teaching of that language being paid for out of the public purse'.[55] The same report also recommended that 'even the youngest children should be assembled at very frequent intervals and taught to salute the flag, thus inculcating loyalty in the children and preparing the soil in which the seeds of civics, as they grow more advanced, could be planted'.[56] Parker's view of education, therefore, entailed a belief that its function was education in national identity as well as more broad educative purposes. Education was yet another method to defend the Union.

Parker introduced a number of Bills as Parliamentary Secretary, including the important Education Act of 1938, which brought Northern Ireland into uniformity with education in England and Wales. Compulsory schooling to the age of fifteen was introduced, along with nursery and technical schools and the acceptance of children's rights to education. Parker guided the Bill through the Commons against opposition to the funding of the increased provision having to be borne by the local authorities.[57] The Bill was part of the government's acceptance that Northern Ireland should move step-by-step with the rest of the United Kingdom, though it would not have been out of the question for the government to have decided to follow the Scottish path of a system separate and different from that in England and Wales. Parker had on occasion raised doubts about the wisdom of always following Westminster because Northern Ireland did have its separate problems, but generally she too was keen to maintain the essential Britishness of governance in Ulster.

During the war years, two developments affected Parker's political career. The first was her dissatisfaction with Andrews as Prime Minister and the role she played in his replacement by Brooke. The second was her resignation from her post as Parliamentary Secretary to the Ministry of Education. Both affected her attitude to national identity and the Union.

The Second World War, like the first, widened the gender divide as women's subordinate role to men became apparent in the delineation between fighting men and waiting women.[58] The UWUC dedicated itself to the war effort in September 1939 as it had done in August 1914. An average 2,000 garments per year were contributed as comforts for the forces and monthly 'At Homes' were held at Unionist head-quarters.[59] Northern Ireland differed from the rest of the United Kingdom, however, because conscription was not imposed. There was the potential for serious political revolt from much of the Catholic minority, which offered allegiance to Éire, which had declared its neu-trality.[60] This did mean that the war effort in Northern Ireland was entirely voluntary, enabling women in Northern Ireland to show their patriotism in equal measure with men. In other ways it emphasized the limited role allotted to women in wartime.

Parker was clear that her role at the Ministry of Education was not crucial to the war effort. She readily saw that educational policy would be retarded by the war.[61] In addition, her responsibility for evacuation and the care of children acted to demonstrate the caring role assigned to women in wartime.[62] Parker declared her support for Craig's wartime leadership and emphasized that she did so 'representing the women of this country'.[63]

There were serious doubts about the Northern Ireland contribution to the war effort. Parker's defence of Craig had come in a debate on all-party government, which was one reflection of criticism. Edmond Warnock, a right-wing Unionist MP, resigned from the government in May 1940 and said that the 'speeches about Ulster pulling her weight … have never carried conviction'.[64] In September he moved a vote of censure against the government. Craig died in November 1940 and was replaced by John Andrews. Born in 1871, he was one of Unionism's 'old guard' and had been in government since 1921. He did not take the opportunity to restructure his cabinet, a failure that smacked of further complacency.

For the next two years, as war crisis followed war crisis, Andrews faced a rumbling revolt within his own party and increasing discontent from outside.[65] The Belfast blitz of April–May 1941, which revealed the inadequacy of air raid precautions, occurred against the background of a cabinet debate on how to secure the safety of the Stormont statue of Lord Carson. The government response to the revelations of corruption within Belfast Corporation was seen as weak and the product of back-bench pressure rather than government initiative.[66] The election of Beattie and Midgley put more pressure on Andrews. He held on, however, with the implication that he held his personal position in higher regard than the war effort. In January 1943 Unionist back-benchers demanded reconstruction of the government and a change of leadership; still Andrews refused to move. In March he survived a vote of confidence when it was withdrawn, but calls for changes within the cabinet were passed. In mid-April, the Ulster Unionist Council backed Andrews. At this point, Dehra Parker and two other junior ministers threatened to resign from the government and following a meeting of Unionist back benchers, Andrews resigned to be replaced by Brooke on 1 May 1943.[67] While much of the 'old guard' was cleared out of the government, Parker remained at Education, her role in the revolt having shown her patriotism.

Some of Parker's opponents used the episode of Andrews' resignation as a stick with which to beat her. The extent of her influence in the crisis is difficult to gauge, but rather than an act of patriotism, Beattie and Henderson argued that it was a product of her overpowering personality and a victory for 'petticoat' government.[68] Henderson said that Parker had

> never been guilty of anything else only creating trouble amongst the Members on all sides of the House and especially the Members of the Opposition. She has been most insulting ... I do not think she could agree with anybody. It is quite true to say that the hon. Lady was the one that created the disaster that overtook the old guard ... The hon. Lady was one of the ringleaders in getting them thrown to the wolves.[69]

Their opportunity came after the resignation of Corkey as Minister of Education in February 1944. Corkey was a Presbyterian clergyman, hostile to Catholic teachers and schools.[70] He saw the war as a battle for Christianity, and education in Christian values as being an essential part of schooling. He praised Protestant elementary school teachers for 'implanting in the minds of ... children a sense of the value of truth, honour, honesty, fidelity to duty, and faith in God ... laying the foundation for the sort of character that has made the British Empire what it is, and the sort of character we are fighting to keep alive in the world to-day'.[71] Parker would not have disagreed with such views but her emphasis at the Ministry was co-operation with teachers and local authorities. All schools in Northern Ireland were compelled to teach Bible instruction, which was a core Unionist demand. However, the too close association of Bible instruction to Protestant Unionism was likely to disrupt the efficacy of the Ministry's deliverance of sound education. In February 1944 Brooke forced Corkey to resign because of his inattention to his ministerial duties. The Ministry had been moved from Belfast to Portrush and Corkey's visits to the Ministry became infrequent. Far from being the opportunity for Parker's promotion, she too came under pressure to resign, which she did before the month was out. Her opposition to Corkey's Presbyterian evangelism had led to the questioning of her commitment to Protestantism.[72] She valued co-operation with local authorities and teachers as the best method of delivering education and was responsible, with a senior civil servant, for drafting the 1947 legislation that repealed guarantees of Bible instruction in schools.

Youth and culture

Between 1944 and 1949 Parker was chairman of the Youth Committee established by the 1944 Youth Welfare Act.[73] She had a long interest in issues affecting young people and particularly considered that the generation of adolescents who had experienced the war needed especial attention because of the strains of war.[74] The attention that she thought necessary confirmed that she viewed most issues through the lens of national identity, for as Parliamentary Secretary for Education she provided extra-statutory funding for the Girls Training Corps, the object of which was to train young women aged between 16 and 18 years for service in the WRNS, ATS and WAAF. The Ministry had been instrumental in the establishment of the Corps and provided its funding, because as Parker explained in the House, 'the G.T.C. does not attract grants from the services like the boys' units'. Parker herself chaired the 'committee of ladies' which ran the Corps.[75]

Parker's concern for and interest in youth was linked to a parallel desire to encourage the diffusion of high culture. Again, her concerns were connected to her sense of national identity. At Education, she encouraged the funding of the Council for the Encouragement of Music and the Arts (CEMA). CEMA was established as a wartime agency to promote the national culture among the working class to stiffen their resolve. As Richard Weight has argued, 'it seemed an ideal way to foster a more refined Britishness'.[76] The body survived the war. In Northern Ireland its connection to loyalism was absolute. In 1946 the liberal Education Minister, Colonel Hall-Thompson, insisted that the national anthem should be played at the end of all CEMA-sponsored events, 'in accordance with the British traditions and cultural interests of Northern Ireland'.[77] This established that the concern of CEMA in Northern Ireland was solely with the loyal Protestant working class. Parker was President of CEMA (NI) between 1949 and 1960. She contributed substantially to 'its distinctly tweedy, west-Brit establishment feel'.[78]

Parker was brought back into the government in 1949 as Minister of Health and Local Government. Both as Minister and President of CEMA (NI), she made the opening speech at Northern Ireland's Festival of the Arts, which formed a major component of the province's contribution to the Festival of Britain in 1951.[79] The relationship between Northern Ireland and the United Kingdom was symbolized by hanging a portrait of Winston Churchill painted by the Ulster artist Sir John Lavery next to a portrait of Lavery painted by Churchill.[80]

Parker wanted to ensure that Northern Ireland's distinctiveness was represented within the context of national unity. She was certainly not averse to allowing elements of Irishness to be present within Ulster unionist culture. She opposed Irish nationalism but could make a distinction between political and cultural Irishness. In the mid-1940s St John Ervine was authorized to write a biography of Sir James Craig. This was designed to be a major event in continuing the development of the Ulster Unionist tradition. The biography became the subject of cabinet discussion because of the vehement denunciations Ervine made of the Éire and Irishness generally. Parker wrote to the author asserting Craig's Irishness. She told Ervine that Craig had described himself to her not as anti-Irish' but as 'anti-Eirean, anti-Republic'. In a subsequent letter, she explained further that she was 'Quite certain, that, whatever his fundamental views or his personal feelings, James was an Irishman, as well as an Ulsterman, and that he would not have cared to have his Biography intermingled with such scathing criticism of Ireland and the Irish, past and present'.[81]

Parker's view of the relationship between her Northern Irish and British identities was that the former provided a regionally distinct contribution to the latter. Such a perspective could also be applied to her feelings about the relationship of Ulster to Irishness. She acted as chairman of the Ancient Monuments Advisory Committee (later Council), which considered Ulster archaeology. Parker was also supportive of Ulster folklife studies, which culminated in the establishment of the Ulster Folk Museum in 1958.[82] While much emphasis was placed on the constant reinforcing of Ulster's essential Britishness, there were also efforts to establish that this was a Britishness imbued with an ancient Irishness. The 1950s saw attempts to develop Ulster history teaching not to subvert the Britishness of history teaching but to augment it. Likewise, Parker was prepared to borrow pictures from the National Gallery in Ireland for exhibition by CEMA in Northern Ireland to display the Irish dimension of Ulster Britishness.[83]

This did not mean that she abandoned her hostility to Roman Catholicism as part of the political aspect of Irish national identity. In 1953 she led the cabinet opposition to the full state funding of a Catholic teacher training college, insisting that only a 65 per cent grant should be provided with a loan making up the remainder.[84] In part, such opposition emerged from her Conservatism, the desire for the state to allow a place for voluntarism (she was always a staunch defender of Protestant voluntary grammar schools). She combined her desire to encourage free enterprise with her conviction in the potential for Northern Ireland to remain united but not uniform with the United Kingdom through the Housing Miscellaneous Provisions Bill. She hoped the Bill would become her political monument.[85] The Bill allowed private landlords to raise their rents if they improved their properties. The Westminster Conservative government supported the sentiment behind the Bill, but the responsible minister in London, Enoch Powell, suggested that Northern Ireland should follow rather than lead. Parker's reputation for formidableness was enhanced by her determination to continue. There was opposition from within the cabinet – Warnock resigned (again) – but she had the support of Brooke and the bill was passed. If Midgley's Ulster Unionism remained linked to his sense of class identity, then so did Parker's. The Act expressed the interests of property-owners, even if self-interest was seen as encouraging improved housing conditions. The Act provoked opposition from the Protestant working class and undoubtedly played a part in the revival of the NILP in the 1950s.

Parker's Unionism was never open to question. She was a consistent and vocal supporter of the Union and the effectiveness of the Unionist Party in defending the constitutional position of Northern Ireland within the United Kingdom. She never sought a political role outside of Northern Ireland. This was not a result of parochialism. Her father had American connections, she had been educated in the United States and she cultivated American friendships. She undertook 'a lifetime of travel' and conversed readily in French and German.[86] She certainly saw Northern Ireland as part of the wider Empire. Parker's development of a distinctive Ulster identity was not in conflict with these wider identities. Unionism provided the setting for her development of a local variant of Britishness. Graham Walker has recently concluded that Ulster Unionism took shape as a form of nationalism and that Ulster national identity developed out of the Irish experience of the

Union.[87] As was seen in chapter 8, the assignment of the description 'nation' to Northern Ireland and 'nationalism' to Ulster Unionist identities is problematic. Northern Ireland saw the development of a distinct regional civil society in an Irish context. Parker played an extensive role in this civil society, with widely ranging interests, from ancient monuments to physical training for youth. She did not see these Ulster bodies as divorcing her from the Union but as encouraging the distinctiveness of Ulster within it.

Parker's contribution to Unionism shows that the Union was not an entirely male construction. The UWUC believed that women had a different role from men in the defence of the Union and that the Union protected women's domestic sphere. Parker shared such beliefs to a great extent. She did not, however, consider that separate women's politics were necessary because Unionists, male and female, shared the single objective of the defence of the Union. She responded to women's issues, as was to be expected in a parliament with so few women – and only a single woman cabinet minister in fifty years – but her commitment to the Union was the foremost part of her political identity.

Ulster at the crossroads: epilogue

With the deteriorating economy in the 1950s, the NILP staged a revival, which the Unionists came to see as the major threat to their own position. In 1958 the NILP won four Belfast seats. This was a challenge to the Unionist Party not to the Union. The NILP was a unionist party as well as a labour party. The Unionist Party was losing its ability to hold the loyalty of the Protestant working class. William Grant, the veteran labour Unionist and cabinet minister, died in 1949. Midgley was a link into the working class, but he was never fully accepted by the Unionist leadership.[88] After 1950, he turned increasingly to anti-Catholicism, perhaps seeking the leadership of the party rather than the leadership of the working-class section of Unionism.

The NILP did not make its breakthrough despite the hopes of the late 1950s and early 1960s. In 1962 the NILP increased its share of the vote by 15 per cent, though it did not win any more seats. The task of Terence O'Neill, who became leader of the Unionist Party and Prime Minister in 1963, was to reconstruct the cross-class Unionist alliance. O'Neill used a rhetoric of modernization to encourage investment in Northern Ireland. His intention was to reduce unemployment, which was the highest in the United Kingdom.[89] As Bew, Patterson and

Gibbon have argued, O'Neill saw this as a political rather than an economic problem. Unemployment was a cause of the loss of working class loyalty to his party: its relief was intended to regain that loyalty.[90] O'Neill wanted to establish the Britishness of Northern Ireland through the integration of Catholics into society, because this would increase the likelihood of investment and improve employment.

There were contradictions entailed in his strategy.[91] As Loughlin has commented, 'O'Neill differed from his predecessors ... [in] that whereas they saw the Union as securing a distinct Ulster, Unionist way of life within the United Kingdom, he saw it as providing standards of "Britishness" which Unionists would have to adopt'.[92] O'Neill's push towards uniformity contradicted the purposes to which devolution had been applied in the past. Economically, O'Neill was successful. Unemployment fell substantially and this achieved his political objective when in 1965 the advance of the NILP was halted, indeed reversed, when it lost two of its four seats.

New problems were arising for which O'Neill did not have solutions. His claim that he was going to apply British standards raised the expectations of the Catholic population. As Vernon Bogdanor has argued 'the political consequence of the establishment of a separate parliament in Northern Ireland was to sever the six counties from common United Kingdom principles of equity and fairness, and to take away from the Catholic minority in Northern Ireland the redress which could have been expected from Parliament at Westminster.'[93] It seemed now that O'Neill was going to address Catholic disadvantage. Unionists had associated themselves with Britishness through a claim to equal citizenship with the other nations of the United Kingdom, while denying the equality of citizenship of Catholics in the province. O'Neill's apparent change of direction made for dynamic politics. It seemed to many Catholics that change was possible. The claim for 'full British democratic standards ... to which they were entitled as British subjects', as Paddy Byrne, vice-president of the Campaign for Democracy in Ulster, demanded, was fundamentally threatening to the Protestant Unionist identity.[94] Having spent forty years seeking the marginalization of the NILP, the Unionist leadership ensured that when sections of the Protestant working class deserted the official party, they would have to move towards a more fundamentalist Protestant politics. This was the trajectory that Midgley had followed from the 1920s to the 1950s. He had not had to break with official Unionism because the stagnant politics of Brooke had encouraged the rise of the NILP but had not necessitated a defence of Protestant privilege. O'Neill joined the Royal Black Preceptory and the Apprentice Boys after becoming Prime Minister, to reassert his Protestantism. Such contradictions made for instability. Pushed by the Labour government at Westminster, which had rediscovered its sympathies for Irish Catholics, and by the civil rights campaign inside the province, O'Neill granted 'one man one vote' [*sic*], the ultimate 'British' measure of democracy in local elections, in early 1969. Giving 'British' rights to people they believed disloyal was too much for many Unionists and O'Neill was forced to resign, being replaced by Chichester-Clark on 1 May. Like O'Neill, he came from landed Unionism, the class to which Parker had belonged. Such individuals were incapable of retaining the loyalty of the urban Protestant people. The crisis continued throughout the summer of 1969 and in August the British army was deployed on the streets of Derry and Belfast to attempt to restore order.

Between 1969 and 1972 governments at Westminster attempted to reconcile aspects of devolution with direct rule. Devolved government in Northern Ireland had meant Protestant supremacy, while Westminster now applied a mixture of political concessions to Catholics with the imposition of a massive security force. This mixture exacerbated the alienation of both sides in Northern Ireland. Chichester-Clark fell in March 1971 to be succeeded by Brian Faulkner, who wanted to reassert the Unionist Party's hegemony over Protestants. In August 1971, the Conservative government at Westminster allowed him to introduce internment, which was directed solely at Catholics. On 30 January 1972, 'Bloody Sunday', British paratroops killed fourteen people on a routine civil rights demonstration in Derry. Within two months, on 24 March 1972, the Northern Ireland parliament was suspended for a year after which time it was abolished. The terms of the Union were now in urgent need of renegotiation.

Conclusion

The United Kingdom created by Acts of Union between the nations of the British Isles was not in the process of crumbling from the moment of its birth. The Union and unionism was pieced together bit by bit, repairing the wear and tear caused by the inevitable tensions of a multi-national polity. There were major challenges. Ireland could not be held within the Union once the majority of its people decided that their nationality could no longer be represented to their satisfaction within the United Kingdom. From the 1880s onwards the Irish electorate returned a majority of MPs who supported devolution. The British parties, the Conservatives and Liberals, differed on the question of how to respond to the claims of Irish nationhood. They did not differ in their belief that their main task was the maintenance of the Union. From Gladstone onwards, though sometimes with little enthusiasm, the Liberals believed that Irishness could be accommodated within the Union by making substantial concessions of political autonomy to Ireland. The Conservatives believed that the Union ought to be politically monolithic. They accepted regional identities but believed they should be subordinated to a single political identity. The dispute between these parties had not been resolved by the time of the First World War, during which the majority of nationalist Ireland was converted to a form of nationalism that was no longer compatible with the continued existence of the Union.

The British government that negotiated Ireland out of the Union was a coalition government presided over by a Welsh Liberal. The leader of the Conservatives was a Canadian Ulster-Scot. Outside Ireland, the political parties acted as a powerful integrative force. They allowed the representation of distinctiveness and acted as an essential mechanism for putting forward the claims of the nations within the United Kingdom.

Relationships within the Union were always subject to negotiation. There was never a moment of tranquility when the Union was fully formed. The individuals discussed in this book constantly interrogated their identities and then sought to readjust the relationships between their national, regional and local identities to fit their political and personal circumstances. Sometimes they had a sense of frustration about the responses to their desires for their nations but they also secured a substantial measure of recognition for the distinctive positions of their nationalities inside the Union. Frequently there seemed to be hesitation and disdain from the English majority as it was politically represented in the House of Commons. Arguments for greater devolution of administrative and executive power, or even consultation, had often to be made again and again before governments responded. The demand for a Secretary of State for Wales was made in the 1930s but the post was not created until the 1960s. In the meantime, however, governments did make numerous concessions to the plural nature of the United Kingdom.

Scotland and Wales were not granted Home Rule between 1918 and the 1970s because devolution was not the political demand of the majority of the electorates in those nations. It is churlish to criticize London governments for not granting the demands of minorities within the national minorities of the United Kingdom. The Scottish and Welsh continued to give their electoral support to British parties, which were multi-national coalitions. These broad church parties, both Conservative and Labour, seemed to offer the best option for securing material and cultural resources on a regional basis. One of those cultural resources was the opportunity and ability to express their national identities.

Northern Ireland was a special case. The demand for nationalism in all-Ireland before 1921 had already sheared Ireland away from British party politics and the devolution of government to Northern Ireland within the United Kingdom confirmed this separation from the political alliances that sought to capture state power at Westminster. British Labour, in particular, was eager to turn separation from the politics of Ulster into divorce. It consistently refused to aid the development of labour politics in the province and, therefore, carries a significant element of responsibility for the failure to draw Northern Irish politics towards issues of social and economic policy and away from ethno-sectarian rivalry. Harry Midgley's journey towards Unionist sectarianism was not solely caused by British Labour's refusal to enter 'Irish' politics, but his options in politics were narrowed by Labour's abandonment of the Ulster working class, Protestant and Catholic.

Support for the Union came in an immense variety of forms and at different levels of commitment. The Unionism of Elliot, Tweedsmuir, Gwilym Lloyd-George, Midgley and Parker was well developed and defined. They consciously chose to call themselves Unionists. They did not arrive at this definition in an instant but considered and constructed their political ideas over substantial periods of time, often in response to specific circumstances. Gwilym Lloyd-George's most clear account of his attitude on the place of Wales within the Union was in response to the campaign for a parliament for Wales led by his sister. The unionism of Johnston, Megan Lloyd George and Edwards was more instrumental. Johnston saw the Union as a convenient constitutional device for securing improvements in the social condition of the Scottish. Edwards wanted Welsh voices to be heard at Westminster. Both operated inside the British Labour Party, making use of the electoral power of the British working class to gain benefits for Scotland and Wales. The creation of the British welfare state in the 1940s confirmed the immense advantages of the Union. It did not, however, stop Edwards and Megan Lloyd George continuing to seek to re-negotiate the political relationship of Wales to the Union.

Unionism was not, therefore, a political creed based on a single class, gender or political affiliation. It was hegemonic in British politics but it was contested and opposed. There were small minorities in Scotland and Wales who wanted such fundamental reform of the Union that its demise would be inevitable. Plaid Cymru and the Scottish National Party did challenge the essential unity of the Union. They were, however, fringe parties from their formation in the 1920s until the 1960s. Even in the 1970s, they only established themselves as significant minorities, able to make a bid for status as second or third parties but not realistically able to capture majorities of the Welsh or Scottish votes. It was not until 1997 that the SNP overtook the Conservative share of the vote in Scotland. Plaid Cymru did not secure more than half the share of the Conservative vote in Wales until after 1997. In both countries, Labour has been able to represent nationality as well as class to the satisfaction of nearly half of the electorate in Wales and around 40 per cent in Scotland. The elections to the Scottish Parliament and Welsh Assembly show that in the context of devolution, voters are more likely to support nationalist parties, but both the SNP and Plaid Cymru's shares of the vote fell from 1999 to 2003.[1]

A further and powerful advantage to the Union was that it enabled small nations to play roles in the world that would have been impossible alone. The Union allowed them to 'punch above their weight' in international relations.[2] In the first half of the century, this role could still be seen as straightforwardly imperial. Elliot was interested in the problems of Empire and the development of the Commonwealth as a third British Empire; Johnston developed his Empire Socialism in the 1920s; Megan Lloyd George championed the Welsh contribution to Empire and Midgley went so far as to form a party that lay its primary emphasis on the Commonwealth. Yet for none of them was the Empire so central as to form the only element of their support for the Union and their differing senses of being British. Their unionism survived the end of Empire. It is difficult not to agree with Keith Robbins that 'To accept [that] the "loss of Empire" played a critical part in determining the degree of unity or disunity is to overemphasize the part that Empire played in establishing ... "British island nationality".'[3] Empire was important but not critical component of Britishness. It is possible to go further, to argue that many Britons saw decolonization as a confirmation of British virtues. The end of Empire might have removed much British international power, but it gave a tremendous stock of good feeling about being British. Decolonization, if it really was not a matter of choice, confirmed that the Empire had always really been about 'helping lame dogs over stiles' towards self-government on the British model. Both Elliot and Tweedsmuir considered their role in decolonization in such light. Both hoped that Britain could retain its influence through the renegotiation of the colonial relationship inside the Commonwealth. The realization that the Commonwealth would be a faded shadow of their hopes involved a less traumatic readjustment than one entailed in considering decolonization as a consequence of Britain's weakness. Tweedsmuir was well able to reconcile the end of Empire with her increasing belief that Britain must align more closely with its neighbours in Europe. She never saw this as entailing abdication from a global role for Britain and, through people like her, Scotland, within the Union. Many of the other individuals discussed here allowed their senses of imperialism to lapse in a fit of absence of mind. Johnston turned his attention from the Empire to Scotland, but imperial decline did not make him a separatist. Gwilym Lloyd-George defended the belligerent action of the Conservative government over Suez. Megan Lloyd George looked for other areas to express Welsh distinctiveness. Edwards still referred to the Commonwealth as the arena for Welshness to express itself in the late 1950s. Midgley's interest in the Commonwealth lapsed when he took responsibility for a domestic ministry in the Northern Ireland government. Evidence for Parker's attitude towards empire and its demise is too sparse to make any tenable interpretation. What can be said with certainty is that the loss of Britain's imperial role did not provoke any of these individuals into sudden or dramatic changes of heart with regard to the Union.[4]

Britain's contribution to the two world wars played a significant part in developing and maintaining the perceptions of the benevolent role that the United Kingdom could exercise in the world. Elliot, Gwilym Lloyd-George, Edwards, and Midgley all served in the forces in the First World War. All enlisted voluntarily. All played their parts in encouraging patriotic efforts in the Second World War. Parker was honoured for her voluntary contribution to the war effort in the Great War, and Megan Lloyd George and Tweedsmuir participated politically and personally in the Second World War. The role of the United Kingdom in fighting autocracy and dictatorship in two wars was brought home to an individual level. If there were any doubts about Britain's global role arising from its imperialism, then its actions in the Second World War swept them aside.

A biographical approach to the relationship between individuals and their nation(s) works well in the case of these politicians to reveal the different levels of intimacy each enjoyed with the Union. Their political lives were played out within the arena of the Union and their politics were expressions of their personal identities formed from multi-layered attachments to place at local, regional, national and Union levels. Combined with geography was the sociology of their identities – gender, class, religion and family contributed to the milieu of Unionism. Each life was 'an exercise in pluralism', as Morgan has called modern British history.[5] There was nothing inevitable in the affiliation of these individuals to the Union. Their commitment to the Union varied substantially. To Parker, it was always the fundamental aspect of her politics. Edwards considered abandoning the Union for separatist nationalism. The integrity of the Union, however, seemed to all of them, in the end, to provide the best means for the maintenance of their distinctive Scottish, Welsh and Northern Irish identities. Unionism was not an imposition from the core but a product of the periphery. It was this feature of unionism that gave the Union such remarkable stability and adaptability.

Notes

Introduction

1. Kenneth O. Morgan, 'England, Britain and the Audit of War,' *Transactions of the Royal Historical Society*, 6th series, 7 (1997), p. 140.
2. For a discussion of the terminology of the British Isles see Norman Davies, *The Isles: A History* (Basingstoke: Papermac, 2000), pp. xxiii–xli.
3. Christopher Harvie, 'The Moment of British Nationalism, 1939–1970', *Political Quarterly*, 71 (2000), pp. 328–40.
4. There are many books that consider English identities. See, for example, Robert Colls, *Identity of England* (Oxford: Oxford University Press, 2002) and Krishnan Kumar, *The Making of English National Identity* (Cambridge: Cambridge University Press, 2003).
5. David Marquand, 'How United is the Modern United Kingdom?' in Alexander Grant and Keith Stringer (eds), *Uniting the Kingdom: The Making of British History* (London: Routledge, 1995), p. 279; David Powell, *Nationhood and Identity: The British State since 1800* (London: IB Tauris, 2002), p. 154.
6. And not only in political thought. The multi-national nature of the UK was evident in the day-to-day lives of all its citizens/subjects. There now numerous books considering the variety of ways in which individuals have identified with the nations of the United Kingdom. As well as books and articles cited in other notes in this introduction see, for example, Keith Robbins, *Nineteenth-Century Britain: England, Scotland, and Wales The Making of a Nation* (Oxford: Oxford University Press, 1989), Raphael Samuel (ed.), *Patriotism: The Making and Unmaking of British National Identity*, 3 volumes (London: Routledge, 1989), Robert Colls, *Identity of England* (Oxford: Oxford University Press, 2002) and Paul Ward, *Britishness since 1870* (London: Routledge, 2004).
7. See John Turner, 'Letting Go: The Conservative Party and the End of the Union with Ireland', in Grant and Skinner, *Uniting the Kingdom* (London: Routledge, 1995) pp. 255–74.
8. John Ramsden, *The Age of Churchill and Eden 1940–1957, A History of the Conservative Party* (London: Longman, 1995), p. 200. Many Liberals 'went over' to the Conservatives as a reflection of their anti-labour politics rather than on the constitutional issue of the Union.
9. See David Howell, *British Workers and the Independent Labour Party 1888–1906* (Manchester: Manchester University Press, 1983), pp. 139, 140, 204–9, for working-class Conservatism in Scotland and Lancashire.
10. For the use of upper and lower case in 'unionism' see the note on terminology in the preliminary pages.
11. See for example Richard J. Finlay, 'Unionism and Dependency Culture: Politics and State Intervention in Scotland, 1918–1997' and James Mitchell, 'Contemporary Unionism', in Catriona M.M. Macdonald (ed.), *Unionist Scotland 1800–1997* (Edinburgh: John Donald, 1998), pp. 101, 117–121.

12. Quoted in Eugenio Biagini, *Gladstone* (Basingstoke: Macmillan, 2000), p. 97. See also Vernon Bogdanor, *Devolution in the United Kingdom* (Oxford: Oxford University Press, 2001), pp. 19–26.
13. For a discussion of these terms see Keith Robbins, 'Core and Periphery in Modern British History', in his *History, Religion and Identity in Modern Britain* (London: Hambledon, 1993), pp. 239–57.
14. Graeme Morton, *Unionist-Nationalism: Governing Urban Scotland, 1830–1860* (East Linton: Tuckwell, 1999), p. 8.
15. I have erred on the side of caution: those classified here as 'English' include Salisbury, Baldwin, Chamberlain, Churchill, Attlee, Eden, Wilson, Heath and Thatcher.
17. The notion of a British World has been explored in a series of conferences organised by Dr Philip Buckner of the Institute of Commonwealth Studies, University of London and in the resultant publications, see P.A. Buckner and Carl Bridge, 'Reinventing the British World', *The Round Table*, 368 (2003), 77–88; Carl Bridge and Kent Fedorowich (eds), *The British World: Diaspora, Culture and Identity* (London: Frank Cass, 2003).
18. Marquand, 'How United is the Modern United Kingdom?' pp. 287–8.
19. Stuart Ball (ed.), *Parliament and Politics in the Age of Churchill and Attlee: The Headlam Diaries 1935–51* (Cambridge: Royal Historical Society, 1999), pp. 214–5.
20. The most important books arguing the crisis paradigm are Tom Nairn, *The Break-up of Britain, Crisis and Neo-Nationalism* (London: New Left Books, 1977), second edition (London: Verso, 1981); Stephen Haseler, *The English Tribe: Identity, Nation and Europe* (Basingstoke: Macmillan, 1996) and Norman Davies, *The Isles: A History* (Basingstoke: Papermac, 2000).
21. Richard Weight, *Patriots: National Identity in Britain 1940–2000* (Basingstoke: Pan, 2003), p. 1.
22. For a discussion of post-devolution historiography see Richard Finlay, 'New Britain, New Scotland, New History? The Impact of Devolution on the Development of Scottish Historiography', *Journal of Contemporary History*, 36 (2001), pp. 383–93.

Chapter 1

1. See, for example, Linda Colley, *Britons: Forging the Nation 1707–1837* (London: Pimlico, 1994).
2. Graeme Morton, *Unionist-Nationalism: Governing Urban Scotland, 1830–1860* (East Linton: Tuckwell, 1999), p. 18.
3. Morton, *Unionist-Nationalism*, pp. 6–10.
4. Frances MacKinnon letters, 25 January 1948 and 23 February 1948, in Arthur Donaldson Papers, Acc. 6038/1/3, National Library of Scotland (NLS).
5. Unsigned letter, no date, Arthur Donaldson Papers, NLS Acc. 6038/1/17.
6. Christopher Harvie, *Scotland and Nationalism: Scottish Society and Politics 1707–1994*, second edition (London: Routledge, 1994), pp. 1–2, portrays McIntyre's election as the prophecy of subsequent nationalist growth from the 1960s onwards. For wartime by-elections in Scotland, see Hutchinson, I.G.C., *Scottish Politics in the Twentieth Century* (Basingstoke: Palgrave, 2001), p. 85.

7. Rita Davis (constituent) to Walter Elliot, 3 March 1953, Walter Elliot Papers, Acc. 6721/6/6, NLS.

8. John Maclean in Scotland opposed the formation of the CPGB demanding a separate party for Scotland. See David Howell, *A Lost Left: Three Studies in Socialism and Nationalism* (Manchester: Manchester University Press, 1986), pp. 155–225.

9. T.C. Smout, 'Scotland 1850–1950', in F.M.L. Thompson (ed.), *The Cambridge Social History of Britain 1750–1950 Volume I Regions and Communities* (Cambridge: Cambridge University Press, 1990), pp. 228–32.

10. Eugenio F. Biagini (ed.), *Citizenship and Community: Liberals, Radicals and Collective Identities in the British Isles, 1865–1931* (Cambridge: Cambridge University Press, 1996), p. 14.

11. See Christopher Harvie, 'Scottish Politics', in A. Dickson and J.H. Treble (eds), *People and Society in Scotland Volume III 1914–1990* (Edinburgh: John Donald, 1992), pp. 244–7.

12. See for example, Jo Grimond, *Memoirs* (London: Heinemann, 1979), pp. 208–9.

13. Michael Keating and David Bleiman, *Labour and Scottish Nationalism* (London: Macmillan, 1979), p. 52.

14. See Paul Ward, 'Nationalism and National Identity in British Politics, c. 1880s to 1914,' in Helen Brocklehurst and Robert Phillips (eds), *History, Identity and the Question of Britain* (Basingstoke: Palgrave, 2004), p. 219.

15. Biagini applies this description to the Liberal and Labour parties: *Citizenship and Community*, p. 2.

16. Richard Finlay, 'Scottish Conservatism and Unionism since 1918', in Martin Francis and Ina Zweiniger-Bargielowska (eds), *The Conservatives and British Society* (Cardiff: University of Wales Press, 1996), p. 112.

17. Hutchinson, I.G.C., 'Scottish Unionism between the Two World Wars', in Catriona M.M. Macdonald (ed.), *Unionist Scotland 1800–1997* (Edinburgh: John Donald, 1998), p. 87.

18. George Pottinger, *The Secretaries of State for Scotland 1926–76* (Edinburgh: Scottish Academic Press, 1979), p. 148.

19. John F. McCaffrey, 'The Origins of Liberal Unionism in the West of Scotland', *Scottish Historical Review*, 50 (1971), pp. 47–71.

20. Quoted in Hutchinson, I.G.C., *A Political History of Scotland 1832–1924* (Edinburgh: John Donald, 1986), p. 198.

21. Jack Brand, *The National Movement in Scotland* (London: Routledge and Kegan Paul, 1978), pp. 59–60.

22. James Kellas, 'The Party in Scotland,' in Anthony Seldon and Stuart Ball (eds), *Conservative Century: The Conservative Party since 1900* (Oxford: Oxford University Press, 1994), pp. 682–3.

23. Vernon Bogdanor, 'Devolution,' in Zig Layton-Henry (ed.), *Conservative Party Politics* (London: Macmillan, 1981), pp. 92–3.

24. For the powers accrued in Scotland since 1885 see Vernon Bogdanor, *Devolution in the United Kingdom* (Oxford: Oxford University Press, 2001), pp. 111–15.

25. Sydney and Olive Checkland, *Industry and Ethos: Scotland 1832–1914* (London: Edward Arnold, 1984), p. 170.

26. This is not to underplay the anxiety over winning elections in a democracy, but in the 1920s this anxiety was based on a fear of class rather than 'Scottish' voting. See David Jarvis, 'British Conservatism and Class Politics in the 1920s', *English Historical Review*, 111 (1996), 59–84, especially pp. 59–60, 64, 70.

27. James J. Smyth, 'Resisting Labour: Unionists, Liberals and Moderates in Glasgow between the Wars', *Historical Journal*, 46 (2003), p. 390. Smyth discusses the ability of militant Protestant candidates to take sizeable chunks of the Unionist vote in municipal elections.

28. Hutchinson, *Scottish Politics*, p. 98; John Ramsden, *The Winds of Change: Macmillan to Heath, 1957–1975* (Harlow: Longman, 1996), p. 66.

29. Finlay, 'Scottish Conservatism', p. 122.

30. On the decline of Unionism in Scotland, see for example David Seawright, *An Important Matter of Principle: The Decline of the Scottish Conservative and Unionist Party* (Aldershot: Ashgate, 1999), and Kellas, 'The Party in Scotland', pp. 677–93.

31. Kellas, 'The Party in Scotland', p. 690.

32. Quoted in Paul Smith (ed.), *Lord Salisbury on Politics: A Selection from his Articles in the Quarterly Review, 1860–1883* (Cambridge: Cambridge University Press, 1972), pp. 347–8.

33. Walter Elliot, Election Address, 1945, Walter Elliot Papers, NLS, Acc. 6721/7/3.

34. Quoted in Thomas Hennessey, *Dividing Ireland: World War 1 and Partition* (London: Routledge, 1998), p. 8.

35. Quoted in James Loughlin, *Ulster Unionism and British National Identity since 1885* (London: Pinter, 1995), p. 30

36. A.J. Balfour, *Nationality and Home Rule* (London: Longmans, Green and Co., 1913), pp. 10–11.

37. John Kendle, *Federal Britain: A History* (London: Routledge, 1997), pp. 72–3. See also Patricia Jalland, 'United Kingdom Devolution 1910–14: Political Panacea or Tactical Diversion?' *Economic History Review*, 4 (1979), pp. 757–85.

38. Neil Evans, 'Introduction: Identity and Integration in the British Isles', in Neil Evans (ed.), *National Identity in the British Isles* (Harlech: Coleg Harlech, 1989), p. 21.

39. Michael Fry, *The Scottish Empire* (Edinburgh: Tuckwell and Birlinn, 2001), p. 496. See also John M. MacKenzie, 'Empire and National Identities: The Case of Scotland', *Transactions of the Royal Historical Society*, 6th series, 8 (1998), pp. 215–31; Richard J. Finlay, 'The Rise and Fall of Popular Imperialism in Scotland 1850–1950', *Scottish Geographical Magazine*, 113 (1997), pp. 13–21; Harvie, *Scotland and Nationalism*, pp. 56–72.

40. Checkland and Checkland, *Industry and Ethos*, p. 169.

41. See Graham Walker, *Thomas Johnston* (Manchester: Manchester University Press, 1988), chapter 3 and also chapter 3 below.

42. John Darwin, 'The Fear of Falling: British Politics and Imperial Decline since 1900', *Transactions of the Royal Historical Society*, 5th series, 36 (1986), p. 42.

Chapter 2

1. Most of the biographical details given here come from Colin Coote, *A Companion of Honour: The Story of Walter Elliot* (London: Collins, 1965).

2. For Lowland Scottishness see Colin Kidd, 'Race, Empire and the Limits of Nineteenth-Century Scottish Nationhood', *Historical Journal*, 46 (2003), pp. 873–92.

3. Coote, *Companion of Honour*, p. 16.

4. Elliot to Katharine Elliot, 11 July 1940, typed extract, Walter Elliot Papers, National Library of Scotland (NLS), Acc. 6721/ 7/1.

5. Elliot to Katharine Elliot, 16 August 1940, Walter Elliot Papers, NLS, Acc. 6721/ 7/1.

6. Elliot to Katharine Elliot, 17 August 1940, Walter Elliot Papers, NLS, Acc. 6721/ 7/1.

7. Elliot to Katharine Elliot, 19 July 1940, Walter Elliot Papers, NLS, Acc. 6721/ 7/1.

8. House of Commons Debates, vol. 487, col. 503, 25 April 1951.

9. Quoted in Coote, *Companion of Honour*, pp. 139–40.

10. For Elliot's war service see his letters to Helen Hamilton, who became his first wife, Walter Elliot Papers, NLS, Acc. 12267/1.

11. *Scots Pictorial*, 17 August 1918.

12. Coote, *Companion of Honour*, p. 48.

13. Coote, *Companion of Honour*, p. 18.

14. Christopher Harvie, 'Scottish Politics', in A. Dickson and J.H. Treble (eds), *People and Society in Scotland Volume III 1914–1990* (Edinburgh: John Donald, 1992), p. 247.

15. George Pottinger, *The Secretaries of State for Scotland 1926–76* (Edinburgh: Scottish Academic Press, 1979), p. 65.

16. Duke of Atholl, *Narrative of the Scottish National War Memorial Scheme* (Edinburgh: privately published, 1923), p. 3. The London war museum became the Imperial War Museum, marking the imperial rather than English contribution to the war.

17. *Report of the Committee on the Utilisation of Edinburgh Castle for the Purpose of a Scottish National War Memorial*, Cd 279, HMSO, 1919; Scottish National War Memorial folder, NLS, Acc. 4714.

18. See Elizabeth M.M. Taylor, *The Politics of Walter Elliot 1929–1936*, unpublished PhD, Edinburgh, 1979.

19. John Ramsden, *The Age of Balfour and Baldwin 1902–1940: A History of the Conservative Party* (London: Longman, 1978), pp. 208–15.

20. Ross McKibbin, 'Class and Conventional Wisdom: The Conservative Party and the "Public" in Inter-war Britain', in his *Ideologies of Class* (Oxford: Oxford University Press, 1991), pp. 259–93.

21. Richard Finlay, 'Scottish Conservatism and Unionism since 1918', in Martin Francis and Ina Zweiniger-Bargielowska (eds), *The Conservatives and British Society* (Cardiff: University of Wales Press, 1996), p. 116.

22. G. Ward-Smith, 'Baldwin and Scotland: More than Englishness', *Contemporary British History*, 15 (2001), pp. 61–82.

23. Walter Elliot, *Toryism and the Twentieth Century* (London: Philip Allan, 1927), p. 4.

24. Elliot, *Toryism*, p. 135.

25. Quoted in Coote, *Companion of Honour*, p. 226.

26. Quoted at http://www2.ebs.hw.ac.uk/edweb/hisc/digest/elli1.html, 16 September 2003.

27. Coote, *Companion of Honour*, p. 41; Elliot, *Toryism*, chapter 2.
28. Broadcast script, 'Calling Australia: A Journey in War-time', 19 March 1942, Walter Elliot Papers, NLS, Acc. 6721/1/3.
29. Graeme Morton, *Unionist-Nationalism: Governing Urban Scotland, 1830–1860* (East Linton: Tuckwell 1999).
30. House of Commons Debates, vol. 493, col. 401, 8 November 1951.
31. Coote, *Companion of Honour*, pp. 93–4.
32. Coote, *Companion of Honour*, p. 87.
33. Hutchinson, I.G.C., *Scottish Politics in the Twentieth Century* (Basingstoke: Palgrave, 2001), pp. 41–2.
34. See Philip Williamson, *National Crisis and National Government: British Politics, the Economy and Empire, 1926–1932* (Cambridge: Cambridge University Press, 1992) for the way in which the United Kingdom's governments considered the economic crisis in imperial terms.
35. Coote, *Companion of Honour*, pp. 116–18. Elliot had preliminary discussions with other young MPs in October 1930 about a parliamentary attack on party politics, see Taylor, *Politics of Walter Elliot*, p. 61.
36. Walter Elliot, Election Address, 1935, Walter Elliot Papers, NLS, Acc. 6721/7/3.
37. Richard J. Finlay, 'National Identity in Crisis: Politicians, Intellectuals and the "End of Scotland", 1920–1939,' *History*, 79 (1994), pp. 242–59.
38. Coote, *Companion of Honour*, p. 15.
39. Finlay, 'National Identity in Crisis.'
40. For arguments against the inevitabilist view of appeasement explained here see R.A.C. Parker, *Chamberlain and Appeasement: British Policy and the Coming of the Second World War* (Basingstoke: Macmillan, 1993).
41. Taylor, *The Politics of Walter Elliot*, pp. 171–8.
42. For pressure on Elliot from Coote and Dugdale see Elliot to Baffy Dugdale, 21 February 1938, Walter Elliot Papers, NLS, Acc. 12198, also quoted in Coote, *Companion of Honour*, p. 156. Through Dugdale, Elliot was a supporter of Zionism. Fry has argued that support for Zionism was part of the Scottish imperial experience and there was much Scottish admiration for the Jews as a small people constructing their own national destiny: *The Scottish Empire* (Edinburgh: Tuckwell and Birlinn, 2001), chapter 30.
43. Coote, *Companion of Honour*, pp. 156–7.
44. Elliot to Baffy Dugdale, 1 January 1938, Walter Elliot Papers, NLS, Acc. 12198.
45. Coote, *Companion of Honour*, p. 157.
46. Elliot to Baffy Dugdale, 28 March 1938, Walter Elliot Papers, NLS, Acc. 12198; Elliot to Baffy Dugdale, 7 October 1938, quoted in Coote, *Companion of Honour*, p. 163.
47. *Baffy: The Diaries of Blanche Dugdale 1936–1947*, ed. N.A. Rose (Mitchell: London, 1973), p. 99.
48. Rose, *Baffy*, pp. 101, 102.
49. See Christopher Hill, *Cabinet Decisions on Foreign Policy: The British Experience October 1938–June 1941* (Cambridge: Cambridge University Press, 1991), p. 92 and A.R. Peters, *Anthony Eden at the Foreign Office 1931–1938* (Aldershot: Gower, 1986).
50. Typed extracts of letters to Katherine Elliot, 1940, Walter Elliot papers, NLS, Acc. 6721/7.

51. 'Cato', *Guilty Men* (London: Victor Gollancz, 1940), p. 19.
52. Coote, *Companion of Honour*, p. 131.
53. Gordon F. Millar, 'Elliot, Walter Elliot (1888–1958)', *Oxford Dictionary of National Biography*, Oxford University Press, 2004 [accessed 20 October 2004: http://www.oxforddnb/view/article/33003].
54. Robert Rhodes James (ed.), *Chips: The Diaries of Sir Henry Channon* (London: Weidenfeld, 1993), p. 248.
55. John Foster, 'The Twentieth Century, 1914–1979', in R.A. Houston and W.W.J. Knox (eds), *The New Penguin History of Scotland From the Earliest Times to the Present Day* (London: Penguin, 2002), p. 450.
56. Quoted in Coote, *Companion of Honour*, pp. 212–13.
57. The broadcasts are collected together in Walter Elliot, *Long Distance* (London: Constable, London, 1943).
58. 'Calling Australia and New Zealand,' 9 July 1942, Walter Elliot Papers, NLS, Acc. 6721/1/3. The celebration of urban Scotland is noteworthy here.
59. Election Address, 1946, Walter Elliot Papers, NLS, Acc. 6721/1/1.
60. *Observer*, 17 November 1946.
61. 'Scottish Administration', Walter Elliot Papers, NLS, Acc. 6721/9/5.
62. Quoted in Finlay, 'Scottish Conservatism', p. 121.
63. John Ramsden, *The Age of Churchill and Eden 1940–1957, A History of the Conservative Party* (London: Longman, 1995), p. 242.
64. House of Commons Debates, vol. 495, col. 969, 11 February 1952.
65. House of Commons Debates, vol. 512, cols. 213–217, 3 March 1953.
66. Linda Colley, *Britons: Forging the Nation* (London: Pimlico, 1994), pp. 11–54; Fry, *The Scottish Empire*, p. 386.
67. Walter Elliot, 'Scottish Politics,' in the Duke of Atholl (ed.), *A Scotsman's Heritage* (London: Alexander Maclehose, 1932), pp. 58–9.
68. John M. MacKenzie, '"The Second City of the Empire": Glasgow – Imperial Municipality,' in Felix Driver and David Gilbert (eds), *Imperial Cities: Landscape, Display and Identity* (Manchester: Manchester University Press, 1999), pp. 215–37.
69. Coote, *Companion of Honour*, p. 53.
70. These escapades are described in Coote, *Companion of Honour*, chapter 4.
71. Coote, *Companion of Honour*, pp. 46–7.
72. See, for example, Norman Davies, *The Isles: A History* (Basingstoke: Papermac, 2000), p. 882.
73. Richard Finlay, 'The Rise and Fall of Popular Imperialism in Scotland 1850–1950', *Scottish Geographical Magazine*, 113 (1997), pp. 19, 21.
74. Stephen Constantine, '"Bringing the Empire Alive": The Empire Marketing Board and Imperial Propaganda 1926–33', in John M. MacKenzie (ed.), *Imperialism and Popular Culture* (Manchester: Manchester University Press, 1986), p. 200.
75. Walter Elliot, 'The New Empire: I. Lessons from the Files', *The Times*, 6 May 1929.
76. Elliot, 'The New Empire: I. Lessons from the Files'.
77. Walter Elliot, 'The New Empire: II. Novelty in Africa', *The Times*, 7 May 1929.
78. Walter Elliot, 'The New Empire: IV. And so to England', *The Times*, 10 May 1929.

79. Elliot, 'The New Empire: IV. And so to England'.
80. See Walter Elliot, 'East Wind – West Wind: Stevenson, Scotland and the South Seas', *Geographical Magazine*, December 1950.
81. Walter Elliot, 'Speech to Federal Assembly, Salisbury', 10 September 1954, Walter Elliot Papers, NLS, Acc. 6721/10/3.
82. For Livingstone in imperialist context see Richard J. Finlay, *A Partnership for Good? Scottish Politics and the Union since 1880* (Edinburgh: John Donald, 1997), chapter 1.
83. Colin MacArthur, 'The Dialectic of National Identity: The Glasgow Empire Exhibition of 1938,' in Tony Bennet, Colin Mercer and Janet Woollacott (eds), *Popular Culture and Social Relations* (Milton Keynes: Open University Press, 1986), pp. 117–34. Quote from p. 130.
84. Elliot to Baffy Dugdale, 16 August 1937, Walter Elliot Papers, NLS, Acc. 12198.
85. Coote, *Companion of Honour*, p. 103.
86. John Grierson, 'Walter Elliot,' July 1963, Walter Elliot Papers, Acc. 6721/7/2 (i), NLS.
87. John Grierson, 'Walter Elliot,' July 1963, Walter Elliot Papers, Acc. 6721/7/2 (i), NLS.
88. Broadcast script, 'The English – How Do They Do It?' 13 December 1948, Walter Elliot Papers, Acc. 6721/7/2 (i), NLS.
89. Walter Elliot, 'The New Empire: I. Lessons from the Files'.
90. Quoted in Coote, *Companion of Honour*, p. 258.
91. Elliot to Katharine Elliot, 20 March 1944, typed extract, Walter Elliot Papers, NLS, Acc. 6721/10/4.
92. Elliot, *Long Distance*, p. 160. For Scotland and the decolonization of Africa see Fry, *The Scottish Empire*, chapter 32.
93. Walter Elliot, 'The New Empire: II. Novelty in Africa'.
94. Quoted in Coote, *Companion of Honour*, p. 265.
95. See John Darwin, *Britain and Decolonization: The Retreat from Empire in the Post-War World* (Basingstoke: Macmillan, 1988), pp. 183–9.
96. Mrs Bell to Walter Elliot, 5 March 1954, Walter Elliot to Mrs Bell, 8 March 1954, Walter Elliot Papers, Acc. 6721/9/2, NLS.
97. See for example House of Commons Debates, vol. 493, col. 391, 8 November 1951.
98. Walter Elliot, 'Speech to Federal Assembly, Salisbury', 10 September 1954, Walter Elliot Papers, NLS, Acc. 6721/10/3.

Chapter 3

1. The best general source for Labour in Scotland is Ian Donnachie, Christopher Harvie and Ian S. Wood (eds), *Forward! Labour Politics in Scotland 1888–1988* (Edinburgh: Polygon, 1989).
2. Graham Walker, *Thomas Johnston* (Manchester: Manchester University Press, 1988) and William Knox (ed.), *Scottish Labour Leaders 1918–1939* (Edinburgh: Mainstream, 1984), pp. 149–58 provide good interpretations of Johnston's life.
3. Walker, *Johnston*, p. 2.

4. Walker, *Johnston*, p. 43; Knox, *Scottish Labour Leaders*, p. 150.
5. Michael Keating and David Bleiman, *Labour and Scottish Nationalism* (London: Macmillan, 1979), chapter 2.
6. For the debates over nation and class within the British labour movement see Paul Ward, *Red Flag and Union Jack: Englishness, Patriotism and the British Left, 1881–1924* (Woodbridge: Royal Historical Society/Boydell, 1998). This was not the only interpretation of the working class relationship to the nation in *The Communist Manifesto*. In the same place, Marx also wrote that 'the struggle of the proletariat is at first a national struggle' and that the proletariat 'must constitute itself as the nation'. He said that *differences* and *antagonisms* between nations would vanish, but not necessarily the nations themselves.
7. *Forward*, 31 May 1924.
8. Thomas Johnston, *Our Scots Noble Families* (Glendarvel: Argyll Publishing, 1999 [1909]), pp. xxxii. Johnston later repudiated the book as 'historically one sided and unjust and quite unnecessarily wounding': *Memories* (London: Collins, 1952), p. 35.
9. Walker, *Johnston*, pp. 10–11.
10. For the new journalism and the social origins of the leaders of the ILP see Carl Levy, 'Education and Self-Education: Staffing the Early ILP', in Carl Levy (ed.), *Socialism and the Intelligentsia 1880–1914* (London: Routledge and Kegan Paul, 1987), pp. 135–210.
11. Rohan McWilliam, *Popular Politics in Nineteenth-Century England* (London: Routledge, 1998), p. 55.
12. For a discussion of 'varieties of populism' in the late nineteenth century see Patrick Joyce, *Visions of the People: Industrial England the Politics of Class, 1848–1914* (Cambridge: Cambridge University Press, 1994), pp. 65–74.
13. See Catriona M.M. Macdonald and E.W. McFarland (eds), *Scotland and the Great War* (Edinburgh: Tuckwell, 1999).
14. *Forward*, 2 October 1915, quoted in Walker, *Johnston*, p. 32.
15. Walker, *Johnston*, pp. 34–5.
16. *Forward*, 5 February 1916, quoted in Walker, *Johnston*, pp. 36–7.
17. T.C. Smout, 'Scotland 1850–1950', in F.M.L. Thompson (ed.), *The Cambridge Social History of Britain 1750–1950 Volume I Regions and Communities* (Cambridge: Cambridge University Press, 1990), p. 235.
18. See for example Iain McLean, *The Legend of Red Clydeside* (Edinburgh: John Donald, 1983).
19. Keating and Bleiman, *Labour and Scottish Nationalism*, pp. 59–62.
20. Thomas Johnston, *The History of the Working Classes in Scotland* (Wakefield: EP Publishing, 1974, reprint of fourth edition, 1946 [1920]), p. 5.
21. John Foster, 'The Twentieth Century, 1914–1979,' in R.A. Houston and W.W.J. Knox (eds), *The New Penguin History of Scotland From the Earliest Times to the Present Day* (London: Penguin, 2002), p. 434.
22. Walker, *Johnston*, pp. 15, 51.
23. Gordon Brown, *Maxton* (Glasgow: Fontana, 1988), pp. 11–17 describes the scene.
24. Johnston, *Memories*, p. 46.
25. Quoted in Knox, *Scottish Labour Leaders*, p. 151. Most of the Clydeside MPs were teetotallers. Johnston's Kirkintilloch exercised the local option and

was 'dry' between the 1920s and 1970s, and Johnston was one of the few who voted for a stern private member's bill on licensing which would have imposed prison sentences on drink traffickers: W.W. Knox, *Industrial Nation: Work, Culture and Society in Scotland 1800–Present* (Edinburgh: Edinburgh University Press, 1999), p. 198.

26. Ward, *Red Flag and Union Jack*, pp. 155–60.
27. Knox, *Scottish Labour Leaders*, p. 151.
28. Johnston, *Memories*, p. 49.
29. For Labour and imperialism in the 1920s and 1930s see Partha Sarathi Gupta, *Imperialism and the British Labour Movement, 1914–1964* (London: Macmillan, 1975) and Stephen Howe, *Anti-Colonialism in British Politics: The Left and the End of Empire, 1918–1964* (Oxford: Clarendon, 1993).
30. Quoted in Knox, *Scottish Labour Leaders*, p. 152.
31. Quoted in Knox, *Scottish Labour Leaders*, p. 152.
32. See G. Douds, 'Tom Johnston in India', *Journal of the Scottish Labour History Society*, 19 (1984), pp. 6–21.
33. Walker, *Johnston*, p. 78.
34. See Antoinette Burton, *Burdens of History: British Feminists, Indian Women, and Imperial Culture, 1865–1915* (Chapel Hill: University of North Carolina Press, 1994).
35. Johnston, *Memories*, p. 72.
36. For his visit to Canada see Johnston, *Memories*, pp. 85–90.
37. *Forward*, 26 July 1924, quoted in Knox, *Scottish Labour Leaders*, p. 152.
38. *Forward*, 23 August 1924, quoted in Walker, *Johnston*, p. 82.
39. It was not only the economics of Empire that developed popular imperialism in Scotland. MacKenzie has pointed out that the imperial missionaries David Livingstone and Mary Slessor were 'celebrated by the auto-didacts of the trade union movement, the working-men's clubs and left-leaning politicians': John M. MacKenzie, 'Empire and National Identities: The Case of Scotland', *Transactions of the Royal Historical Society*, 6th series, 8 (1998), p. 226.
40. Douds, 'Tom Johnston in India', p. 7.
41. Walker, *Johnston*, p. 70.
42. House of Commons Debates, vol. 206, cols. 865–74, 13 May 1927.
43. Keating and Bleiman, *Labour and Scottish Nationalism*, pp. 104–7.
44. Arthur Woodburn, quoted in Knox, *Industrial Nation*, p. 243.
45. Knox, *Scottish Labour Leaders*, p. 154. See Johnston's *The Financiers and the Nation* (1934).
46. For different interpretations of the place of planning in Scottish politics see Richard J. Finlay, 'Continuity and Change: Scottish Politics 1900–45,' in T.M. Devine and R.J. Finlay (eds), *Scotland in the Twentieth Century* (Edinburgh: Edinburgh University Press, 1996), pp. 80–81 and Foster, 'The Twentieth Century,' pp. 448–9.
47. Walker, *Johnston*, p. 125.
48. See Jack Brand, *The National Movement in Scotland* (London: Routledge and Kegan Paul, 1978), p. 52.
49. 'Scottish Home Rule and Administrative Devolution', Thomas Johnston Papers, Acc. 5862/8, National Library of Scotland.
50. 'Scottish Home Rule and Administrative Devolution', Thomas Johnston Papers, Acc. 5862, National Library of Scotland.

51. For Labour debates over appeasement and preparation for war see Paul Ward, 'Preparing for the People's War: Labour and Patriotism in the 1930s,' *Labour History Review*, 67 (2002), pp. 171–85.

52. Knox, *Scottish Labour Leaders*, p. 154.

53. Foster, 'The Twentieth Century,' p. 453.

54. Winston Churchill, quoted in *The Times*, 14 May 1943.

55. Churchill was heard to say 'Ah, here comes the King of Scotland' as Johnston approached him: T.M. Devine, *The Scottish Nation 1700–2000* (London: Allen Lane, 1999), p. 552.

56. Johnston, *Memories*, p. 148.

57. Its members were Lord Alness, Sir Archibald Sinclair, Walter Elliot, John Colville and Ernest Brown.

58. Michael Lynch, *Scotland: A New History* (London, Century, 1991), pp. 436–7.

59. 'Scotland at War,' typescript in Thomas Johnston papers, Acc. 5862/9.

60. Quoted in *Report of the Official Committee on the Machinery of Government, on the Machinery of Government in Scotland*, 24 December 1943, in Ian Levitt (ed.), *The Scottish Office: Depression and Reconstruction 1919–1959* (Edinburgh: Scottish History Society, 1992), p. 101.

61. *Report of the Official Committee on the Machinery of Government*, in Levitt, *The Scottish Office*, p. 101.

62. Walker, *Johnston*, pp. 163–6.

63. Walker, *Johnston*, p. 173.

64. See Richard J. Finlay, 'Scotland in the Twentieth Century: In Defence of Oligarchy?' *Scottish Historical Review*, 73 (1994), 103–12.

65. Quoted in Murray G.H. Pittock, *Scottish Nationality* (Basingstoke: Palgrave, 2001), p. 112.

66. Walker, *Johnston*, p. 158.

67. Johnston, *Memories*, p. 195.

68. Richard Weight, *Patriots: National Identity in Britain, 1940–2000* (Basingstoke: Pan, 2003), p. 203.

69. Smout, 'Scotland 1850–1950,' p. 241.

70. Quoted in Ben Pimlott (ed.), *The Second World War Diary of Hugh Dalton, 1940–45* (London: Jonathan Cape/BLPES, 1986), p. 224.

71. *Daily Record*, 13 March 1944.

Chapter 4

1. House of Commons Debates, vol. 536, col. 983, 1 February 1955.

2. See Helen Corr, 'Where is the Lass o'Pairts?: Gender, Identity and Education in Nineteenth Century Scotland', in Dauvit Broun, R.J. Finlay and Michael Lynch (eds), *Image and Identity: The Making and Re-making of Scotland through the Ages* (Edinburgh: John Donald, 1998), pp. 220–8.

3. Hutchinson, I.G.C., 'Scottish Unionism between the Two World Wars', in Catriona M.M. Macdonald (ed.), *Unionist Scotland 1800–1997* (Edinburgh: John Donald, 1998), p. 77.

4. See 2nd Baron Tweedsmuir Papers, National Library of Scotland (NLS), Acc. 11628/17a–c.

5. For the films see *The Times*, 24 March 1949. See also unattributed press cutting, 1947, in 2nd Baron Tweedsmuir Papers, NLS, Acc. 11628/226.
6. See Ina Zweiniger-Bargielowska, *Austerity in Britain: Rationing, Controls and Consumption, 1939–1955* (Oxford: Oxford University Press, 2000), pp. 214–30.
7. This was the post for which Elliot was considered.
8. Quoted in G.E. Maguire, *Conservative Women: A History of Women and the Conservative Party, 1874–1997* (Basingstoke: Macmillan, 1998), p. 171.
9. James Mitchell, *Conservatives and the Union: A Study of Conservative Party Attitudes to Scotland* (Edinburgh: Edinburgh University Press, 1990), p. 31.
10. Harold Macmillan, *Tides of Fortune 1945–1955* (London: Macmillan, 1969), p. 211.
11. Oliver Poole to Lady Priscilla Tweedsmuir, 7 August 1959, Lady Priscilla Tweedsmuir Papers, NLS, Dep. 337/24/3. These boxes have now been re-catalogued under the Accession no. 11884.
12. 'Political Notes', 1945, Lady Priscilla Tweedsmuir Papers, NLS, Acc. 11884/262.
13. 'Political Notes', 1945, Lady Priscilla Tweedsmuir Papers, NLS, Acc. 11884/262.
14. 'General Election Broadcast on Behalf of the Conservative and Unionist Party', 28 September 1959, Lady Priscilla Tweedsmuir Papers, NLS, Dep. 337/24.
15. 'Political Notes', 1945, Lady Priscilla Tweedsmuir Papers, NLS, Acc. 11884/262.
16. Mitchell, *Conservatives and the Union*, p. 36.
17. 'General Election Campaign, September–October 1964, Speeches', Lady Priscilla Tweedsmuir Papers, NLS, Acc. 11884/21.
18. 'General Election Campaign, September–October 1964, Speeches', Lady Priscilla Tweedsmuir Papers, NLS, Acc. 11884/21.
19. 'Speech at dinner for Vice-President of the Commission of the European Communities', 3 February 1972, ' Lady Priscilla Tweedsmuir Papers, NLS, Acc. 11884/29.
20. Election Address, North Aberdeen, 1945, Lady Priscilla Tweedsmuir Papers, NLS, Dep. 337/1.
21. 'General Election October 1959, Campaign Speech Notes and Briefs, Eve of Poll Meeting', 7 October 1959, Lady Priscilla Tweedsmuir Papers, NLS, Acc. 11884/16.
22. 'General Election Broadcast on Behalf of the Conservative and Unionist Party', 28 September 1959, Lady Priscilla Tweedsmuir Papers, NLS, Dep. 337/24.
23. Mitchell, *Conservatives and the Union*, pp. 49–50.
24. Mitchell, *Conservatives and the Union*, p. 34.
25. The seat was won back for the Conservatives by Lt-Col. Colin Mitchell of the Argyll and Sutherland Highland Regiment. He was defending an imperial military career in which he had been criticized for his role in policing in Aden and he also fought to prevent the loss of a distinct Scottish identity for his regiment. As late as 1970, therefore, imperial Conservatism could turn the tide in some parts of Scotland: Michael Fry, *The Scottish Empire* (Edinburgh: Tuckwell and Birlinn, 2001), p. 491.
26. See John Ramsden, *The Winds of Change: Macmillan to Heath, 1957–1975* (Harlow: Longman, 1996), pp. 268, 306.
27. Mitchell, *Conservatives and the Union*, pp. 10–11.

28. Hutchinson, I.G.C., *Scottish Politics in the Twentieth Century* (Basingstoke: Palgrave, 2001), p. 119.
29. Richard Crossman recorded Heath making this comment, quoted in Mitchell, *Conservatives and the Union*, p. 55.
30. Richard Finlay, 'Scottish Conservatism and Unionism since 1918', in Martin Francis and Ina Zweiniger-Bargielowska (eds), *The Conservatives and British Society* (Cardiff: University of Wales Press, 1996), p. 121.
31. Quoted in Ramsden, *Winds of Change*, pp. 405–6.
32. Mitchell, *Conservatives and the Union*, p. 55.
33. David Seawright, *An Important Matter of Principle: The Decline of the Scottish Conservative and Unionist Party* (Aldershot: Ashgate, 1999), p. 124.
34. James G. Kellas, 'Scottish Nationalism', in David Butler and Michael Pinto-Duchinsky (eds), *The British General Election of 1970* (London: Macmillan, 1971), pp. 446–62.
35. George Pottinger, *The Secretaries of State for Scotland 1926–76* (Edinburgh: Scottish Academic Press, 1979), p. 174.
36. See Bogdanor, *Devolution in the United Kingdom*, pp. 133–6.
37. Notes for speech, General Election, October 1974, Lady Priscilla Tweedsmuir Papers, NLS, Acc. 11884/29.
38. 'General Election Campaign, September–October 1964, Speeches', Lady Priscilla Tweedsmuir Papers, NLS, Acc. 11884/21.
39. Janet Adam Smith, *John Buchan: A Biography* (London: Rupert Hart Davis, 1965).
40. Lord Tweedsmuir, *Always a Countryman*, second edition (Robert Hale, London, 1971 [1955]).
41. 'The Scottish Race', 2nd Lord Tweedsmuir Papers, NLS, Acc. 11628/251.
42. House of Commons Debates, vol. 480, col. 1450, 13 November 1951.
43. House of Commons Debates, vol. 536, col. 979, 1 February 1955. See also Lady Tweedsmuir, 'Problème de Migration Mondiale', address to the University of Strasbourg, 2nd Baron Tweedsmuir Papers, NLS, Acc. 11628/125.
44. *The Empire Club of Canada Speeches 1960–1961*, Toronto, The Empire Club Foundation, 1960, at http://www.empireclubfoundation.com, 2 December 2003.
45. For hunting as masculine, see John M. MacKenzie, 'The Imperial Pioneer and Hunter and the Masculine Stereotype in Late Victorian and Edwardian Times', in J.A. Mangan and James Walvin (eds), *Manful Assertions: Masculinities in Britain since 1800* (London: Routledge, 1991), pp. 178–98.
46. Lord Tweedsmuir, *One Man's Happiness* (London: Robert Hale, 1968), p. 79.
47. 'Journal: Canada, British Columbia, September–October 1955', p. 5, Lady Priscilla Tweedsmuir Papers, NLS, Acc. 11884/133.
48. Journal: Canada, British Columbia, September–October 1955', p. 6, Lady Priscilla Tweedsmuir Papers, NLS, Acc. 11884/133.
49. Journal: Canada, British Columbia, September–October 1955', p. 11, Lady Priscilla Tweedsmuir Papers, NLS, Acc. 11884/133.
50. Mary A. Procida, 'Good Sports and Right Sorts: Guns, Gender, and Imperialism in British India', *Journal of British Studies*, 40 (2001), p. 455.
51. There are many affectionate sketches in the private correspondence between them.

52. 'Political and Personal Journal 1965–66, entry for 4 December 1966', Lady Priscilla Tweedsmuir Papers, NLS, Acc. 11884/230.

53. 'Political and Personal Journal 1965–66, entry for 22 July 1966', Lady Priscilla Tweedsmuir Papers, NLS, Acc. 11884/230.

54. House of Commons Debates, vol. 716, cols. 1238–48, 19 July 1965.

55. 'Political and Personal Journal 1965–66, entry for 22 July 1966', Lady Priscilla Tweedsmuir Papers, NLS, Acc. 11884/230.

56. Lady Tweedsmuir, 'Problème de Migration Mondiale', address to the University of Strasbourg, 2nd Baron Tweedsmuir Papers, NLS, Acc. 11628/125.

57. 'Speech at dinner for Vice-President of the Commission of the European Communities', 3 February 1972, ' Lady Priscilla Tweedsmuir Papers, NLS, Acc. 11884/29.

58. House of Lords Debates, vol. 333, cols. 1346, 25 July 1972.

59. House of Lords Debates, vol. 335, cols. 467–8, 14 September 1972.

60. See for example Lord Willis, House of Lords Debates, vol. 328, cols. 1250–1, 2 March 1972, who pointed out that the population of Iceland was the same as that of Southampton at 208,000.

61. House of Lords Debates, vol. 328, cols. 1257, 2 March 1972.

62. See Christopher Hill and Christopher Lloyd, 'The Foreign Policy of the Heath Government', in Stuart Ball and Anthony Seldon (eds), *The Heath Government 1970–74: A Reappraisal* (London: Longman, 1996), pp. 285–314.

63. *Evening Standard*, 11 July 1972.

64. *Daily Mail*, 5 December 1972.

65. Quoted in Bogdanor, *Devolution in the United Kingdom*, p. 137.

66. Bogdanor, *Devolution in the United Kingdom*, p. 190.

67. One in five of those who voted continued to support the Conservatives.

Chapter 5

1. See Geraint H. Jenkins and Mari A. Williams (eds), *'Let's Do Our Best for the Ancient Tongue': The Welsh Language in the Twentieth Century* (Cardiff: University of Wales Press, 2000).

2. D. Hywell Davies, *The Welsh Nationalist Party 1925–1945: A Call to Nationhood* (Cardiff: University of Wales Press, 1983), p. 55; Kenneth O. Morgan, *Rebirth of a Nation: A History of Modern Wales* (Oxford: Oxford University Press, 1982), pp. 206–7.

3. Sir E. Vincent Evans papers, Talks and Lectures c. 1890–1930, N12, National Library of Wales.

4. Davies, *The Welsh Nationalist Party*, pp. 193–4, 194n; National Eisteddfod Court, *Yr Eisteddfod/The Eisteddfod*, n.p., n.d.

5. Morgan, *Rebirth*, pp. 254–5; Davies, *The Welsh Nationalist Party*, pp. 154–66.

6. Davies, *The Welsh Nationalist Party*, pp. 237, 248.

7. Morgan, *Rebirth*, p. 393. Alan Butt Philip, *The Welsh Question: Nationalism in Welsh Politics 1945–1970* (Cardiff: University of Wales Press, 1975) argues that Plaid Cymru's influence was stronger and 'far from confined to party politics', p. 317.

8. Kenneth O. Morgan, 'Lloyd George and Welsh Liberalism,' in his *Modern Wales: Politics, Places and People* (Cardiff: University of Wales Press, 1995), pp. 400–18.

9. Morgan, 'Lloyd George and Welsh Liberalism,' p. 410.
10. John S. Ellis, 'Reconciling the Celt: British National Identity, Empire, and the 1911 Investiture of the Prince of Wales', *Journal of British Studies*, 37 (1998), pp. 391–418. Quote from p. 396.
11. George Thomas, Viscount Tonypandy, *My Wales* (London: Century, 1986), pp. 101–2.
12. Morgan, *Rebirth*, p. 181.
13. Morgan, 'Lloyd George and Welsh Liberalism,' pp. 413–14.
14. The Liberal vote recovered somewhat in the 1970s. It did not substantially increase the number of Liberals MPs. In 1983 the Liberal/SDP Alliance won 23.2 per cent of the vote but only two MPs in Wales.
15. See for example Chris Williams, *Capitalism, Community and Conflict: The South Wales Coalfield 1898–1947* (Cardiff: University of Wales Press, 1998).
16. Morgan, *Rebirth*, pp. 97–8.
17. See Thomas, *My Wales*, with its photographs by Lord Snowden, which represents the way in which the Welshness of a 'British' politician was formulated.
18. J. Graham Jones, 'The Parliament for Wales Campaign, 1950–1956,' *Welsh History Review*, 16 (1992–3), p. 221.
19. Jones, 'Parliament for Wales Campaign,' pp. 207–36.
20. Morgan, *Modern Wales*, p. 16.
21. Kenneth O. Morgan, 'Power and the Glory: War and Reconstruction, 1939–1951,' in Duncan Tanner, Chris Williams and Deian Hopkin (eds), *The Labour Party in Wales, 1900–2000* (Cardiff: University of Wales Press, 2000), p. 178.
22. For Davies, see Morgan, *Rebirth*, p. 281.
23. James Griffiths, *Pages from Memory* (London: J.M. Dent, 1969), p. 1.
24. Peter Stead, 'The Labour Party and the Claims of Wales,' in John Osmond (ed.), *The National Question Again: Welsh Political Identity in the 1980s* (Llandusyl: Gomer, 1985), pp. 99–123, provides a good discussion of Labour's moves towards devolution from the 1940s to 1970s.
25. Morgan, *Rebirth*, pp. 105–12.
26. Quoted in Gervase Phillips, 'Dai Bach Y Soldiwr: Welsh Soldiers in the British Army, 1914–1918,' *Llafur*, 6 (1993), p. 102.
27. Mervyn Jones, *A Radical Life: The Biography of Megan Lloyd George* (London: Hutchinson, 1991), p. 11; John Grigg, *Lloyd George: From Peace to War 1912–1916* (London: Methuen, 1985), p. 402.
28. See Kenneth O. Morgan, 'England, Britain and the Audit of War,' *Transactions of the Royal Historical Society*, 6th series, 1997, vol. 7, p. 150.
29. Brian Davies, 'Empire and Identity: The "Case" of Dr William Price', in David Smith (ed.), *A People and a Proletariat: Essays in the History of Wales 1780–1980* (London: Pluto, 1980), pp. 86–7.
30. Aled Jones and Bill Jones, 'The Welsh World and the British Empire, c. 1851–1939: An Exploration', in Carl Bridge and Kent Fedorowich (eds), *The British World: Diaspora, Culture and Identity* (London: Frank Cass, 2003), pp. 57–81.
31. D. Andrews and J. Howell, 'Transforming into a Tradition: Rugby and the Making of Imperial Wales, 1890–1914', in A. Ingham and J. Loy (eds), *Sport in Social Development: Traditions, Transitions, and Transformations* (Champaign, Ill., Human Kinetics, 1993), p. 79.

32. Griffiths, *Pages from Memory*, p. 92.
33. Griffiths, *Pages from Memory*, p. 119.
34. See Richard Finlay, '"For or Against?" Scottish Nationalists and the British Empire, 1919–39', *Scottish Historical Review*, 71 (1992), pp. 184–206.
35. Saunders Lewis, 'The case for Welsh nationalism', *The Listener*, 13 May 1936, p. 915.
36. See for example H.W.J. Edwards, *What is Welsh Nationalism?* Second edition (Cardiff: Plaid Cymru, 1954) and F. Ridley quoted in Peter Berresford Ellis (ed.), *The Creed of Celtic Revolution* (London: Medusa, 1969), p. 14.

Chapter 6

1. Gwilym chose to hyphenate his name to Lloyd-George, establishing some superficial measure of independence from his father's name.
2. Mervyn Jones, *A Radical Life: The Biography of Megan Lloyd George* (London: Hutchinson, 1991), p. 22. Richard, the eldest son, and Olwen, the eldest daughter did not enter politics.
3. Viscount Gwynedd, *Dame Margaret: The Life Story of His Mother* (London: George Allen and Unwin, 1947), p. 21. He wrote of his mother: 'In a word, she was Wales' (p. 32).
4. Richard was born in 1889, Mair Eluned was born in 1890 (but died in 1907), and Olwen was born in 1892.
5. John Grigg, *Lloyd George: The People's Champion 1902–1911* (London: Eyre Methuen, 1978), p. 54.
6. G.R. Searle, *The Liberal Party: Triumph and Disintegration 1886–1929*, second edition (Basingstoke: Palgrave, 2001), p. 72.
7. J. Graham Jones, 'Major Gwilym Lloyd-George, First Viscount Tenby (1894–1967),' *National Library of Wales Journal*, 32 (2001), p. 177. This essay provides the fullest account of Lloyd-George's political life. See also Kenneth O. Morgan on Lloyd-George in the *Dictionary of National Biography*.
8. Unpublished autobiography, Gwilym Lloyd-George Papers, National Library of Wales (NLW), MS 23671C, f. 9.
9. She did later become a weekly boarder at a school in Wimbledon and later at Garratt's Hall school, Banstead. Grigg, *Lloyd George: From Peace to War*, p. 74, 402.
10. Quoted in Jones, *A Radical Life*, p. 38. In fact, Megan did not get on with Margot Asquith.
11. Megan's perspective on Lloyd George's fall is given in a letter to her sister Olwen on 25 October 1922. She wrote 'Tada had wonderful receptions both at Manchester & Leeds & made wonderful speeches in both places. The people are absolutely with him, altho' very tired of the government, more particularly because of its being a coalition than anything else. Whatever happens Tada will be in power. He will be tremendous in opposition – & Bonar [Law] knows it,' Kenneth O. Morgan (ed.), *Lloyd George Family Letters 1885–1936* (Cardiff and London: University of Wales Press and Oxford University Press, 1973), p. 197.
12. For Megan's adoption for Anglesey see Jones, *A Radical Life*, pp. 74–5.

13. For Gwilym's account see 'Autobiography', NLW, MS 23671C, ff. 42. See also A. Lentin, *Lloyd George and the Lost Peace: From Versailles to Hitler, 1919–1940* (Basingstoke: Palgrave, 2001), chapter 5.

14. J. Graham Jones, 'A Breach in the Family: The Lloyd Georges', *Journal of Liberal Democrat History*, 25 (1999–2000), pp. 34–39.

15. 'Autobiography', notes, NLW, MS 23671C.

16. See Jones, 'Major Gwilym Lloyd-George', p. 179.

17. *The Times*, 20 May 1929, p. 15.

18. Jones, 'Major Gwilym Lloyd-George', pp. 178–81.

19. 'Autobiography', NLW, MS 23671C, ff. 2–3.

20. Mrinalini Sinha, 'Britishness, Clubbability, and the Colonial Public Sphere: The Genealogy of an Imperial Institution in Colonial India', *Journal of British Studies*, 40 (2001), pp. 489–521 (quotes from pp. 494, 496). For the club as the site of the amateur but effective defence of Empire see Richard Usborne, *Clubland Heroes* (London: Hutchinson, 1983 [1953]).

21. Lloyd-George, 'Autobiography,' NLW, MS 23671C, ff. 15, 18.

22. Lloyd-George, 'Autobiography,' NLW, MS 23671C, ff. 15, 18.

23. Morgan, *Dictionary of National Biography*, p. 666; Ben Pimlott (ed.), *The Second World War Diary of Hugh Dalton* (London: Jonathan Cape, 1986), pp. 527, 562–3; Jones, 'A Breach in the Family', p. 38.

24. Lloyd-George, 'Autobiography,' NLW, MS 23671C, f. 21.

25. Lloyd-George, 'Autobiography,' NLW, MS 23671C, f. 28.

26. Lloyd-George, 'Autobiography,' NLW, MS 23671C, f. 14.

27. Lloyd-George, 'Autobiography,' NLW, MS 23671C, f. 39.

28. Jones, 'Major Gwilym Lloyd-George', p. 186.

29. See for example his speech opening a British Restaurant at Willesden, where he said the Ministry's policy was 'getting people to return to the simple foods which are the foundation of health – the simple foods that once made the peasantry of England the finest and sturdiest in the world,' Gwilym Lloyd-George Papers, NLW, MS 23669E.

30. Jones, 'Breach in the Family', p. 38.

31. Jones, 'Major Gwilym Lloyd-George', p. 190.

32. This paragraph is based on Jones, 'Major Gwilym Lloyd George', p. 192.

33. Roy Douglas, *The History of the Liberal Party 1895–1970* (London: Sidgwick and Jackson, 1971), p. 249.

34. Churchill to Mrs Cox, 11 October 1951, copy, Letters to Gwilym Lloyd-George 1914–68, NLW, MS 23668E.

35. Gwilym Lloyd-George, Election Address 1951, NLW, ex 1972.

36. *The Times*, 13 September 1951, quoted in Jones, 'Major Gwilym Lloyd George', p. 194.

37. Jones, 'Major Gwilym Lloyd George', pp. 194–5.

38. J. Graham Jones, 'The Parliament for Wales Campaign 1950–1956,' *Welsh History Review*, 16 (1992–3), p. 209. See also Alan Butt Philip, *The Welsh Question: Nationalism in Welsh Politics 1945–1970* (Cardiff: University of Wales Press, 1975), p. 295.

39. The following paragraph relies heavily on Felix Aubel, 'The Conservatives in Wales, 1880–1935,' in Martin Francis and Ina Zweiniger-Bargielowska (eds), *The Conservatives and British Society* (Cardiff: University of Wales Press, 1996), pp. 96–110. The quote is from p. 97.

40. Aubel, 'The Conservatives in Wales', p. 101.
41. Aubel, 'The Conservatives in Wales', pp. 105–6.
42. Aubel, 'The Conservatives in Wales', p. 106.
43. Indeed in 1979 the Conservatives captured Anglesey. For a sense of Conservative optimism in the 1970s and 1980s see Chris Butler, 'The Conservative Party in Wales: Remoulding a Radical Tradition,' and Donald Walters, 'The Reality of Conservatism,' in John Osmond (ed.), *The National Question Again: Welsh Political Identity in the 1980s* (Llandusyl: Gomer, 1985), pp. 155–66, 210–21.
44. Jones, 'Parliament for Wales Campaign,' p. 215.
45. For the full debate see House of Commons Debates, vol. 537, cols 2439–528, 4 March 1955.
46. House of Commons Debates, vol. 537, cols 2468–71, 4 March 1955.
47. Speech at Freedom of the City of Cardiff, 28 October 1956, Gwilym Lloyd-George Papers, NLW, MS 23669E, ff. 39–52.
48. His father had become an earl in 1944, shortly before his death. David Lloyd George feared that he would not retain his parliamentary seat and saw the Lords as the only alternative method to raise his voice about post-war issues. Megan was opposed to his acceptance of the earldom.
49. Jones, *A Radical Life*, p. 54.
50. Letter to *The Times*, 17 May 1966.
51. Quoted in Jones, 'Major Gwilym Lloyd-George', pp. 181–2.
52. Jones, *A Radical Life*, p. 103.
53. Douglas, *History of the Liberal Party*, p. 245
54. Jones, *A Radical Life*, p. 248.
55. Morgan (ed.), *Lloyd George Family Letters*, pp. 208, 209.
56. Kenneth O. Morgan, *Rebirth of a Nation: A History of Modern Wales* (Oxford: Oxford University Press, 1982), p. 243.
57. Megan received 49.4 per cent, Labour 28.4 per cent and the Conservative secured 22.2 per cent. In the heart of Welsh Wales, one in five voters supported the Unionists. In 1931, in the context of the national crisis and no Labour candidate, the Conservative got 41.7 per cent and Megan got 58.3 per cent.
58. Quoted in Jones, *A Radical Life*, p. 85.
59. *South Wales Echo and Evening Express*, 28 May 1947, in Press Cuttings, February 1945 to November 1951, Megan Lloyd George Papers, NLW, MS 20941E. These indexed press cuttings files provide an excellent source for Megan Lloyd George's speeches in Wales.
60. Quoted in Jones, *A Radical Life*, p. 223.
61. For the Liberals in the 1920s, see Searle, *The Liberal Party*, chapter 9.
62. Quoted in Jones, *A Radical Life*, pp. 113–14.
63. See J. Graham Jones, 'Dame Margaret Lloyd George, The Norway Debate and the Fall of Neville Chamberlain', *The National Library of Wales Journal*, 31 (1999–2000), pp. 423–32 and Foot's Letter to *The Times*, 17 May 1966.
64. The relationship forms a major theme in Mervyn Jones' biography of Megan, *A Radical Life*.
65. Emyr Price, *Megan Lloyd George* (Caernarfon: Gwynedd Archives Service, 1983), p. 45.

66. Quoted in Jones, *A Radical Life*, pp. 209–10.
67. Jones, 'Parliament for Wales Campaign,' pp. 207–36, especially pp. 213–14.
68. See Butt Philip, *The Welsh Question*, p. 257n.
69. Campaign for a Parliament for Wales (Aberystwyth, nd.), quoted in Butt Philip, *The Welsh Question*, p. 257.
70. Jones, 'Parliament for Wales Campaign,' pp. 227–8.
71. House of Commons Debates, vol. 537, col. 2469, 4 March 1955.
72. Jones, 'Parliament for Wales Campaign,' p. 228.
73. Philip, *The Welsh Question*, p. 76.
74. The following is compiled from Jones, 'Parliament for Wales Campaign,' pp. 229–33 and Butt Philip, *The Welsh Question*, pp. 258–60.
75. Jones, 'Parliament for Wales Campaign,' p. 230.
76. See her published statement on joining Labour, quoted in Jones, *A Radical Life*, p. 248.
77. Quoted in Jones, *A Radical Life*, p. 234.
78. Deirdre Beddoe, 'Images of Welsh Women', in Tony Curtis (ed.), *Wales: The Imagined Nation Studies in Cultural and National Identity* (Bridgend: Poetry Wales Press, 1986), p. 227.
79. The two pioneering historical studies were J.A. Mangan and James Walvin (eds), *Manliness and Morality: Middle-Class Masculinity in Britain and America, 1800–1940* (Manchester: Manchester University Press, 1987) and Michael Roper and John Tosh (eds), *Manful Assertions: Masculinities in Britain since 1800* (London: Routledge, 1991). See also Martin Francis, 'The Domestication of the Male? Recent Research on Nineteenth- and Twentieth-Century British Masculinity', *Historical Journal*, 45 (2002), pp. 637–52.
80. Obituary, *The Times*, 15 February 1967.
81. Thelma Cazalet-Keir, *From the Wings: An Autobiography* (London: The Bodley Head, 1967), p. 126.
82. Morgan, 'Lloyd George and Welsh Liberalism', pp. 400–1.
83. Morgan, 'Lloyd George and Welsh Liberalism', pp. 413–14.
84. Jones, 'Major Gwilym Lloyd-George', p. 185.
85. Lloyd-George, 'Autobiography,' NLW, MS 23671C, f. 9.
86. Obituary, *The Times*, 15 February 1967.
87. Lloyd-George, 'Autobiography,' NLW, MS 23671C, f. 12.
88. Quoted in Grigg, *Lloyd George: From Peace to War*, pp. 169, 171.
89. Morgan, *Dictionary of National Biography*, p. 664; See also Jones, 'Major Gwilym Lloyd-George', p. 178.
90. For the letters, written in a mixture of English and Welsh, see 'Lloyd George Family Letters,' NLW, MS 23657E. The quote comes from the letter dated 12 March 1916.
91. *The Times*, 15 February 1967.
92. Morgan, *Dictionary of National Biography*, p. 666.
93. Beddoe, 'Images of Welsh Women'. This is effectively the identity that Richard assigned to Margaret Lloyd George, see Gwynedd, *Dame Margaret*.
94. Jones, *A Radical Life*, p. 44.
95. Quoted in Jones, *A Radical Life*, p. 61.
96. Quoted in Jones, *A Radical Life*, p. 61.

97. Undated *New York Tribune* press cutting, Megan Lloyd George, Notes of Tour, NLW, MS 23265D, f. 117. Megan received a number of letters from men she had never met declaring their love for her.

98. Price, *Megan Lloyd George*, p. 21.

99. See Lesley A. Hall, 'Impotent Ghosts from No Man's Land, Flappers' Boyfriends or Crypto-Patriarchs? Men, Sex and Social Change in 1920s Britain', *Social History*, 21 (1996), pp. 54–70. The press attention combined hostility with fascination.

100. 'Broadcast speech,' 13 May 1929, Megan Lloyd George Papers, NLW, MS 20483C.

101. Quoted in Jones, *A Radical Life*, pp. 74–5.

102. Jones, *A Radical Life*, p. 75.

103. See Foot's letter to *The Times*, 17 May 1966.

104. *Daily Mail*, 1 November 1935, in Press Cuttings, 1935–1937, Megan Lloyd George Papers, NLW, MS 20488E. Welsh was not of course 'a strange tongue' in the context of rural mid- and north Wales.

105. House of Commons Debates, vol. 385, col. 784, 25 November 1942.

106. Quoted in Jones, *A Radical Life*, p. 179.

107. Jones, *A Radical Life*, p, 148.

108. *Daily Sketch*, 7 June 1940, *Caernarvon and Denbigh Herald*, 25 October 1940, in Press Cuttings, 1 June 1939 to 31 December 1942, Megan Lloyd George Papers, NLW, MS 204490E.

109. Grigg, *Lloyd George: People's Champion*, p. 52.

110. Morgan, *Rebirth*, p. 45.

111. Gwyn A. Williams, *When was Wales? A History of the Welsh* (Harmondsworth: Penguin, 1985), chapter 10.

112. David Lloyd George, *Patriotism and Free Trade*, 1904, in David Feldman, 'Nationality and Ethnicity', in Paul Johnson (ed.), *Twentieth-Century Britain* (London: Longman, 1994), pp. 137–8.

113. Andrew S. Thompson, *Imperial Britain: The Empire in British Politics c. 1880–1932* (Harlow: Pearson, 2000), p. 170.

114. Grigg, *Lloyd George: From Peace to War*, p. 110.

115. See for example, Miles Taylor, 'Imperium et Libertas? Rethinking the Radical Critique of Imperialism during the Nineteenth Century', *Journal of Imperial and Commonwealth History*, 19 (1991), pp. 1–23.

116. Notes of Tour, NLW, MS 23265D, f. 3.

117. Notes of Tour, NLW, MS 23265D, f. 23.

118. *North Wales Chronicle*, 21 May 1937 in Press Cuttings May 1937 to September 1939, Megan Lloyd George Papers, NLW, MS 20489E.

119. *North Wales Chronicle*, 21 May 1937 in Press Cuttings May 1937 to September 1939, Megan Lloyd George Papers, NLW, MS 20489E.

120. *North Wales Chronicle*, 23 October 1936, in Press Cuttings, 1935–1937, Megan Lloyd George Papers, NLW, MS 20488E.

121. Quoted by John Holt, letter to *The Times*, 29 April 1955. Holt, a Liverpool Conservative, was criticising Megan's decision to join Labour.

122. Quoted in Brian Brivati, *Hugh Gaitskell* (London: Richard Cohen, 1996), p. 277.

123. The Conservatives did not field a candidate.

124. Lloyd-George, 'Autobiography,' NLW, MS 23671C, f. 15; 'Notes for speech on foreign policy,' Gwilym Lloyd-George Papers, NLW, MS 23669E.
125. See Lord Beloff, 'The Crisis and Its Consequences for the British Conservative Party', in William Roger Louis and Roger Owen (eds), *Suez 1956: The Crisis and Its Consequences* (Oxford: Clarendon, 1991), pp. 319–34.
126. Speech on Suez, October 1956, Gwilym Lloyd-George Papers, NLW, MS 23669E.
127. 'Speech on Suez,' St Pancras Town Hall, 3 December 1956, Gwilym Lloyd-George Papers, NLW, MS 23669E.
128. Lloyd-George, 'Autobiography,' NLW, MS 23671C, f. 10.
129. Speech at Freedom of the City of Cardiff, 28 October 1956, Gwilym Lloyd-George Papers, NLW, MS 23669E, ff. 39–52.

Chapter 7

1. Richard Weight, *Patriots: National Identity in Britain, 1940–2000* (Basingstoke: Pan, 2003), p. 127.
2. Huw T. Edwards, *Hewn from the Rock* (Cardiff: Western Mail and TWW, 1967). It had previously been published in two volumes in Welsh, as *Tros y Tresi* (1956) and *Troi'r Drol* (1963).
3. Edwards, *Hewn from the Rock*, p. 12.
4. Edwards, *Hewn from the Rock*, p. 15.
5. Edwards, *Hewn from the Rock*, pp. 42–3, 44–45. See Kenneth O. Morgan, *Rebirth of a Nation: A History of Modern Wales* (Oxford: Oxford University Press, 1982), pp. 145–9 for the deterioration of industrial relations.
6. Edwards, *Hewn from the Rock*, pp. 42–3, 45.
7. Edwards, *Hewn from the Rock*, p. 46.
8. ILP, *Annual Conference Report*, 1915, p. 10.
9. Paul Ward, *Red Flag and Union Jack: Englishness, Patriotism and the British Left, 1881–1924* (Woodbridge: Royal Historical Society/Boydell, 1998), p. 127.
10. Gervase Phillips, 'Dai Bach Y Soldiwr: Welsh Soldiers in the British Army, 1914–1918,' *Llafur*, 6 (1993), pp. 94–105.
11. Edwards, *Hewn from the Rock*.
12. Edwards, *Hewn from the Rock*, p. 58.
13. Edwards, *Hewn from the Rock*, p. 78.
14. See D.W. Howell and C. Baber, 'Wales', in F.M.L. Thompson (ed.), *The Cambridge Social History of Britain 1750–1950 Volume I Regions and Communities* (Cambridge: Cambridge University Press, 1990), pp. 307–9.
15. Edwards, *Hewn from the Rock*, pp. 92–3.
16. 'Flintshire Election Special: Cyril O. Jones,' Huw T. Edwards Papers C3, National Library of Wales (NLW). The leaflet is headed 'Gleanings by H.T. Edwards.'
17. Edwards, *Hewn from the Rock*, p. 109.
18. Kenneth O. Morgan, *Modern Wales: Politics, Places and People* (Cardiff: University of Wales Press, 1995), p. 18.
19. Kenneth O. Morgan, 'Power and the Glory: War and Reconstruction, 1939–1951,' in Duncan Tanner, Chris Williams and Deian Hopkin (eds),

The Labour Party in Wales, 1900–2000 (Cardiff: University of Wales Press, 2000), p. 178.

20. See, for example, Steven Fielding, Peter Thompson and Nick Tiratsoo, *'England Arise!' The Labour Party and Popular Politics in 1940s Britain* (Manchester: Manchester University Press, 1995) and Ralph Miliband, *Parliamentary Socialism*, second edition (London: Merlin, 1972).

21. See R. Merfyn Jones and Ioan Rhys Jones, 'Labour and the Nation,' in Tanner, Williams and Hopkin, *The Labour Party in Wales*, pp. 248–9.

22. Huw T. Edwards, *What I Want for Wales* (Carmarthen: Druid Press, 1949), p. 4. This pamphlet was a reprint of an article published in January 1944. It embarrassed Edwards because he had criticized 'the cant and hypocrisy' of Welsh religion. As chairman of the Council of Wales such comments were politically uncomfortable.

23. Edwards, *What I Want for Wales*, p. 4.

24. Quoted in Jones and Jones, 'Labour and the Nation,' pp. 249–50.

25. Jones and Jones, 'Labour and the Nation', pp. 249–50.

26. Huw T. Edwards, 'The Problems of Wales,' Huw T. Edwards Papers A4/1, NLW.

27. Huw T. Edwards, 'The Problems of Wales,' Huw T. Edwards Papers A4/1, NLW.

28. Huw T. Edwards, 'An Open Letter to the Prime Minister and the Cabinet,' Huw T. Edwards Papers A4/3, NLW.

29. Huw T. Edwards, 'An Open Letter to the Prime Minister and the Cabinet,' Huw T. Edwards Papers A4/3, NLW.

30. Morgan, *Modern Wales*, p. 13.

31. 'Council for Wales and Monmouthshire, Note on Constitution', c. 1952, Huw T. Edwards Papers C4, NLW.

32. Mervyn Jones, *A Radical Life: The Biography of Megan Lloyd George* (London: Hutchinson, 1991), p. 235; Edwards, *Hewn from the Rock*, p. 125.

33. Morgan, 'Power and the Glory,' p. 181.

34. Jones and Jones, 'Labour and the Nation,' p. 251.

35. 'Notes of Speeches 1945–51,' Huw T. Edwards Papers C3, NLW.

36. Edwards, *Hewn from the Rock*, p. 129.

37. Edwards, *Hewn from the Rock*, p. 149.

38. Huw T. Edwards to Sir David Maxwell-Fyfe, 4 July 1952, Huw T. Edwards Papers A2/67, NLW.

39. Huw T. Edwards to Henry Brooke, 13 November 1957, Huw T. Edwards Papers A2/124, NLW.

40. Edwards, *Hewn from the Rock*, p. 150.

41. Jones and Jones, 'Labour and the Nation,' p. 251.

42. 'Personal Statement by Alderman H.T. Edwards', 24 October 1958, Huw T. Edwards Papers E10, NLW.

43. 'Personal Statement by Alderman H.T. Edwards', 24 October 1958, Huw T. Edwards Papers E10, NLW.

44. Peter Stead, 'The Labour Party and the Claims of Wales,' in John Osmond (ed.), *The National Question Again: Welsh Political Identity in the 1980s* (Llandusyl: Gomer, 1985), p. 106.

45. Alan Butt Philip, *The Welsh Question: Nationalism in Welsh Politics 1945–1970* (Cardiff: University of Wales Press, 1975), p. 282.

46. Quoted in Butt Philip, *The Welsh Question*, p. 283.
47. *The Times*, 7 August 1959.
48. Edwards, *Hewn from the Rock*, p. 165.
49. Weight, *Patriots*, p. 127.
50. Duncan Tanner, 'Facing the Challenge: Labour and Politics 1970–2000,' in Tanner, Williams and Hopkin, *The Labour Party in Wales*, p. 268.
51. Edwards, *Hewn from the Rock*, p. 165.
52. Edwards, *Hewn from the Rock*. This is the title of chapter 2 of Book II.
53. Gwynfor Evans to Huw T. Edwards, 15 February 1959, Huw T. Edwards Papers A1/521, NLW.
54. Huw T. Edwards to Lord Kilmuir, 9 October 1958, Huw T. Edwards Papers A2/127, NLW.
55. Edwards, *Hewn from the Rock*, p. 167.
56. Welsh Board of Directors TWW Ltd, *Wales: Today and Tomorrow: A Symposium of Views* (n.p.: TWW, 1960), p. 1.
57. See D. Gareth Evans, *A History of Wales 1906–2000* (Cardiff: University of Wales Press, 2000), pp. 264–78 for cultural activities and Welsh in the post-war period. Evans points out that by the 1980s monoglot English speakers in Wales were poorly served by the TV channels, with only 24 hours a week of English language programmes being produced for the four-fifths of the population who are English-speaking (p. 277).
58. Morgan, *Rebirth*, pp. 383–4.
59. Results from Morgan, *Rebirth*, pp. 381, 385.
60. Edwards, *Hewn from the Rock*, p. 157.
61. Huw T. Edwards to Ray [?], 15 June 1962, Huw T. Edwards to Emrys Roberts, n.d., Huw T. Edwards Papers A2/144, A2/132, NLW.
62. Huw T. Edwards to Gwynfor Evans, 6 October 1962, Huw T. Edwards Papers A2/145, NLW.
63. George Brown to Huw T. Edwards, 24 June 1964; Harold Wilson to Huw T. Edwards, 7 October 1964, Huw T. Edwards Papers A1/797, A1/806, NLW.
64. James Griffiths, *Pages from Memory* (London: J.M. Dent, 1969).
65. Edwards, *Hewn from the Rock*, p. 236.
66. Huw T. Edward to Eirene White, 25 March 1968, Huw T. Edwards Papers A2/162, NLW.
67. 'Notes of Speeches, 1945–51,' Huw T. Edwards Papers, C6, NLW.
68. Edwards, *Hewn from the Rock*, p. 144.
69. 'Visits to USA 1958 and Patagonia 1965,' Huw T. Edwards Papers C10, NLW. See also Edwards, *Hewn from the Rock*, chapters 8 and 9 for East Germany and Russia, chapters 6 and 7 for the USA.
70. 'This Capital Business,' Talks on Radio folder, Huw T. Edwards Papers, E4, NLW.
71. *Official Programme Souvenir of the Festival of Wales May–Oct. 1968*, NLW ex. 1047.
72. Weight, *Patriots*, p. 277.
73. Edwards to Winston Churchill, 25 June 1945, Huw T. Edwards Papers, A2/2, NLW. He turned down subsequent honours, see e.g. Edwards to D.H.F. Ricket, 11 May 1950, Huw T. Edwards Papers, A2/46, NLW.
74. Edwards to William Whitely, 20 February 1947, Huw T. Edwards Papers, A2/10, NLW.

75. Edwards to F. Blaise Gillie, 10 October 1958, Huw T. Edwards Papers, A2/128, NLW.
76. Edwards to H.A. Strutt, 8 September 1952, Huw T. Edwards Papers, A2/69, NLW.
77. Edwards to H.A. Strutt, 24 October 1952, Huw T. Edwards Papers, A2/71, NLW.
78. See Griffiths, *Pages from Memory*, pp. 183–4.
79. Jones, *A Radical Life*, p. 320; Morgan, *Rebirth*, p. 386.
80. Quoted in Weight, *Patriots*, p. 412.
81. Griffiths, *Pages from Memory*, p. 202: 'I watched the children at play and was delighted to see how well they looked. What a transformation higher living standards, supplemented by the expansion of the social services, have wrought in children's physique. The mid-morning milk and the midday school meal are some of the best investments the nation ever made. I am proud of these children of the Welfare State.'
82. Butt Philip, *The Welsh Question*, pp. 286–7.
83. Morgan, *Rebirth*, pp. 390–1.
84. George Thomas, Viscount Tonypandy, *My Wales* (London: Century, 1986), p. 104.
85. Butt Philip, *The Welsh Question*, p. 292.
86. Edwards, *Hewn from the Rock*, p. 235.

Chapter 8

1. House of Commons Debates, vol. 127, cols 989–90, 29 March 1920, in Patrick Buckland, *Irish Unionism 2: Ulster Unionism and the Origins of Northern Ireland, 1886–1922* (Dublin: Gill and Macmillan, 1973), pp. 116–17.
2. Gillian McIntosh, *The Force of Culture: Unionist Identities in Twentieth-Century Ireland* (Cork: Cork University Press, 1999), pp. 1–2.
3. Following James Loughlin, I use 'statelet' not in a pejorative sense but because 'it seems appropriate to an entity which, while having many of the attributes of independence, lacked constitutional independence': *The Ulster Question since 1945* (Basingstoke: Macmillan, 1998), p. xii.
4. Quoted in Jonathan Bardon, *A History of Ulster* (Belfast: Blackstaff, 1992), p. 513. See also David Officer, 'In Search of Order, Permanence and Stability: Building Stormont, 1921–32', in Richard English and Graham Walker (eds), *Unionism in Modern Ireland: New Perspectives on Politics and Culture* (Basingstoke: Macmillan, 1996), pp. 130–47 and James Loughlin, 'Consolidating "Ulster": Regime Propaganda and Architecture in the Inter-war Period', *National Identities*, 1 (1999), pp. 161–77.
5. Jack Santino, *Signs of War and Peace* (New York: Palgrave, 2001).
6. D. George Boyce and Alan O'Day, 'The Union: Introduction', in D. George Boyce and Alan O'Day (eds), *Defenders of the Union: A Survey of British and Irish Unionism since 1801* (London: Routledge, 2001), p. 7.
7. This section is based on, among other works, Paul Bew, *Ideology and the Irish Question: Ulster Unionism and Irish Nationalism 1912–1916* (Oxford: Clarendon, 1994); D. George Boyce, *Nationalism in Ireland*, second edition (London: Routledge, 1991) and Alvin Jackson, *Ireland 1798–1998: Politics and War* (Oxford: Blackwell, 1999).

8. See Thomas Hennessey, *Dividing Ireland: World War 1 and Partition* (London: Routledge, 1998), p. 22.
9. Speech in Manchester 14 March 1915, press cutting, National Library of Ireland, MS7450.
10. For a repudiation of the 'place apart' epithet see D. George Boyce, 'Northern Ireland: A Place Apart?' in Eamonn Hughes (ed.), *Culture and Politics in Northern Ireland 1960–1990* (Milton Keynes: Open University Press, 1991), pp. 13–25.
11. Patrick Buckland, *The Factory of Grievances: Devolved Government in Northern Ireland 1921–39* (Dublin: Gill and Macmillan, 1979), p. 30.
12. For the argument that the nationalist parties in Northern Ireland were in fact frequently Catholic parties see Michael Farrell, *Northern Ireland: The Orange State* (London: Pluto, 1976), p. 116.
13. Eamon Phoenix, *Northern Nationalism: Nationalist Politics, Partition and the Catholic Minority in Northern Ireland 1890–1940* (Belfast: Ulster Historical Foundation, 1994).
14. Alvin Jackson, 'Irish Unionism, 1870–1922', in Boyce and O'Day, *Defenders of the Union*, p. 121. See also Patrick Buckland, *Irish Unionism 1: The Anglo-Irish and the New Ireland, 1885–1922* (Dublin: Gill and Macmillan, 1972).
15. Patrick Buckland, *Irish Unionism 1885–1922* (London: Historical Association, 1973), pp. 39–40.
16. D.G. Boyce, '"The Marginal Britons": The Irish,' in Robert Colls and Philip Dodd (eds), *Englishness: Politics and Culture 1880–1920* (London: Croom Helm, 1986), p. 233.
17. See Keith Jeffery (ed.), *'An Irish Empire'? Aspects of Ireland and the British Empire* (Manchester: Manchester University Press, 1996).
18. Quoted in Buckland, *Irish Unionism 2*, p. xxx.
19. This withdrawal was never complete.
20. F.S.L. Lyons, *Ireland since the Famine* (London: Fontana, 1973), p. 221.
21. Alvin Jackson, 'Unionist Myths 1912–1985', *Past and Present*, 136 (1992), p. 164.
22. The gendered nature of Ulster Unionism is discussed in chapter 10 below.
23. This section relies on James Loughlin, *Ulster Unionism and British National Identity since 1885* (London: Pinter, 1995), pp. 78–84 and Keith Jeffery, *Ireland and the Great War* (Cambridge: Cambridge University Press, 2000), pp. 56–7, 133–4. See also Adrian Gregory and Senia Paseta (eds), *Ireland and the Great War: 'A War to Unite Us All?'* (Manchester: Manchester University Press, 2002).
24. Loughlin, *Ulster Unionism*, p. 83.
25. David W. Miller, *Queen's Rebels: Ulster Loyalism in Historical Perspective* (Dublin: Gill and Macmillan, 1978).
26. Loughlin, *Ulster Unionism*, p. 228.
27. Graham Walker, *A History of the Ulster Unionist Party: Protest, Pragmatism and Pessimism* (Manchester: Manchester University Press, 2004), p. 284.
28. Arthur Aughey, *Under Siege: Ulster Unionism and the Anglo-Irish Agreement* (London: Hurst, 1989), chapter 1.
29. See Ian McBride, 'Ulster and the British Problem', in English and Walker, *Unionism in Modern Ireland*, pp. 1–18 and Paul Ward, *Britishness since 1870* (London: Routledge, 2004). As a contemporary example, Aughey's

defence of Unionism happily takes up Bikhu Parekh's reworking of British-ness as a civic identity that can accommodate ethnic identities: *Under Siege*, p. 18.

30. Patrick Buckland, 'A Protestant State: Unionists in Government, 1921–39', in Boyce and O'Day, *Defenders of the Union*, p. 218.

31. *Belfast Telegraph*, 23 November 1959, in Andrew Gailey, *Crying in the Wilderness: Jack Sayers, A Liberal Editor in Ulster, 1939–1969* (Belfast: Institute of Irish Studies, Queen's University Belfast, 1995), p. 57. See also Walker, *A History of the Ulster Unionist Party*.

32. Andrew Gailey, 'The Destructiveness of Constructive Unionism: Theories and Practice, 1890s–1960s', in Boyce and O'Day, *Defenders of the Union*, pp. 227–50.

33. Gailey, 'The Destructiveness of Constructive Unionism', p. 236.

34. Thomas Hennessey, *A History of Northern Ireland 1920–1996* (Basingstoke: Macmillan, 1997), p. 11.

35. See Buckland, *Factory of Grievances*, p. 72.

36. Quoted in Hennessey, *History of Northern Ireland*, p. 64.

37. Paul Bew, Peter Gibbon and Henry Patterson, *Northern Ireland 1921–1994: Political Forces and Social Classes* (London: Serif, 1995). See also Bob Purdie, 'The Demolition Squad: Bew, Gibbon and Patterson on the Northern Ireland State', in Seán Hutton and Paul Stewart (eds), *Ireland's Histories: Aspects of State, Society and Ideology* (London: Routledge, 1991), pp. 164–76.

38. British Conservatives also feared the working class electorate after 1918 for the same reasons, see David Jarvis, 'British Conservatism and Class Politics in the 1920s', *English Historical Review*, 111 (1996), pp. 59–84.

39. Bew, Gibbon and Patterson, *Northern Ireland*, p. 56.

40. Loyal and patriotic workers, often ex-servicemen, were important in post-war politics throughout the British Empire, see for example Raymond Evans, *Loyalty and Disloyalty: Social Conflict on the Queensland Homefront, 1914–1918* (Sydney: Allen and Unwin, 1987).

41. Bardon, *History of Ulster*, p. 479.

42. Hennessey, *A History of Northern Ireland*, pp. 45–6.

43. Hennessey, *A History of Northern Ireland*, p. 15. Craig used this slogan in 1921.

44. Hennessey, *A History of Northern Ireland*, p. 45.

45. Brian Barton, 'Northern Ireland: The Impact of War, 1939–45', in Brian Girvin and Geoffrey Roberts (eds), *Ireland and the Second World War: Politics, Society and Remembrance* (Dublin: Four Courts, 2000), p. 74.

46. *Belfast Newsletter*, 27 November 1947, quoted in Bew, Gibbon and Patterson, *Northern Ireland*, pp. 103–4.

47. Quoted in Hennessey, *History of Northern Ireland*, p. 98. See also Brian Barton, 'The Impact of World War II on Northern Ireland and Belfast-London Relations', in Peter Catterall and Sean McDougall (ed.), *The Northern Ireland Question in British Politics* (Basingstoke: Macmillan, 1996), pp. 61–66 and Peter Rose, *How the Troubles Came to Northern Ireland* (Basingstoke: Palgrave, 2001), pp. 1–8.

48. Churchill's comment in vol. 2 of his *History of the Second World War*, quoted in Loughlin, *Ulster Unionism*, p. 139.

49. Loughlin, *The Ulster Question*, p. 23.

50. Bew, Gibbon and Patterson, *Northern Ireland*, chapter 3.
51. Bardon, *History of Ulster*, p. 689.

Chapter 9

1. There was also a Conservative inheritance within the Labour Party, which had less sympathy for Irish nationalism. See Martin Pugh, 'The Rise of Labour and the Political Culture of Conservatism, 1890–1945', *History*, 87 (2002), pp. 514–37.
2. Michael Farrell, *Northern Ireland: The Orange State* (London: Pluto, 1976) is an influential narrative of working-class Unionism as the product of the manipulation of capitalist and landowning interests. For a discussion of the schools of labour historiography in Northern Ireland see Terry Cradden, *Trade Unionism, Socialism and Partition: The Labour Movement in Northern Ireland 1939–1953* (Belfast: December, 1993), chapter 1.
3. Henry Patterson, *Class Conflict and Sectarianism: The Protestant Working Class and the Belfast Labour Movement 1868–1920* (Belfast: Blackstaff, 1980), p. xi.
4. Austen Morgan, *Labour and Partition: The Belfast Working Class 1905–23* (London: Pluto, 1991) p. 324.
5. Speech in Portadown, *Belfast Telegraph*, 25 February 1957. This episode is discussed later in this chapter.
6. Graham Walker, *The Politics of Frustration: Harry Midgley and the Failure of Labour in Northern Ireland* (Manchester: Manchester University Press, 1985). I owe a great debt to Walker's book.
7. Winston Churchill's successful leadership during the Second World War acted to rehabilitate his political reputation despite his leaving the Conservative Party in 1903 and the Liberal Party in the 1920s.
8. See for example, E. Rumpf and A.C. Hepburn, *Nationalism and Socialism in Twentieth Century Ireland* (Liverpool: Liverpool University Press, 1977), p. 200.
9. The appendices on 'Individuals' and 'Organisations' in Farrell, *Northern Ireland* provide a valuable source for the varied organizational forms of nationalism and unofficial Unionism in the six counties.
10. Walker, *The Politics of Frustration*, p. 3.
11. For Walker see Morgan, *Labour and Partition*, chapter 4.
12. *Irish News*, 15 January 1906, quoted in Patterson, *Class Conflict and Sectarianism*, pp. 55–6.
13. Walker, *The Politics of Frustration*, p. 7; John Gray, 'Turncoat or Evangel? Harry Midgley and Ulster Labour', *Saothar*, 12 (1987), pp. 58–62.
14. Paul Ward, *Red Flag and Union Jack: Englishness, Patriotism and the British Left, 1881–1924* (Woodbridge: Royal Historical Society/Boydell, 1998), p. 145.
15. Labour Party National Executive Committee Minutes, 16 October 1917.
16. The scheme failed through disputes with anti-war socialists and confusion about what was to be commemorated. The sheer number of appeals for public subscriptions in the immediate post-war period must also have had an impact. See Ward, *Red Flag and Union Jack*, p. 169.

17. Thomas Hennessey, *Dividing Ireland: World War 1 and Partition* (London: Routledge, 1998) provides a nuanced interpretation of the impact of war on national identities in Ireland.
18. Harry Midgley, *Thoughts from Flanders* (Belfast: privately published, 1924), p. 35.
19. Midgley, *Thoughts from Flanders*, pp. 20–1.
20. C. Fitzpatrick, 'Nationalising the Ideal: Labour and Nationalism in Ireland, 1909–1923', in Eugenio Biagini (ed.), *Citizenship and Community: Liberals, Radicals and Collective Identities in the British Isles, 1865–1931* (Cambridge: Cambridge University Press, 1996), pp. 276–304.
21. Farrell, *Northern Ireland*, p. 27.
22. Walker, *The Politics of Frustration*, p. 18.
23. Quoted in Farrell, *Northern Ireland*, p. 67.
24. Walker, *The Politics of Frustration*, p. 20.
25. Walker, *Politics of Frustration*, p. 20.
26. *Forward*, 13 October 1923, quoted in Walker, *The Politics of Frustration*, p. 28.
27. Farrell, *Northern Ireland*, p. 107; Walker, *The Politics of Frustration*, p. 31.
28. Walker, *The Politics of Frustration*, p. 50.
29. Walker, *The Politics of Frustration*, p. 30. For Labour's emphasis of its war service see Ward, *Red Flag and Union Jack*, pp. 169–70.
30. Geoffrey Bell, *Troublesome Business: The Labour Party and the Irish Question* (London: Pluto, 1982), pp. 38–9.
31. Ward, *Red Flag and Union Jack*, p. 186.
32. Terry Cradden, 'Labour in Britain and the Northern Ireland Labour Party, 1900–70', in Peter Catterall and Sean McDougall (ed.), *The Northern Ireland Question in British Politics* (Basingstoke: Macmillan, 1996), p. 74. For the imperial standard, see also Ward, *Red Flag and Union Jack*, p. 70.
33. Cradden, 'Labour in Britain and the NILP', p. 75.
34. For the state of the Northern Irish economy and the outdoor relief riots see Jonathan Bardon, *A History of Ulster* (Belfast: Blackstaff, 1992), pp. 526–9.
35. Farrell, *Northern Ireland*, pp. 125–32, discusses the campaign and riots as an example of working class unity around a single economic issue.
36. Thomas Hennessey, *A History of Northern Ireland 1920–1996* (Basingstoke: Macmillan, 1997), p. 61.
37. *Forward*, 22 October 1932, quoted in Walker, *The Politics of Frustration*, p. 63.
38. Northern Ireland House of Commons Debates, vol. 17, col. 147, 22 November 1934.
39. Bardon, *A History of Ulster*, p. 541.
40. See, for example, Farrell, *Northern Ireland*, pp. 136–42; Bardon, *A History of Ulster*, pp. 538–9.
41. Gray, 'Turncoat or Evangel?' p. 12. Farrell provides a hostile view of Midgley in 1935, suggesting that his holiday of that year was conveniently timed to remove him from the need to make a political statement on events: *Northern Ireland*, p. 146n.
42. See, for example, his declaration that 'a sectarian nature is not confined to one side of this House,' Northern Ireland House of Commons Debates, vol. 17, col. 141, 22 November 1934. In the same debate he accused the nationalists of seeking to drive him from public life: col. 142.

43. Quoted in Walker, *The Politics of Frustration*, p. 99. See also Harry Midgley, *Give Labour a Chance* (Belfast: NILP, 1937), pp. 4, 6.
44. Gray, 'Turncoat or Evangel?' p. 12.
45. Harry Midgley, *Spain: The Press, the Pulpit and the Truth* (Belfast: privately published, 1936).
46. Walker, *The Politics of Frustration*, p. 106.
47. In 1933 he won the seat with 4893 votes to the Unionists' 3685. In 1938 the result was Unionist 3578; Nationalist 2891; NILP (Midgley) 1923.
48. Alvin Jackson, 'Irish Unionists and the Empire, 1880–1920: Classes and Masses', in Keith Jeffery (ed.), *'An Irish Empire'? Aspects of Ireland and the British Empire* (Manchester: Manchester University Press, 1996), pp. 123–47.
49. Sonya O. Rose, *Which People's War? National Identity and Citizenship in Wartime Britain* (Oxford: Oxford University Press, 2003), chapter 7, picks the reality of the 'people's war' apart. See also Wendy Webster, *Englishness and Empire, 1939–65* (Oxford: Oxford University Press, forthcoming).
50. Harry Midgley, 'Northern Ireland Reactions to the First Year of War', draft typescript of radio broadcast, Harry Midgley Papers, Public Record Office of Northern Ireland (PRONI), D/4089/3/1/1.
51. Harry Midgley, 'Northern Ireland Reactions to the First Year of War', draft typescript of radio broadcast, Harry Midgley papers, PRONI, D/4089/3/1/1.
52. Harry Midgley, 'Personal Reactions to First Year of War', broadcast script, 27 September 1940, PRONI, D/4089/3/1/3.
53. Graham Walker, 'The Commonwealth Labour Party in Northern Ireland, 1942–7', *Irish Historical Studies*, 24 (1984), pp. 69–90, provides a very full account of Midgley's estrangement from the NILP. See also Walker, *The Politics of Frustration*, chapter 7.
54. Hennessey, *A History of Northern Ireland*, pp. 91–2.
55. James Loughlin, *Ulster Unionism and British National Identity since 1885* (London: Pinter, 1995), p. 132.
56. For the air raids see Bardon, *A History of Ulster*, pp. 568–73; for the political crisis see Brian Barton, 'Northern Ireland: The Impact of War, 1939–45', in Brian Girvin and Geoffrey Roberts (eds), *Ireland and the Second World War: Politics, Society and Remembrance* (Dublin: Four Courts Press, 2000), pp. 47–75.
57. Quoted in Walker, *The Politics of Frustration*, p. 126.
58. Walker, *The Politics of Frustration*, p. 129.
59. The 'Declaration' is reproduced in Walker, *The Politics of Frustration*, pp. 222–3.
60. Quoted in Walker, *The Politics of Frustration*, p. 135.
61. Because of his expulsion from the NILP he was removed from his post in the National Union of Distributive and Allied Workers. He replied 'That such action should be taken against one whose only crime has been that he has endeavoured to build up closer association between Northern Ireland and Great Britain in the stress of war's adversity is almost beyond comprehension': Harry Midgley to J. Hallsworth, 18 February 1943, Harry Midgley papers, PRONI, D/4089/1/1/5.
62. Quoted in Walker, 'The Commonwealth Labour Party', p. 71.
63. Northern Ireland House of Commons Debates, vol. 26, col. 228, 9 March 1943.

64. Hennessey, *A History of Northern Ireland*, p. 92.
65. Bardon, *A History of Ulster*, p. 579.
66. Walker, 'The Commonwealth Labour Party', p. 75.
67. Quoted in Paul Bew, Peter Gibbon and Henry Patterson, *Northern Ireland 1921–1994: Political Forces and Social Classes* (London: Serif, 1995), pp. 92–3.
68. Bew, Gibbon and Patterson, *Northern Ireland*, p. 96.
69. Harry Midgley, 'Election Address, June 1945', Harry Midgley papers, PRONI, D/4089/4/1/25.
70. Hennessey, *A History of Northern Ireland*, p. 94, Bew, Gibbon and Patterson, *Northern Ireland*, pp. 97–101.
71. Walker, 'The Commonwealth Labour Party', p. 88.
72. *Belfast Newsletter*, 27 September 1947, quoted in Farrell, *Northern Ireland*, p. 192.
73. Farrell, *Northern Ireland*, p. 193.
74. Farrell, *Northern Ireland*, p. 194.
75. *Belfast Telegraph*, 1 July 1947, quoted in Walker, 'The Commonwealth Labour Party', p. 88.
76. Harry Midgley, 'Election Address', October 1953, Harry Midgley Papers, PRONI, D/4089/4/1/32.
77. *The Voice of Ulster*, October 1947, Harry Midgley Papers, PRONI, D/4089/4/1/30.
78. 'Points from a speech at St Anne's Unionist Association', 28 November 1947, Harry Midgley papers, PRONI, D/4089/3/5/1.
79. See for example Northern Ireland House of Commons Debates, vol. 30, cols. 2039–42, 15 October 1946.
80. Northern Ireland House of Commons Debates, vol. 17, col. 138, 22 November 1934.
81. For a detailed discussion of education in Northern Ireland see Michael McGrath, *The Catholic Church and Catholic Schools in Northern Ireland: The Price of Faith* (Dublin: Irish Academic Press, 2000).
82. Patrick Shea, *Voices and the Sound of Drums: An Irish Autobiography* (Belfast: Blackstaff, 1981), p. 162. Shea was a Catholic Unionist and senior civil servant.
83. Michael McGrath, 'The Narrow Road: Harry Midgley and Catholic Schools in Northern Ireland', *Irish Historical Studies*, XXX (1997), pp. 429–51.
84. Walker, *The Politics of Frustration*, chapter 10 argues that Midgley was even-handed.
85. Walker, *The Politics of Frustration*, p. 182.
86. 'Points from speech to Bangor Unionists,' 20 March 1952, Harry Midgley papers, PRONI, D/4089/3/9/5.
87. See Loughlin, *Ulster Unionism*, pp. 163–7.
88. Farrell, *Northern Ireland*, p. 204.
89. Hennessey, *A History of Northern Ireland*, pp. 101–7.
90. Henry Patterson, 'Party versus Order: Ulster Unionism and the Flags and Emblems Act', *Contemporary British History*, 12 (1999), pp. 105–29.
91. *Northern Whig*, 20 October 1951, quoted in Patterson, 'Party versus Order', p. 117.
92. Walker, *The Politics of Frustration*, p. 206.
93. *Belfast Telegraph*, 28 February 1957, cutting, Harry Midgley papers, PRONI, D/4089/6/25/11.

94. *Belfast Telegraph*, 29 April 1957, cutting, Harry Midgley Papers, PRONI, D/4089/6/25/11.

Chapter 10

1. Ronald MacNeill, *Ulster's Stand for the Union* (London: John Murray, 1922), p. 37.
2. There are some notable exceptions. See Diane Urquhart, *Women in Ulster Politics 1890–1940: A History Not Yet Told* (Dublin: Irish Academic Press, 2000; Janice Holmes and Diane Urquhart (eds), *Coming Into the Light: The Work, Politics and Religion of Women in Ulster* (Belfast: Institute of Irish Studies, Queen's University Belfast, 1994).
3. Alvin Jackson, 'Irish Unionism, 1870–1922', in D. George Boyce and Alan O'Day (eds), *Defenders of the Union: A Survey of British and Irish Unionism since 1801* (London: Routledge, 2001), p. 127.
4. See Margaret Ward, *Unmanageable Revolutionaries: Women and Irish Nationalism* (London: Pluto, 1983) and Susan Kingsley Kent, *Gender and Power in Britain 1640–1990* (London: Routledge, 1999), pp. 263–6.
5. For clarity this chapter uses Parker's final surname throughout. For a brief biography see R.A. Wilford, 'Parker, Dame Dehra (1882–1963)', *Oxford Dictionary of National Biography*, Oxford University Press, 2004 [accessed 20 October 2004: http://www.oxforddnb.com/view/article/58268].
6. Urquhart, *Women in Ulster Politics*, pp. 182–97 examines Parker's political career up to 1940. My chapter could not have been written without Urquhart's research and analysis. Art Byrne and Sean McMahon, *Great Northerners* (Dublin: Poolbeg, 1991), pp. 194–5 has a two-page outline of Parker's life, which argues that 'she was immensely influential and ensured that when she resigned in 1960, her seat was won by her grandson, Major James Chichester-Clark. The story is also told that she directed that Terence O'Neill, to whom she was related, should succeed Brookeborough as premier and that he in turn should be followed by Chichester-Clarke (which was exactly what happened).' Given that Unionism was becoming increasingly more difficult to control in the 1960s and early 1970s these are unlikely scenarios.
7. See Paul Ward, *Britishness since 1870* (London: Routledge, 2004), chapter 2.
8. See Jon Lawrence, 'Class and Gender in the Making of Urban Toryism, 1880–1914', *English Historical Review*, 108 (1993), pp. 628–52.
9. See Jose Harris, *Private Lives, Public Spirit: Britain 1870–1914* (London: Penguin, 1994), pp. 27–8.
10. Ian McBride, 'Ulster and the British problem', in R. English and G. Walker (eds), *Unionism in Modern Ireland: New Perspectives on Politics and Culture* (Basingstoke: Macmillan, 1996), p. 7.
11. Urquhart, *Women in Ulster Politics*, p. 51.
12. Jackson points out that the leadership of Ulster Unionism passed away from landed families in the Edwardian period and the role of these families became symbolic: Jackson, 'Irish Unionism', p. 121.
13. Quoted in Urquhart, *Women in Ulster Politics*, pp. 52–3.
14. Ulster Women's Unionist Council minutes, Annual Meeting, 18 January 1912, 'Statement: Ulster's Objections to Home Rule', PRONI, D/1089/1/3.

The minutes of the UWUC and its executive are published in Diane Urquhart (ed.), *The Minutes of the Ulster Women's Unionist Council and Executive Committee* (Dublin: Women's History Project and Irish Manuscripts Commission, 2001).

15. Urquhart, *Women in Ulster Politics*, p. 61.
16. MacNeill, *Ulster's Stand for the Union*, p. 37; Urquhart, *Women in Ulster Politics*, p. 57.
17. Diane Urquhart, '"The Female of the Species is More Deadlier than the Male"? The Ulster Women's Unionist Council, 1911–40', in Holmes and Urquhart, *Coming into the Light*, p. 96.
18. See e.g. UWUC minutes, Annual Meeting, 18 January 1912, PRONI, D/1089/1/3.
19. Quoted in Nancy Kinghan, *United We Stood: The Official History of the Ulster Women's Unionist Council 1911–1974* (Belfast: Appletree, 1975), pp. 16–17.
20. Quoted in Kinghan, *United We Stood*, p. 21.
21. Northern Ireland House of Commons Debates, vol. 8, col. 2905, 15 November 1927. She was opposing a private member's bill for the equalization of suffrage at 21. See Urquhart, *Women in Ulster Politics*, pp. 187–8.
22. Northern Ireland House of Commons Debates, vol. 8, col. 2906, 15 November 1927.
23. See, for example, UWUC Executive Committee minutes, 17 February 1914, PRONI, D/1098/1/2.
24. Kinghan, *United We Stood*, pp. 32–3. Sphagnum moss, from Irish peat bogs, was beneficial in the treatment of wounds.
25. UWUC Executive Committee minutes, 8 February 1916, PRONI, D/1098/1/2.
26. For the UWUC's list see UWUC Annual Report 1918, PRONI, D/1098/1/3. See also Paul Ward, 'Empire and Everyday: Britishness and Imperialism in Women's Lives in the Great War', British World conference, University of Calgary, July 2003.
27. *The Times*, 29 November 1963.
28. Nicoletta F. Gullace, *"The Blood of Our Sons": Men, Women and the Renegotiation of British Citizenship during the Great War* (New York: Palgrave Macmillan, 2002).
29. See the circular letter from John M. Hamill, secretary of the UWUC, 4 June 1918 appealing for funds to ensure the registration of all unionist women, UWUC Executive Committee minutes, PRONI, D/1098/1/2. See also Urquhart, 'The Female of the Species', p. 109.
30. UWUC Executive Committee minutes, 25 January 1921, quoted in Urquhart, 'The Female of the Species', p. 109. See also Urquhart, *Women in Ulster Politics*, p. 73.
31. UWUC Executive Committee minutes, 2 November 1920 and 7 December 1920, PRONI D/1098/1/2. In fact, due to her husband's illness and death she did not travel to London on this occasion. Her only son had died in 1920.
32. UWUC Executive Committee minutes, Annual Report 1926 and meeting 5 April 1927, PRONI, D.1098/1/2.
33. Maedhbh McNamara and Paschal Mooney, *Women in Parliament: Ireland 1918–2000* (Dublin: Wolfhound, 2000), p. 222.
34. Speech in Belfast, 1927, quoted in Urquhart, *Women in Ulster Politics*, p. 188.

35. Northern Ireland House of Commons Debates, vol. 4, col. 10, 11 March 1924.
36. South Down and south Armagh, close to the border with the Irish Free State had Catholic majorities.
37. See Patrick Buckland, *The Factory of Grievances: Devolved Government in Northern Ireland 1921–39* (Dublin: Gill and Macmillan, 1979), p. 232.
38. Northern Ireland House of Commons Debates, vol. 2, cols. 1046–7, 17 October 1922. See Bardon, *A History of Ulster*, pp. 499–500; Hennessey, *A History of Northern Ireland*, p. 44.
39. Michael Farrell, *Northern Ireland: The Orange State* (London: Pluto, 1976), pp. 83–5 provides a damning critique of gerrymandering.
40. See, for example, Northern Ireland House of Commons Debates, vol. 4, col. 13, 11 March 1921.
41. Northern Ireland House of Commons Debates, vol. 8, cols. 4119–20, 8 December 1927.
42. Northern Ireland House of Commons Debates, vol. 27, col. 266, 22 February 1944.
43. Graham Walker, *A History of the Ulster Unionist Party: Protest, Pragmatism and Pessimism* (Manchester: Manchester University Press, 2004), pp. 124–5. See also John A. Oliver, *Working at Stormont: Memoirs* (Dublin: Institute of Public Administration, 1978), p. 79.
44. Northern Ireland House of Commons Debates, vol. 27, col. 277, 22 February 1944.
45. Northern Ireland House of Commons Debates, vol. 4, col. 11, 11 March 1921; vol. 8, col. 4120, 8 December 1927.
46. Northern Ireland House of Commons Debates, vol. 8, col. 4116, 8 December 1927.
47. Northern Ireland House of Commons Debates, vol. 17, cols. 133–4, 22 November 1934.
48. Northern Ireland House of Commons Debates, vol. 17, cols. 135, 22 November 1934.
49. Northern Ireland House of Commons Debates, vol. 30, cols. 3804–5, 14 January 1947. See also Buckland, *Factory of Grievances*, p. 229.
50. Northern Ireland House of Commons Debates, vol. 17, cols. 135–6, 22 November 1934.
51. The siege mentality was ever present. The UWUC, of which Parker was still a vice-chairman, decided that 'peace and tranquility have been the keynote' of 1927, but warned 'let us not be lulled into any feeling of false security. We must never relax our vigilance': UWUC Executive Committee minutes, annual report, 1927, PRONI, D/1098/1/2.
52. Oliver, *Working at Stormont*, p. 79. As is implied here, Oliver argued that Northern Ireland's civil servants wanted reconciliation of the Catholic population to stabilize the state. This application of 'British' standards was another variant of unionism.
53. This was a comment made by Professor Reverend Robert Corkey, Minister of Education, on Parker as his Parliamentary Secretary, quoted in Urquhart, *Women in Ulster Politics*, p. 195.
54. In 1949 she faced a Nationalist candidate who secured 39.1 per cent of the vote to Parker's 60.9 per cent. The Unionist candidate, Parker's grandson

and later Prime Minister of Northern Ireland, J.D. Chichester-Clark held the seat unopposed until 1969 when he faced the People's Democracy candidate Bernadette Devlin, who secured 38.7 per cent of the vote to Chichester-Clark's 61.3 per cent.

55. Report (Final) of the Committee on Educational Services, Cmd. 15, 1923, quoted in Michael McGrath, *The Catholic Church and the Catholic Schools in Northern Ireland: The Price of Faith* (Dublin: Irish Academic Press, 2000), pp. 54–5.
56. Quoted in McGrath, *The Catholic Church*, p. 98.
57. This paragraph is based on Urquhart, *Women in Ulster Politics*, p. 196. See also McNamara and Mooney, *Women in Parliament*, p. 222.
58. See, for example, Lucy Noakes, *War and the British: Gender and National Identity 1939–1991* (London: IB Tauris, 1998).
59. Kinghan, *United We Stood*, p. 65.
60. Anti-fascism and unemployment encouraged about 42,000 Éire citizens to serve in the British Army during the war. 38,000 men and women from Northern Ireland enlisted: Hennessey, *A History of Northern Ireland*, p. 90.
61. See her statement on the Ministry of Education estimates: Northern Ireland House of Commons Debates, vol. 23, cols. 1290–8, 29 May 1940.
62. See, for example, Harold L. Smith, 'The Effect of War on the Status of Women', in Harold L. Smith (ed.), *War and Social Change: British Society and the Second World War* (Manchester: Manchester University Press, 1986), pp. 208–29.
63. Northern Ireland House of Commons Debates, vol. 23, cols. 1673–4, 25 June 1940. She made no mention of the divisions between Northern Irish women.
64. Quoted in Bardon, *A History of Ulster*, p. 561.
65. See Brian Barton, 'Northern Ireland: The Impact of War, 1939–45', in Brian Girvin and Geoffrey Roberts (eds), *Ireland and the Second World War: Politics, Society and Remembrance* (Dublin: Four Courts, 2000), pp. 47–75.
66. Bardon, *A History of Ulster*, p. 578.
67. Barton, 'Northern Ireland: The Impact of War', pp. 57–8.
68. Northern Ireland House of Commons Debates, vol. 27, cols. 265–6, 22 February 1944.
69. Northern Ireland House of Commons Debates, vol. 27, col. 270, 22 February 1944.
70. Rev. William Corkey, *The Church of Rome and Irish Unrest: How Hatred of Britain is Taught in Irish Schools* (Edinburgh: William Bishop, 1913).
71. Northern Ireland House of Commons Debates, vol. 23, col. 1301, 29 May 1940.
72. See R.J. Lawrence, *The Government of Northern Ireland: Public Finance and Public Services 1921–1964* (Oxford: Clarendon, 1965), p. 118n.
73. htttp://proni.nics.gov.uk/education/ed15.htm, 23 November 2003.
74. Northern Ireland House of Commons Debates, vol. 23, col. 1297, 29 May 1940.
75. Northern Ireland House of Commons Debates, vol. 26, cols. 130, 3 March 1943.
76. Richard Weight, *Patriots: National Identity in Britain 1940–2000* (Basingstoke: Pan, 2003), p. 40.

77. Quoted in McGrath, *The Catholic Church*, p. 147.
78. Ian Hill, 'Arts Administration', in Mark Carruthers and Stephen Douds (eds), *Stepping Stones: The Arts in Ulster 1971–2001* (Belfast: Blackstaff, 2001), pp. 215–17.
79. The main part of the Festival in Northern Ireland was the Farm and Factory Exhibition. See Becky E. Conekin, *'Autobiography of a Nation': The 1951 Festival of Britain* (Manchester: Manchester University Press, 2003), pp. 68–9.
80. *The Times*, 4 May 1951.
81. Quoted in Gillian McIntosh, *The Force of Culture: Unionist Identities in Twentieth Century Ireland* (Cork: Cork University Press, 1999), pp. 149, 154.
82. See E. Estyn Evans, 'Folklife Studies in Northern Ireland', *Journal o f the Folklore Institute*, 2 (1965), pp. 355–63. See also Cab 4/950, 21 October 1954, Cab 4/962, 3 February 1955, PRONI. For Unionist anxieties over the Republic's claim to the history of the whole island see James Loughlin, *Ulster Unionism and British National Identity since 1885* (London: Pinter, 1995), p. 169.
83. Cab 4/884, October 1952, PRONI.
84. McGrath, *The Catholic Church*, p. 134.
85. Terence O'Neill, *The Autobiography of Terence O'Neill: Prime Minister of Northern Ireland 1963–1969* (London: Rupert Hart-Davies, 1972), p. 34.
86. Oliver, *Working at Stormont*, p. 79. The absence of private papers for Parker means that her foreign travel remains closed to historical study.
87. Walker, *A History of the Ulster Unionist Party*, p. 284.
88. Walker, *A History of the Ulster Unionist Party*, p. 140.
89. In 1960 unemployment in Scotland was 3.4 per cent of the workforce while that in Northern Ireland was 6.7 per cent: Paul Bew, Peter Gibbon and Henry Patterson, *Northern Ireland 1921–1994: Political Forces and Social Classes* (London: Serif, 1995), p. 118.
90. Bew, Gibbon and Patterson, *Northern Ireland*, pp. 113–14.
91. Some of the following section is based on Feargal Cochrane, '"Meddling at the Crossroads": The Decline and Fall of Terence O'Neill within the Unionist Community', in Richard English and Graham Walker (eds), *Unionism in Modern Ireland: New Perspectives on Politics and Culture* (Basingstoke: Macmillan, 1996), pp. 148–68.
92. Loughlin, *Ulster Unionism*, p. 181.
93. Vernon Bogdanor, *Devolution in the United Kingdom* (Oxford: Oxford University Press, 2001), p. 81.
94. Quoted in Hennessey, *A History of Northern Ireland*, p. 135.

Conclusion

1. In Scotland, the SNP received about 28 per cent of the vote in 1999 and 22 per cent in 2003. In Wales, Plaid Cymru got 29.5 per cent in 1999 and 20.5 per cent in 2003.
2. I owe this phrase to the anonymous reader of my book proposal for Palgrave.
3. Keith Robbins, 'This Grubby Wreck of Old Glories": The United Kingdom and the End of the British Empire', in his *History, Religion and Identity in Modern Britain* (London: Hambledon, 1993), p. 292.

4. Enoch Powell might be considered as an example of an English politician deeply disturbed by the end of empire, but he was never representative in more than individual aspects of his outbursts. He consoled himself that 'The nationhood of the mother country remained unaltered through it all [Empire], almost unconscious of the strange fantastic structure built around her': quoted in Michael Fry, *The Scottish Empire* (Edinburgh: Tuckwell and Birlinn, 2001), p. 497.
5. Kenneth O. Morgan, 'England, Britain and the Audit of War,' *Transactions of the Royal Historical Society*, 6th series, 7 (1997), p. 140.

Bibliography

Primary Sources

Manuscript Sources
National Library of Scotland
Arthur Donaldson Papers, Acc. 6038.
Thomas Johnston Papers, Acc. 5862.
Walter Elliot and 'Baffy' Dugdale Letters, Acc. 12198.
Walter Elliot Papers, Acc. 6721.
Walter Elliot Papers, Acc. 12267.
Scottish National War Memorial folder, Acc. 4714.
The Scottish Secretariat, Acc. 3721.
2nd Baron Tweedsmuir Papers, National Library of Scotland, Acc. 11628.
Lady Priscilla Tweedsmuir Papers, Acc. 11884 (formerly Dep. 337).

Public Record Office of Northern Ireland
Cab 4 files.
Harry Midgley Papers, D/4089.
Ulster Women's Unionist Council Executive Committee minutes, D/1098/1/2.
Ulster Women's Unionist Council minutes, D/1089/1/3.

National Library of Wales
Huw T. Edwards Papers.
Sir E. Vincent Evans Papers.
Lloyd-George Family Letters, MS 23657E.
Gwilym Lloyd-George Papers, MS 23671C, MS 23669E.
Letters to Gwilym Lloyd-George 1914–68, MS 23668E.
Megan Lloyd George Papers, MS 20941E, MS 20483C, MS 20488E, MS 20489E, MS 20490E.
Megan Lloyd George, Notes of Tour, MS 23265D.

Government and Institutional Sources
House of Commons Debates.
House of Lords Debates.
ILP, *Annual Conference Report*, 1915.
Labour Party National Executive Committee Minutes (microfilm).
National Library of Ireland, Volume of Press Cuttings MS 7450.
Northern Ireland House of Commons Debates.
Diane Urquhart (ed.), *The Minutes of the Ulster Women's Unionist Council and Executive Committee* (Dublin: Women's History Project and Irish Manuscripts Commission, 2001).
Welsh Board of Directors TWW Ltd. *Wales: Today and Tomorrow: A symposium of Views* (n.p.: TWW, 1960).

Published Diaries, Memoirs and Letters

Ball, Stuart (ed.), *Parliament and Politics in the Age of Churchill and Attlee: The Headlam Diaries 1935–51* (Cambridge: Royal Historical Society, 1999).

Cazalet-Keir, Thelma, *From the Wings: An Autobiography* (London: The Bodley Head, 1967).

Edwards, Huw T., *Hewn from the Rock* (Cardiff: Western Mail and TWW, 1967).

Gailey, Andrew, *Crying in the Wilderness: Jack Sayers, A Liberal Editor in Ulster, 1939–1969* (Belfast: Institute of Irish Studies, Queen's University Belfast, 1995).

Griffiths, James, *Pages from Memory* (London: J.M. Dent, 1969).

Grimond, Jo, *Memoirs* (London: Heinemann, 1979).

Viscount Gwynedd, *Dame Margaret: The Life Story of His Mother* (London: George Allen and Unwin, 1947).

Johnston, Thomas, *Memories* (London: Collins, 1952).

Macmillan, Harold, *Tides of Fortune 1945–1955* (London: Macmillan, 1969).

Morgan, Kenneth O. (ed.), *Lloyd George Family Letters 1885–1936* (Cardiff and London: University of Wales Press and Oxford University Press, 1973).

Oliver, John A., *Working at Stormont: Memoirs* (Dublin: Institute of Public Administration, 1978).

O'Neill, Terence, *The Autobiography of Terence O'Neill: Prime Minister of Northern Ireland 1963–1969* (London: Rupert Hart-Davies, 1972).

Pimlott, Ben (ed.), *The Second World War Diary of Hugh Dalton* (London: Jonathan Cape, 1986).

Rhodes James, Robert (ed.), *Chips: The Diaries of Sir Henry Channon* (London: Weidenfeld, 1993).

Rose, N.A. (ed.), *Baffy: The Diaries of Blanche Dugdale 1936–1947* (London: Mitchell, 1973).

Shea, Patrick, *Voices and the Sound of Drums: An Irish Autobiography* (Belfast: Blackstaff, 1981).

Thomas, George, Viscount Tonypandy, *My Wales* (London: Century, 1986).

Tweedsmuir, Lord, *Always a Countryman*, second edition (London: Robert Hale, 1971 [1955]).

Tweedsmuir, Lord, *One Man's Happiness* (London: Robert Hale, 1968).

Contemporary Books and Articles

'Cato', *Guilty Men* (London: Victor Gollancz, 1940).

Atholl, Duke of, *Narrative of the Scottish National War Memorial Scheme* (Edinburgh: privately published, 1923).

Balfour, A.J., *Nationality and Home Rule* (London: Longmans, Green and Co., 1913).

Corkey, Rev. William, *The Church of Rome and Irish Unrest: How Hatred of Britain is Taught in Irish Schools* (Edinburgh: William Bishop, 1913).

Edwards, Huw T., *What I Want for Wales* (Carmarthen: Druid Press, 1949).

Edwards, H.W.J., *What is Welsh Nationalism?* Second edition (Cardiff: Plaid Cymru, 1954).

Elliot, Walter, 'East Wind – West Wind: Stevenson, Scotland and the South Seas,' *Geographical Magazine*, December 1950.

Elliot, Walter, 'Scottish Politics,' in the Duke of Atholl (ed.), *A Scotsman's Heritage* (London: Alexander Maclehose, 1932).

Elliot, Walter, 'The New Empire: I. Lessons from the Files,' *The Times*, 6 May 1929.

Elliot, Walter, 'The New Empire: II. Novelty in Africa,' *The Times*, 7 May 1929.
Elliot, Walter, 'The New Empire: IV. And so to England,' *The Times*, 10 May 1929.
Elliot, Walter, *Long Distance* (London: Constable, 1943).
Elliot, Walter, *Toryism and the Twentieth Century* (London: Philip Allan, 1927).
Johnston, Thomas, *Our Scots Noble Families* (Glendarvel: Argyll Publishing, 1999 [1909]).
Johnston, Thomas, *The History of the Working Classes in Scotland* (Wakefield: EP Publishing, 1974, reprint of fourth edition, 1946 [1920]).
Johnston, Thomas, *The Financiers and the Nation* (London: Methuen, 1934).
Lewis, Saunders, 'The Case for Welsh Nationalism,' *The Listener*, 13 May 1936.
Midgley, Harry, *Give Labour a Chance* (Belfast: NILP, 1937).
Midgley, Harry, *Spain: The Press, the Pulpit and the Truth* (Belfast: privately published, 1936).
Midgley, Harry, *Thoughts from Flanders* (Belfast: privately published, 1924).
National Eisteddfod Court, *Yr Eisteddfod/The Eisteddfod*, (n.p., n.d.)
Pottinger, George, *The Secretaries of State for Scotland 1926–76* (Edinburgh: Scottish Academic Press, 1979).
Smith, Paul (ed.), *Lord Salisbury on Politics: A Selection from his Articles in the Quarterly Review, 1860–1883* (Cambridge: Cambridge University Press, 1972).
The Empire Club of Canada Speeches 1960–1961, Toronto, The Empire Club Foundation, 1960, at http://www.empireclubfoundation.com, 2 December 2003.

Newspapers (some of these were consulted from press clippings files).

The Times
Forward
Scots Pictorial, 17 August 1918.
Observer, 17 November 1946.
Belfast Telegraph, 25 February 1957.
Evening Standard, 11 July 1972.
Daily Mail, 5 December 1972.
Daily Record, 13 March 1944.

Secondary Sources

Adam Smith, Janet, *John Buchan: A Biography* (London: Rupert Hart Davis, 1965).
Andrews, David and Jeremy Howell, 'Transforming into a Tradition: Rugby and the Making of Imperial Wales, 1890–1914', in Ian G. Ingham and John W. Loy (eds), *Sport in Social Development: Traditions, Transitions, and Transformations* (Champaign, Ill., Human Kinetics, 1993), pp. 77–96.
Aubel, Felix, 'The Conservatives in Wales, 1880–1935,' in Martin Francis and Ian Zweiniger-Bargielowska (eds), *The Conservatives and British Society* (Cardiff: University of Wales Press, 1996), pp. 96–110.
Aughey, Arthur, *Under Siege: Ulster Unionism and the Anglo-Irish Agreement* (London: Hurst, 1989).

Aughey, Arthur, *Nationalism, Devolution and the Challenge to the United Kingdom* (London: Pluto, 2001).

Bardon, Jonathan, *A History of Ulster* (Belfast: Blackstaff, 1992).

Barton, Brian, 'Northern Ireland: The Impact of War, 1939–45', in Brian Girvin and Geoffrey Roberts (eds), *Ireland and the Second World War: Politics, Society and Remembrance* (Dublin: Four Courts, 2000), pp. 47–75.

Barton, Brian, 'The Impact of World War II on Northern Ireland and Belfast-London Relations', in Peter Catterall and Sean McDougall (ed.), *The Northern Ireland Question in British Politics* (Basingstoke: Macmillan, 1996), pp. 47–70.

Beddoe, Deirdre, 'Images of Welsh Women', in Tony Curtis (ed.), *Wales: The Imagined Nation Studies in Cultural and National Identity* (Bridgend: Poetry Wales Press, 1986), pp. 227–38.

Bell, Geoffrey, *Troublesome Business: The Labour Party and the Irish Question* (London: Pluto, 1982).

Beloff, Lord, 'The Crisis and Its Consequences for the British Conservative Party', in William Roger Louis and Roger Owen (eds), *Suez 1956: The Crisis and Its Consequences* (Oxford: Clarendon, 1991), pp. 319–34.

Bew, Paul, *Ideology and the Irish Question: Ulster Unionism and Irish Nationalism 1912–1916* (Oxford: Clarendon, 1994).

Bew, Paul, Peter Gibbon and Henry Patterson, *Northern Ireland 1921–1994: Political Forces and Social Classes* (London: Serif, 1995).

Biagini, Eugenio F. (ed.), *Citizenship and Community: Liberals, Radicals and Collective Identities in the British Isles, 1865–1931* (Cambridge: Cambridge University Press, 1996).

Biagini, Eugenio, *Gladstone* (Basingstoke: Macmillan, 2000).

Bogdanor, Vernon, 'Devolution,' in Layton-Henry, Zig (ed.), *Conservative Party Politics* (London: Macmillan, 1981), pp. 75–94.

Bogdanor, Vernon, *Devolution in the United Kingdom* (Oxford: Oxford University Press, 2001).

Boyce, D. George, '"The Marginal Britons": The Irish,' in Robert Colls and Philip Dodd (eds), *Englishness: Politics and Culture 1880–1920* (London: Croom Helm, 1986), pp. 230–53.

Boyce, D. George, 'Northern Ireland: A Place Apart?' in Eamonn Hughes (ed.), *Culture and Politics in Northern Ireland 1960–1990* (Milton Keynes: Open University Press, 1991), pp. 13–25.

Boyce, D. George, *Nationalism in Ireland*, second edition (London: Routledge, 1991).

Boyce, D. George and Alan O'Day (eds), *Defenders of the Union: A Survey of British and Irish Unionism since 1801* (London: Routledge, 2001).

Brand, Jack, *The National Movement in Scotland* (London: Routledge and Kegan Paul, 1978).

Bridge, Carl and Kent Fedorowich (eds), *The British World: Diaspora, Culture and Identity* (London: Frank Cass, 2003).

Brivati, Brian, *Hugh Gaitskell* (London: Richard Cohen, 1996).

Brown, Gordon, *Maxton* (Glasgow: Fontana, 1988).

Buckland, Patrick, *Irish Unionism 1: The Anglo-Irish and the New Ireland, 1885–1922* (Dublin: Gill and Macmillan, 1972).

Buckland, Patrick, *Irish Unionism 1885–1922* (London: Historical Association, 1973).

Buckland, Patrick, *Irish Unionism 2: Ulster Unionism and the Origins of Northern Ireland, 1886–1922* (Dublin: Gill and Macmillan, 1973).

Buckland, Patrick, *The Factory of Grievances: Devolved Government in Northern Ireland 1921–39* (Dublin: Gill and Macmillan, 1979).

Buckland, Patrick, 'A Protestant State: Unionists in Government, 1921–39', in D. George Boyce and Alan O'Day (eds), *Defenders of the Union: A Survey of British and Irish Unionism since 1801* (London: Routledge, 2001), pp. 211–26.

Buckner, P.A. and Carl Bridge, 'Reinventing the British World', *The Round Table*, 368 (2003), pp. 77–88.

Burton, Antoinette, *Burdens of History: British Feminists, Indian Women, and Imperial Culture, 1865–1915* (Chapel Hill: University of North Carolina Press, 1994).

Butler, Chris, 'The Conservative Party in Wales: Remoulding a Radical Tradition', in John Osmond (ed.), *The National Question Again: Welsh Political Identity in the 1980s* (Llandusyl: Gomer, 1985), pp. 155–66.

Butt Philip, Alan, *The Welsh Question: Nationalism in Welsh Politics 1945–1970* (Cardiff: University of Wales Press, 1975).

Byrne, Art and Sean McMahon, *Great Northerners* (Dublin: Poolbeg, 1991).

Checkland, Sydney and Olive, *Industry and Ethos: Scotland 1832–1914* (London: Edward Arnold, 1984).

Cochrane, Feargal, '"Meddling at the Crossroads": The Decline and Fall of Terence O'Neill within the Unionist Community', in Richard English and Graham Walker (eds), *Unionism in Modern Ireland: New Perspectives on Politics and Culture* (Basingstoke: Macmillan, 1996), pp. 148–68.

Colley, Linda, *Britons: Forging the Nation 1707–1837* (London: Pimlico, 1994).

Colls, Robert, *Identity of England* (Oxford: Oxford University Press, 2002).

Conekin, Becky E., *'Autobiography of a Nation': The 1951 Festival of Britain* (Manchester: Manchester University Press, 2003).

Constantine, Stephen, '"Bringing the Empire Alive": The Empire Marketing Board and Imperial Propaganda 1926–33,' in MacKenzie, John M. (ed.), *Imperialism and Popular Culture* (Manchester: Manchester University Press, 1986), pp. 192–231.

Coote, Colin, *A Companion of Honour: The Story of Walter Elliot* (London: Collins, 1965).

Corr, Helen, 'Where is the Lass o'Pairts?: Gender, Identity and Education in Nineteenth Century Scotland,' in Dauvit Broun, Finlay, R.J. and Lynch, Michael (eds), *Image and Identity: The Making and Re-making of Scotland through the Ages* (Edinburgh: John Donald, 1998), pp. 220–8.

Cradden, Terry, *Trade Unionism, Socialism and Partition: The Labour Movement in Northern Ireland 1939–1953* (Belfast: December, 1993).

Cradden, Terry, 'Labour in Britain and the Northern Ireland Labour Party, 1900–70', in Peter Catterall and Sean McDougall (ed.), *The Northern Ireland Question in British Politics* (Basingstoke: Macmillan, 1996), pp. 71–87.

Darwin, John, 'The Fear of Falling: British Politics and Imperial Decline since 1900', *Transactions of the Royal Historical Society*, 5th series, 36 (1986), pp. 27–43.

Darwin, John, *Britain and Decolonisation: The Retreat from Empire in the Post-War World* (Basingstoke: Macmillan, 1988).

Davies, Brian, 'Empire and Identity: The "Case" of Dr William Price', in David Smith (ed.), *A People and a Proletariat: Essays in the History of Wales 1780–1980* (London: Pluto, 1980), pp. 72–93.

Davies, D. Hywell, *The Welsh Nationalist Party 1925–1945: A Call to Nationhood* (Cardiff: University of Wales Press, 1983).

Davies, Norman, *The Isles: A History* (Basingstoke: Papermac, 2000).

Devine, T.M. and Finlay R.J. (eds), *Scotland in the Twentieth Century* (Edinburgh: Edinburgh University Press, 1996).

Devine, T.M., *The Scottish Nation 1700–2000* (London: Allen Lane, 1999).

Donnachie, Ian, Christopher Harvie and Ian S. Wood (eds), *Forward! Labour Politics in Scotland 1888–1988* (Edinburgh: Polygon, 1989).

Douds, G., 'Tom Johnston in India', *Journal of the Scottish Labour History Society*, 19 (1984), pp. 6–21.

Douglas, Roy, *The History of the Liberal Party 1895–1970* (London: Sidgwick and Jackson, 1971).

Elliott, Sydney, *Northern Ireland Parliamentary Election Results 1921–1972* (Chichester: Political Reference Publications, 1973).

Ellis, John S., 'Reconciling the Celt: British National Identity, Empire, and the 1911 Investiture of the Prince of Wales', *Journal of British Studies*, 37 (1998), pp. 391–418.

English, Richard, and Graham Walker (eds), *Unionism in Modern Ireland: New Perspectives on Politics and Culture* (Basingstoke: Macmillan, 1996).

Evans, E. Estyn, 'Folklife Studies in Northern Ireland', *Journal of the Folklore Institute*, 2 (1965), pp. 355–63.

Evans, Neil, 'Introduction: Identity and Integration in the British Isles', in Neil Evans (ed.), *National Identity in the British Isles* (Harlech: Coleg Harlech, 1989), pp. 6–22.

Evans, Raymond, *Loyalty and Disloyalty: Social Conflict on the Queensland Homefront, 1914–1918* (Sydney: Allen and Unwin, 1987).

Evans, Gareth D., *A History of Wales 1906–2000* (Cardiff: University of Wales Press, 2000).

Farrell, Michael, *Northern Ireland: The Orange State* (London: Pluto, 1976).

Feldman, David, 'Nationality and Ethnicity', in Paul Johnson (ed.), *Twentieth-Century Britain* (London: Longman, 1994), pp. 127–48.

Fielding, Steven, Peter Thompson and Nick Tiratsoo, *'England Arise!' The Labour Party and Popular Politics in 1940s Britain* (Manchester: Manchester University Press, 1995).

Finlay, Richard J., '"For or Against?" Scottish Nationalists and the British Empire, 1919–39', *Scottish Historical Review*, 71 (1992), pp. 184–206.

Finlay, Richard J., 'National Identity in Crisis: Politicians, Intellectuals and the "End of Scotland", 1920–1939,' *History*, 79 (1994), pp. 242–59.

Finlay, Richard J., 'Scotland in the Twentieth Century: In Defence of Oligarchy?' *Scottish Historical Review*, LXXIII (1994), pp. 103–12.

Finlay, Richard J., 'Continuity and Change: Scottish Politics 1900–45,' in T.M. Devine and R.J. Finlay (eds), *Scotland in the Twentieth Century* (Edinburgh: Edinburgh University Press, 1996), pp. 64–84.

Finlay, Richard J., 'Scottish Conservatism and Unionism since 1918', in Martin Francis and Ina Zweiniger-Bargielowska (eds), *The Conservatives and British Society* (Cardiff: University of Wales Press, 1996), pp. 111–26.

Finlay, Richard J., *A Partnership for Good? Scottish Politics and the Union since 1880* (Edinburgh: John Donald 1997).

Finlay, Richard J., 'Unionism and Dependency Culture: Politics and State Intervention in Scotland, 1918–1997', in Catriona M.M. Macdonald (ed.), *Unionist Scotland 1800–1997* (Edinburgh: John Donald, 1998), pp. 100–16.

Finlay, Richard J., 'The Rise and Fall of Popular Imperialism in Scotland 1850–1950', *Scottish Geographical Magazine,* 113 (1997), pp. 13–21.

Finlay, Richard, 'New Britain, New Scotland, New History? The Impact of Devolution on the Development of Scottish Historiography', *Journal of Contemporary History,* 36 (2001), pp. 383–93.

Foster, John, 'The Twentieth Century, 1914–1979,' in R.A. Houston and W.W.J. Knox (eds), *The New Penguin History of Scotland From the Earliest Times to the Present Day* (London: Penguin, 2002), pp. 417–93.

Francis, Martin, 'The Domestication of the Male? Recent Research on Nineteenth- and Twentieth-Century British Masculinity', *Historical Journal,* 45 (2002), pp. 637–52.

Fry, Michael, *The Scottish Empire* (Edinburgh: Tuckwell and Birlinn, 2001).

Gailey, Andrew, 'The Destructiveness of Constructive Unionism: Theories and Practice, 1890s–1960s', in D. George Boyce and Alan O'Day (eds), *Defenders of the Union: A Survey of British and Irish Unionism since 1801* (London: Routledge, 2001), pp. 227–50.

Gray, John, 'Turncoat or Evangel? Harry Midgley and Ulster Labour', *Saothar,* 12 (1987), pp. 58–62.

Gregory, Adrian, and Senia Paseta (eds), *Ireland and the Great War: 'A War to United Us All?'* (Manchester: Manchester University Press, 2002).

Grigg, John, *Lloyd George: The People's Champion 1902–1911* (London: Eyre Methuen, 1978).

Grigg, John, *Lloyd George: From Peace to War 1912–1916* (London: Methuen, 1985).

Gullace, Nicoletta F., *"The Blood of Our Sons": Men, Women and the Renegotiation of British Citizenship during the Great War* (New York: Palgrave Macmillan, 2002).

Gupta, Partha Sarathi, *Imperialism and the British Labour Movement, 1914–1964* (London: Macmillan, 1975).

Hall, Lesley A., 'Impotent Ghosts from No Man's Land, Flappers' Boyfriends or Crypto-Patriarchs? Men, Sex and Social Change in 1920s Britain', *Social History,* 21 (1996), pp. 54–70.

Harris, Jose, *Private Lives, Public Spirit: Britain 1870–1914* (London: Penguin, 1994).

Harvie, Christopher, 'Scottish Politics', in A. Dickson and J.H. Treble (eds), *People and Society in Scotland Volume III 1914–1990* (Edinburgh: John Donald, 1992), pp. 241–60.

Harvie, Christopher, *Scotland and Nationalism: Scottish Society and Politics 1707–1994,* second edition (London: Routledge, 1994).

Harvie, Christopher, 'The Moment of British Nationalism, 1939–1970', *Political Quarterly,* 71 (2000), pp. 328–40.

Haseler, Stephen, *The English Tribe: Identity, Nation and Europe* (Basingstoke: Macmillan, 1996).

Hennessey, Thomas, *A History of Northern Ireland 1920–1996* (Basingstoke: Macmillan, 1997).

Hennessey, Thomas, *Dividing Ireland: World War 1 and Partition* (London: Routledge, 1998).

Hill, Christopher and Christopher Lloyd, 'The Foreign Policy of the Heath Government,' in Stuart Ball and Anthony Seldon (eds), *The Heath Government 1970–74: A Reappraisal* (London: Longman, 1996), pp. 285–314.

Hill, Christopher, *Cabinet Decisions on Foreign Policy: The British Experience October 1938–June 1941* (Cambridge: Cambridge University Press, 1991).

Hill, Ian, 'Arts Administration', in Mark Carruthers and Stephen Douds (eds), *Stepping Stones: The Arts in Ulster 1971–2001* (Belfast: Blackstaff, 2001).

Holmes, Janice, and Diane Urquhart (eds), *Coming Into the Light: The Work, Politics and Religion of Women in Ulster* (Belfast: Institute of Irish Studies, Queen's University Belfast, 1994).

Howe, Stephen, *Anti colonialism in British Politics: The Left and the End of Empire, 1918–1964* (Oxford: Clarendon, 1993).

Howell, David, *British Workers and the Independent Labour Party 1888–1906* (Manchester: Manchester University Press, 1983).

Howell, David, *A Lost Left: Three Studies in Socialism and Nationalism* (Manchester: Manchester University Press, 1986).

Howell, D.W. and C. Baber, 'Wales', in F.M.L. Thompson (ed.) *The Cambridge Social History of Britain 1750–1950 Volume I Regions and Communities* (Cambridge: Cambridge University Press, 1990), pp. 281–354.

htttp://proni.nics.gov.uk/education/ed15.htm, 23 November 2003.

Hutchinson, I.G.C., *A Political History of Scotland 1832–1924* (Edinburgh: John Donald, 1986).

Hutchinson, I.G.C., 'Scottish Unionism between the Two World Wars', in Catriona M.M. Macdonald (ed.), *Unionist Scotland 1800–1997* (Edinburgh: John Donald, 1998).

Hutchinson, I.G.C., *Scottish Politics in the Twentieth Century* (Basingstoke: Palgrave, 2001), pp. 73–99.

Jackson, Alvin, 'Irish Unionism, 1870–1922', in D. George Boyce and Alan O'Day (eds), *Defenders of the Union: A Survey of British and Irish Unionism since 1801* (London: Routledge, 2001), pp. 115–36.

Jackson, Alvin, 'Irish Unionists and the Empire, 1880–1920: Classes and Masses', in Keith Jeffery (ed.), *'An Irish Empire'? Aspects of Ireland and the British Empire* (Manchester: Manchester University Press, 1996), pp. 123–47.

Jackson, Alvin, 'Unionist Myths 1912–1985', *Past and Present*, 136 (1992), pp. 164–85.

Jackson, Alvin, *Ireland 1798–1998: Politics and War* (Oxford: Blackwell, 1999).

Jalland, Patricia 'United Kingdom Devolution 1910–14: Political Panacea or Tactical Diversion?' *Economic History Review*, 4 (1979), pp. 757–85.

Jarvis, David, 'British Conservatism and Class Politics in the 1920s', *English Historical Review*, 111 (1996), pp. 59–84.

Jeffery, Keith, *Ireland and the Great War* (Cambridge: Cambridge University Press, 2000).

Jeffery, Keith (ed.), *'An Irish Empire'? Aspects of Ireland and the British Empire* (Manchester: Manchester University Press, 1996).

Jenkins, Geraint H. and Mari A. Williams (eds), *'Let's Do Our Best for the Ancient Tongue': The Welsh Language in the Twentieth Century* (Cardiff: University of Wales Press, 2000).

Jones, Aled and Bill Jones, 'The Welsh World and the British Empire, c. 1851–1939: An Exploration', in Carl Bridge and Kent Fedorowich (eds), *The British World: Diaspora, Culture and Identity* (London: Frank Cass, 2003), pp. 57–81.

Jones, J. Graham, 'The Parliament for Wales Campaign, 1950–1956,' *Welsh History Review*, 16 (1992–3), pp. 207–36.

Jones, J. Graham, 'A Breach in the Family: The Lloyd Georges', *Journal of Liberal Democrat History*, 25 (1999–2000), pp. 34–39.

Jones, J. Graham, 'Dame Margaret Lloyd George, The Norway Debate and the Fall of Neville Chamberlain', *The National Library of Wales Journal*, 31 (1999–2000), pp. 423–32.

Jones, J. Graham, 'Major Gwilym Lloyd-George, First Viscount Tenby (1894–1967),' *National Library of Wales Journal*, 32 (2001), pp. 177–204.

Jones, Mervyn, *A Radical Life: The Biography of Megan Lloyd George* (London: Hutchinson, 1991).

Jones, R. Merfyn and Ioan Rhys Jones, 'Labour and the Nation,' in Duncan Tanner, Chris Williams and Deian Hopkin (eds), *The Labour Party in Wales, 1900–2000* (Cardiff: University of Wales Press, 2000), pp. 241–63.

Joyce, Patrick, *Visions of the People: Industrial England the Politics of Class, 1848–1914* (Cambridge: Cambridge University Press, 1994).

Keating, Michael and David Bleiman, *Labour and Scottish Nationalism* (London: Macmillan, 1979).

Kellas, James, 'The Party in Scotland,' in Seldon, Anthony and Ball, Stuart (eds), *Conservative Century: The Conservative Party since 1900* (Oxford: Oxford University Press, 1994), pp. 671–93.

Kellas, James G. 'Scottish Nationalism', in David Butler and Michael Pinto-Duchinsky (eds), *The British General Election of 1970* (London: Macmillan, 1971), pp. 446–62.

Kendle, John, *Federal Britain: A History* (London: Routledge, 1997).

Kent, Susan Kingsley, *Gender and Power in Britain 1640–1990* (London: Routledge, 1999).

Kidd, Colin, 'Race, Empire and the Limits of Nineteenth-Century Scottish Nationhood', *Historical Journal*, 46 (2003), pp. 873–92.

Kinghan, Nancy, *United We Stood: The Official History of the Ulster Women's Unionist Council 1911–1974* (Belfast: Appletree, 1975).

Knox, W.W., *Industrial Nation: Work, Culture and Society in Scotland 1800–Present* (Edinburgh: Edinburgh University Press, 1999).

Knox, William (ed.), *Scottish Labour Leaders 1918–1939* (Edinburgh: Mainstream, 1984).

Kumar, Krishan, *The Making of English National Identity* (Cambridge: Cambridge University Press, 2003).

Lawrence, Jon, 'Class and Gender in the Making of Urban Toryism, 1880–1914', *English Historical Review*, 108 (1993), pp. 628–52.

Lawrence, R.J., *The Government of Northern Ireland: Public Finance and Public Services 1921–1964* (Oxford: Clarendon, 1965).

Lentin, A., *Lloyd George and the Lost Peace: From Versailles to Hitler, 1919–1940* (Basingstoke: Palgrave, 2001).

Levitt, Ian (ed.), *The Scottish Office: Depression and Reconstruction 1919–1959* (Edinburgh: Scottish History Society, 1992).

Levy, Carl, 'Education and Self-Education: Staffing the Early ILP', in Carly Levy (ed.), *Socialism and the Intelligentsia 1880–1914* (London: Routledge and Kegan Paul, 1987) pp. 135–210.

Loughlin, James, *Ulster Unionism and British National Identity since 1885* (London: Pinter, 1995).

Loughlin, James, 'Consolidating "Ulster": Regime Propaganda and Architecture in the Inter-war Period', *National Identities*, 1 (1999), pp. 161–77.

Loughlin, James, *The Ulster Question since 1945* (Basingstoke: Macmillan, 1998).

Lynch, Michael (ed.), *The Oxford Companion to Scottish History* (Oxford: Oxford University Press, 2001).

Lynch, Michael, *Scotland: A New History* (London: Century, 1991).

Lyons, F.S.L., *Ireland since the Famine* (London: Fontana, 1973).

MacArthur, Colin, 'The Dialectic of National Identity: The Glasgow Empire Exhibition of 1938,' in Bennet, Tony, Mercer, Colin, and Woollacott, Janet (eds), *Popular Culture and Social Relations* (Milton Keynes: Open University Press, 1986), pp. 117–34.

Macdonald, Catriona M.M. (ed.), *Unionist Scotland 1800–1997* (Edinburgh: John Donald, 1998).

Macdonald, Catriona M.M. and E.W. McFarland (eds), *Scotland and the Great War* (Edinburgh: Tuckwell, 1999).

MacKenzie, John M., '"The Second City of the Empire": Glasgow – Imperial Municipality,' in Felix Driver and David Gilbert (eds), *Imperial Cities: Landscape, Display and Identity* (Manchester: Manchester University Press, 1999), pp. 215–37.

MacKenzie, John M., 'The Imperial Pioneer and Hunter and the Masculine Stereotype in Late Victorian and Edwardian Times', in J.A. Mangan and James Walvin (eds), *Manful Assertions: Masculinities in Britain since 1800* (London: Routledge, 1991), pp. 178–98.

MacKenzie, John M., 'Empire and National Identities: The Case of Scotland', *Transactions of the Royal Historical Society*, 6th series, 8 (1998), pp. 215–31.

MacNeill, Ronald, *Ulster's Stand for the Union* (London: John Murray, 1922).

Maguire, G.E., *Conservative Women: A History of Women and the Conservative Party, 1874–1997* (Basingstoke: Macmillan, 1998).

Mangan, J.A., and James Walvin (eds), *Manliness and Morality: Middle-Class Masculinity in Britain and America, 1800–1940* (Manchester: Manchester University Press, 1987).

Marquand, David, 'How United is the Modern United Kingdom?', in Alexander Grant and Keith Stringer (eds), *Uniting the Kingdom: The Making of British History* (London: Routledge, 1995), pp. 277–91.

McBride, Ian, 'Ulster and the British Problem', in Richard English and Graham Walker, *Unionism in Modern Ireland* (London: Routledge, 2004), pp. 1–18

McCaffrey, John F., 'The Origins of Liberal Unionism in the West of Scotland', *Scottish Historical Review*, 50 (1971), pp. 47–71.

McGrath, Michael, 'The Narrow Road: Harry Midgley and Catholic Schools in Northern Ireland', *Irish Historical Studies*, XXX (1997), pp. 429–51.

McGrath, Michael, *The Catholic Church and Catholic Schools in Northern Ireland: The Price of Faith* (Dublin: Irish Academic Press, 2000).

McIntosh, Gillian, *The Force of Culture: Unionist Identities in Twentieth-Century Ireland* (Cork: Cork University Press, 1999).

McKibbin, Ross, 'Class and Conventional Wisdom: The Conservative Party and the "Public" in Inter-war Britain', in his *Ideologies of Class* (Oxford: Oxford University Press, 1991), pp. 259–93.

McLean, Iain, *The Legend of Red Clydeside* (Edinburgh: John Donald, 1983).

McNamara, Maedhbh and Paschal Mooney, *Women in Parliament: Ireland 1918–2000* (Dublin: Wolfhound, 2000).

McWilliam, Rohan, *Popular Politics in Nineteenth-Century England* (London: Routledge, 1998).

Miliband, Ralph, *Parliamentary Socialism*, second edition (London: Merlin, 1972).

Millar, Gordon F., 'Elliot, Walter Elliot (1888–1958)', *Oxford Dictionary of National Biography*, Oxford University Press, 2004 [accessed 20 October 2004: http://www.oxforddnb/view/article/33003].

Miller, David W., *Queen's Rebels: Ulster Loyalism in Historical Perspective* (Dublin: Gill and Macmillan, 1978).

Mitchell, James, *Conservatives and the Union: A Study of Conservative Party Attitudes to Scotland* (Edinburgh: Edinburgh University Press, 1990).

Mitchell, James, 'Contemporary Unionism', in Catriona M.M. Macdonald (ed.), *Unionist Scotland 1800–1997* (Edinburgh: John Donald, 1998), pp. 117–39.

Morgan, Austen, *Labour and Partition: The Belfast Working Class 1905–23* (London: Pluto, 1991).

Morgan, Kenneth O., *Rebirth of a Nation: A History of Modern Wales* (Oxford: Oxford University Press, 1982).

Morgan, Kenneth O., 'Lloyd George and Welsh Liberalism,' in his *Modern Wales: Politics, Places and People* (Cardiff: University of Wales Press, 1995), pp. 400–18.

Morgan, Kenneth O., 'England, Britain and the Audit of War,' *Transactions of the Royal Historical Society*, 6th series, 7 (1997), pp. 131–53.

Morgan, Kenneth O., 'Power and the Glory: War and Reconstruction, 1939–1951,' in Duncan Tanner, Chris Williams and Deian Hopkin (eds), *The Labour Party in Wales, 1900–2000* (Cardiff: University of Wales Press, 2000), pp. 166–88.

Morton, Graeme, *Unionist-Nationalism: Governing Urban Scotland, 1830–1860* (East Linton: Tuckwell, 1999).

Nairn, Tom, *The Break-up of Britain, Crisis and Neo-Nationalism* (London: New Left Books, 1977), second edition (London: Verso, 1981).

Noakes, Lucy, *War and the British: Gender and National Identity 1939–1991* (London: IB Tauris, 1998).

Officer, David, 'In Search of Order, Permanence and Stability: Building Stormont, 1921–32', in Richard English and Graham Walker (eds), *Unionism in Modern Ireland: New Perspectives on Politics and Culture* (Basingstoke: Macmillan, 1996), pp. 130–47.

Parker, R.A.C., *Chamberlain and Appeasement: British Policy and the Coming of the Second World War* (Basingstoke: Macmillan, 1993).

Patterson, Henry, *Class Conflict and Sectarianism: The Protestant Working Class and the Belfast Labour Movement 1868–1920* (Belfast: Blackstaff, 1980).

Patterson, Henry, 'Party versus Order: Ulster Unionism and the Flags and Emblems Act', *Contemporary British History*, 12 (1999), pp. 105–29.

Peters, A.R., *Anthony Eden at the Foreign Office 1931–1938* (Aldershot: Gower, 1986).

Phillips, Gervase, 'Dai Bach Y Soldiwr: Welsh Soldiers in the British Army, 1914–1918,' *Llafur*, 6 (1993), pp. 94–105.

Phoenix, Eamon, *Northern Nationalism: Nationalist Politics, Partition and the Catholic Minority in Northern Ireland 1890–1940* (Belfast: Ulster Historical Foundation, 1994).

Pittock, Murray G.H., *Scottish Nationality* (Basingstoke: Palgrave, 2001).

Powell, David, *Nationhood and Identity: The British State since 1800* (London: IB Tauris, 2002).

Price, Emyr, *Megan Lloyd George* (Caernarfon: Gwynedd Archives Service, 1983).

Procida, Mary A., 'Good Sports and Right Sorts: Guns, Gender, and Imperialism in British India,' *Journal of British Studies*, 40 (2001), pp. 454–88.

Pugh, Martin, 'The Rise of Labour and the Political Culture of Conservatism, 1890–1945', *History*, 87 (2002), pp. 514–37.

Purdie, Bob, 'The Demolition Squad: Bew, Gibbon and Patterson on the Northern Ireland State', in Seán Hutton and Paul Stewart (eds), *Ireland's Histories: Aspects of State, Society and Ideology* (London: Routledge, 1991), pp. 164–76.

Ramsden, John, *The Age of Balfour and Baldwin 1902–1940: A History of the Conservative Party* (London: Longman, 1978).

Ramsden, John, *The Age of Churchill and Eden 1940–1957, A History of the Conservative Party* (London: Longman, 1995).

Ramsden, John, *The Winds of Change: Macmillan to Heath, 1957–1975* (Harlow: Longman, 1996).

Robbins, Keith, *Nineteenth-Century Britain: England, Scotland, and Wales: The Making of a Nation* (Oxford: Oxford University Press, 1989).

Robbins, Keith, 'Core and Periphery in Modern British History', in his *History, Religion and Identity in Modern Britain* (London: Hambledon, 1993), pp. 239–57.

Roper, Michael, and John Tosh (eds), *Manful Assertions: Masculinities in Britain since 1800* (London: Routledge, 1991).

Rose, Peter, *How the Troubles Came to Northern Ireland* (Basingstoke: Palgrave, 2001).

Rose, Sonya O., *Which People's War? National Identity and Citizenship in Wartime Britain* (Oxford: Oxford University Press, 2003).

Rumpf, E. and A.C. Hepburn, *Nationalism and Socialism in Twentieth Century Ireland* (Liverpool: Liverpool University Press, 1977).

Samuel, Raphael (ed.), *Patriotism: The Making and Unmaking of British National Identity*, 3 volumes (London: Routledge, 1989).

Santino, Jack, *Signs of War and Peace* (New York: Palgrave, 2001).

Searle, G.R., *The Liberal Party: Triumph and Disintegration, 1886–1929*, second edition (Basingstoke: Palgrave, 2001).

Seawright, David, *An Important Matter of Principle: The Decline of the Scottish Conservative and Unionist Party* (Aldershot: Ashgate, 1999).

Sinha, Mrinalini, 'Britishness, Clubbability, and the Colonial Public Sphere: The Genealogy of an Imperial Institution in Colonial India', *Journal of British Studies*, 40 (2001), pp. 489–521.

Smith, Harold L., 'The Effect of War on the Status of Women', in Harold L. Smith (ed.), *War and Social Change: British Society and the Second World War* (Manchester: Manchester University Press, 1986), pp. 208–29.

Smith, Janet A., *John Buchan: A Biography* (London: Rupert Hart Davis, 1965).

Smout, T.C., 'Scotland 1850–1950', in Thompson, F.M.L. (ed.), *The Cambridge Social History of Britain 1750–1950 Volume I Regions and Communities* (Cambridge: Cambridge University Press, 1990), pp. 209–80.

Smyth, James J., 'Resisting Labour: Unionists, Liberals and Moderates in Glasgow between the Wars', *Historical Journal*, 46 (2003), pp. 375–401.

Stead, Peter, 'The Labour Party and the Claims of Wales,' in John Osmond (ed.), *The National Question Again: Welsh Political Identity in the 1980s* (Llandusyl: Gomer, 1985), pp. 99–123.

Taylor, Miles, 'Imperium et Libertas? Rethinking the Radical Critique of Imperialism during the Nineteenth Century', *Journal of Imperial and Commonwealth History*, 19 (1991), pp. 1–23.

Thompson, Andrew S., *Imperial Britain: The Empire in British Politics c. 1880–1932* (Harlow: Pearson, 2000).

Turner, John, 'Letting Go: The Conservative Party and the End of the Union with Ireland', in Alexander Grant and Keith Stringer (eds), *Uniting the Kingdom: The Making of British History* (London: Routledge, 1995), pp. 255–74.

Urquhart, Diane, '"The Female of the Species is More Deadlier than the Male"? The Ulster Women's Unionist Council, 1911–40', in Janice Holmes and Diane Urquhart (eds), *Coming Into the Light: The Work, Politics and Religion of Women in Ulster* (Belfast: Institute of Irish Studies, Queen's University Belfast, 1994), pp. 93–123.

Urquhart, Diane, *Women in Ulster Politics 1890–1940: A History Not Yet Told* (Dublin: Irish Academic Press, 2000).

Usborne, Richard, *Clubland Heroes* (London: Hutchinson, 1983 [1953]).

Walker, Graham, 'The Commonwealth Labour Party in Northern Ireland, 1942–7', *Irish Historical Studies*, 24 (1984), pp. 69–90.

Walker, Graham, *The Politics of Frustration: Harry Midgley and the Failure of Labour in Northern Ireland* (Manchester: Manchester University Press, 1985).

Walker, Graham, *Thomas Johnston* (Manchester: Manchester University Press, 1988).

Walker, Graham, *A History of the Ulster Unionist Party: Protest, Pragmatism and Pessimism* (Manchester: Manchester University Press, 2004).

Walters, Donald, 'The Reality of Conservatism', in John Osmond (ed.), *The National Question Again: Welsh Political Identity in the 1980s* (Llandusyl: Gomer, 1985), pp. 210–21.

Ward, Margaret, *Unmanageable Revolutionaries: Women and Irish Nationalism* (London: Pluto, 1983).

Ward, Paul, *Red Flag and Union Jack: Englishness, Patriotism and the British Left, 1881–1924* (Woodbridge: Royal Historical Society/Boydell, 1998).

Ward, Paul, 'Preparing for the People's War: Labour and Patriotism in the 1930s,' *Labour History Review*, 67 (2002), pp. 171–85.

Ward, Paul, *Britishness since 1870* (London: Routledge, 2004).

Ward, Paul, 'Nationalism and National Identity in British Politics, c. 1880s to 1914', in Helen Brocklehurst and Robert Phillips (eds), *History, Identity and the Question of Britain* (Basingstoke: Palgrave 2004), pp. 213–23.

Ward-Smith, G., 'Baldwin and Scotland: More than Englishness', *Contemporary British History*, 15 (2001), pp. 61–82.

Webster, Wendy, *Englishness and Empire, 1939–65* (Oxford: Oxford University Press, forthcoming).

Weight, Richard, *Patriots: National Identity in Britain 1940–2000* (Basingstoke: Pan, 2003).

Who Was Who (London: Adam and Charles Black, various years).

Wilford, R.A., 'Parker, Dame Dehra (1882–1963)', *Oxford Dictionary of National Biography*, Oxford University Press, 2004 [accessed 20 October 2004: http://www.oxforddnb/view/article/58268].

Williams, Chris, *Capitalism, Community and Conflict: The South Wales Coalfield 1898–1947* (Cardiff: University of Wales Press, 1998).

Williams, Gwyn A., *When was Wales? A History of the Welsh* (Harmondsworth: Penguin, 1985).

Williamson, Philip, *National Crisis and National Government: British Politics, the Economy and Empire, 1926–1932* (Cambridge: Cambridge University Press, 1992).

Zweiniger-Bargielowska, Ina, *Austerity in Britain: Rationing, Controls and Consumption, 1939–1955* (Oxford: Oxford University Press, 2000).

Unpublished theses and papers

Taylor, Elizabeth M.M., *The Politics of Walter Elliot 1929–1936*, unpublished PhD, Edinburgh, 1979.

Ward, Paul, 'Empire and Everyday: Britishness and Imperialism in Women's Lives in the Great War', British World conference, University of Calgary, July 2003.

Index